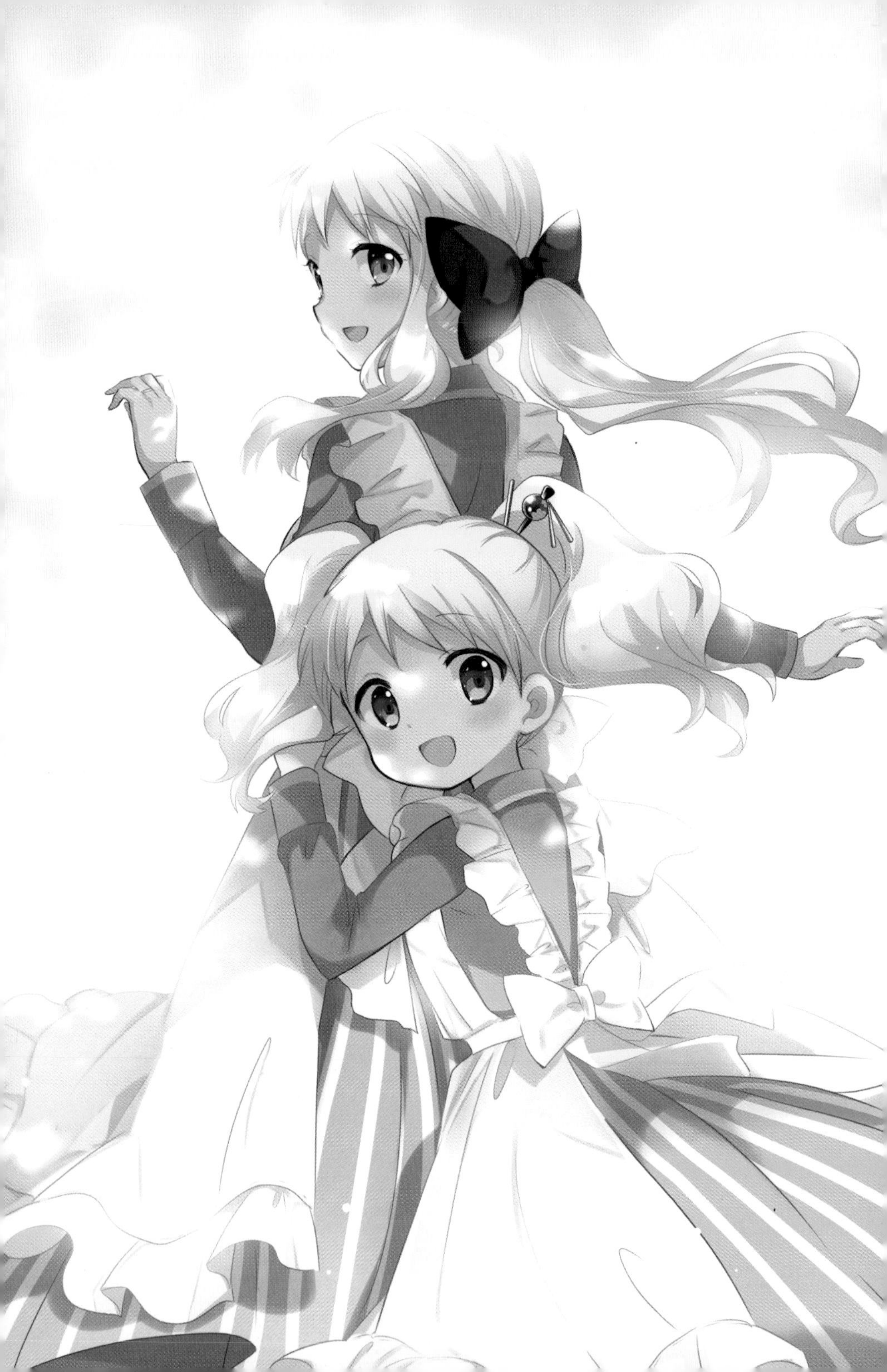

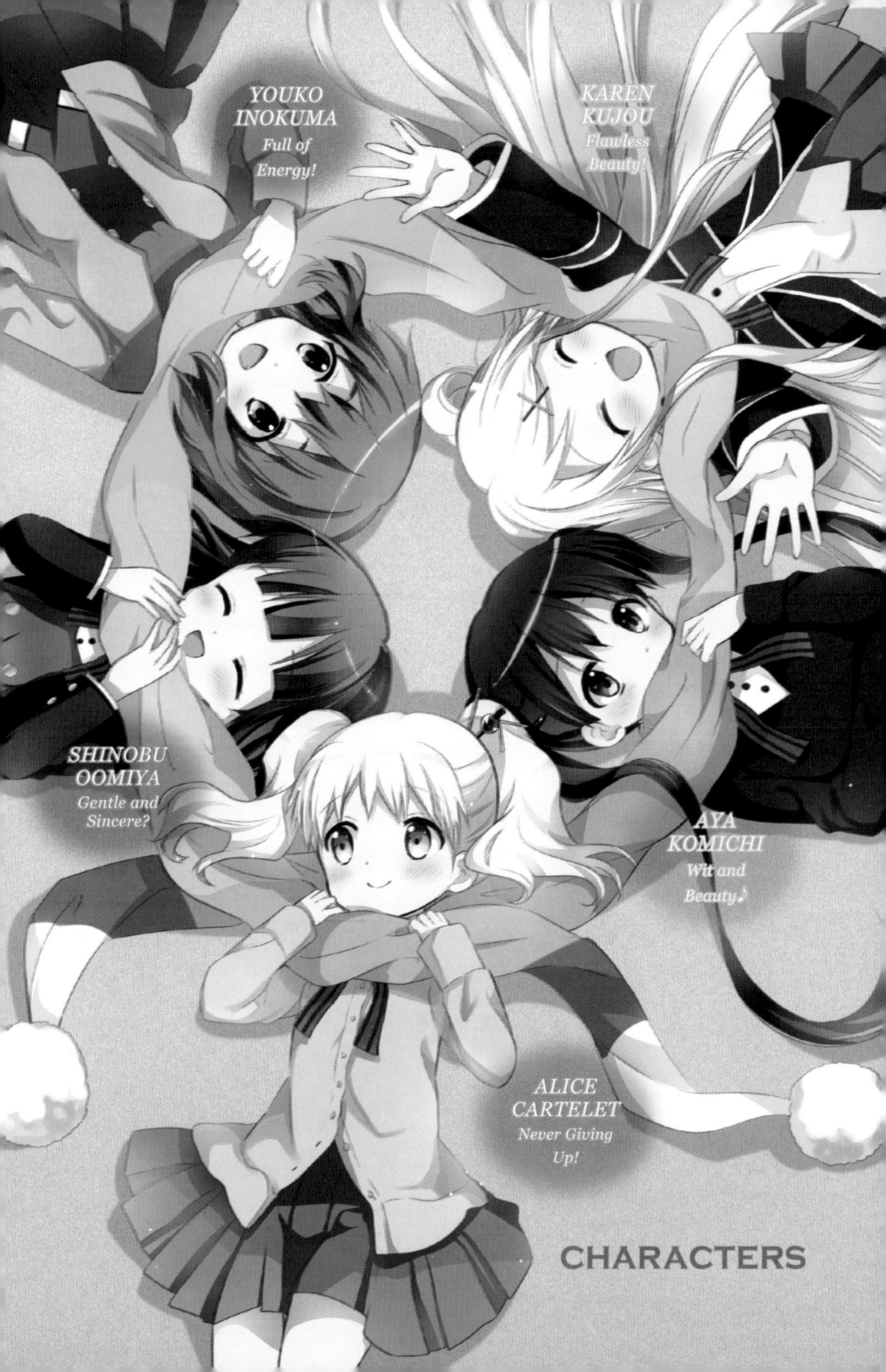
YOUKO INOKUMA
Full of Energy!
KAREN KUJOU
Flawless Beauty!
SHINOBU OOMIYA
Gentle and Sincere?
AYA KOMICHI
Wit and Beauty♪
ALICE CARTELET
Never Giving Up!
CHARACTERS

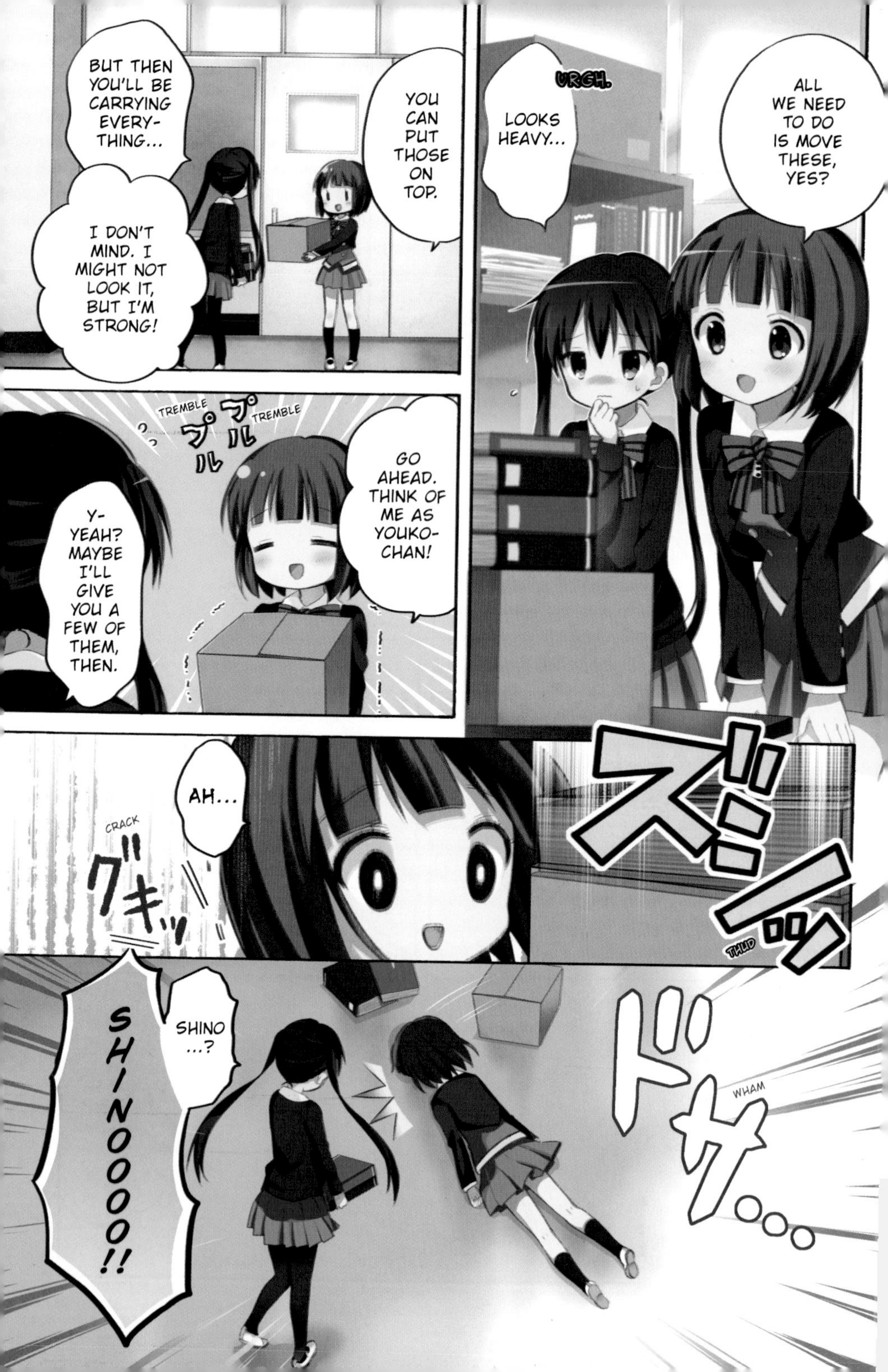
ALL WE NEED TO DO IS MOVE THESE, YES?
URGH.
LOOKS HEAVY...
YOU CAN PUT THOSE ON TOP.
BUT THEN YOU'LL BE CARRYING EVERY-THING...
I DON'T MIND. I MIGHT NOT LOOK IT, BUT I'M STRONG!
GO AHEAD. THINK OF ME AS YOUKO-CHAN!
プルプル
TREMBLE TREMBLE
Y-YEAH? MAYBE I'LL GIVE YOU A FEW OF THEM, THEN.
ズシッ
THUD
AH...
グキッ
CRACK
ドサ…
WHAM
SHINO...?
SHINOOOOOO!!

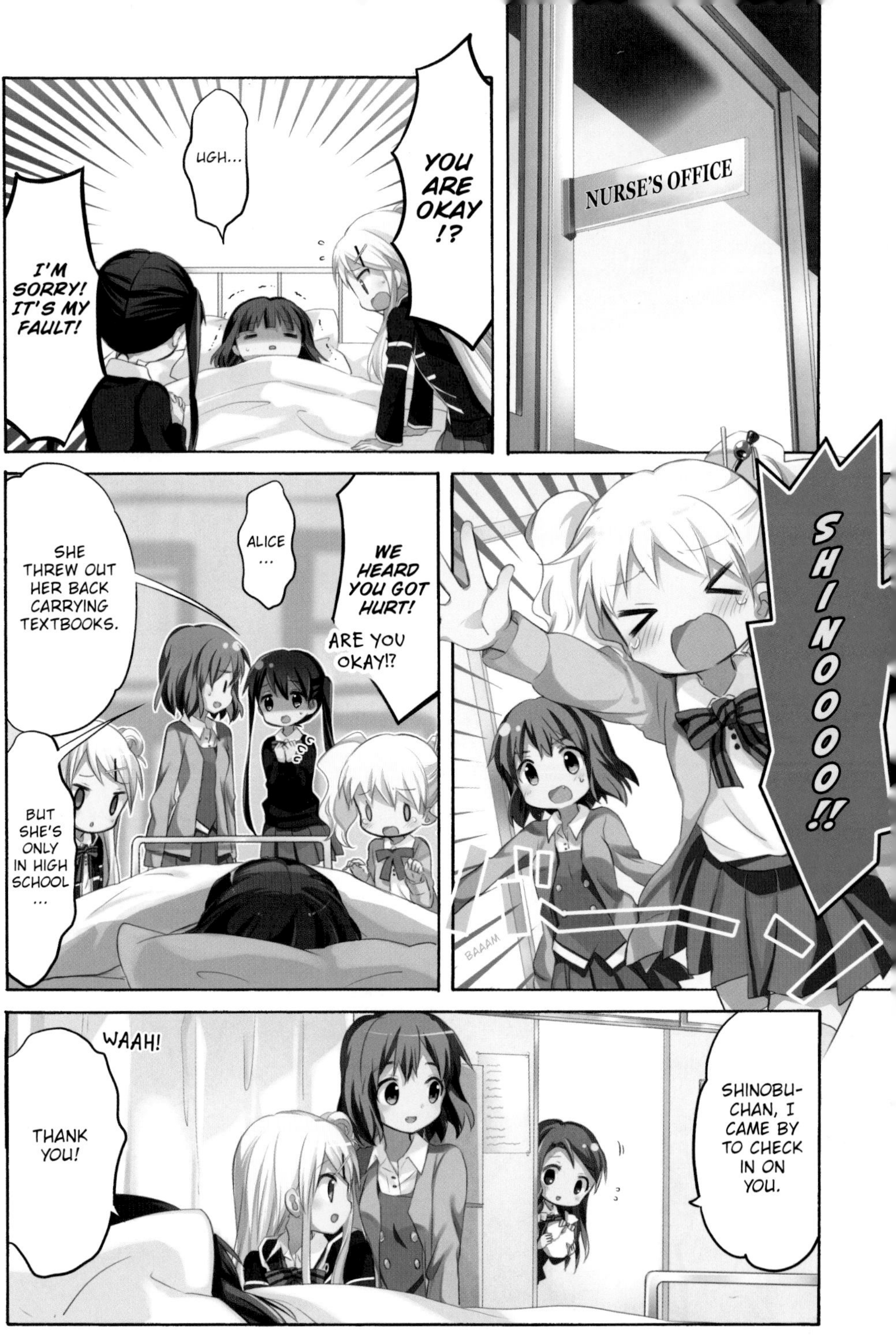
NURSE'S OFFICE
YOU ARE OKAY!?
UGH...
I'M SORRY! IT'S MY FAULT!
SHINOOOOOO!!
BAAAM
WE HEARD YOU GOT HURT!
ARE YOU OKAY!?
ALICE...
SHE THREW OUT HER BACK CARRYING TEXTBOOKS.
BUT SHE'S ONLY IN HIGH SCHOOL...
SHINOBU-CHAN, I CAME BY TO CHECK IN ON YOU.
WAAH!
THANK YOU!

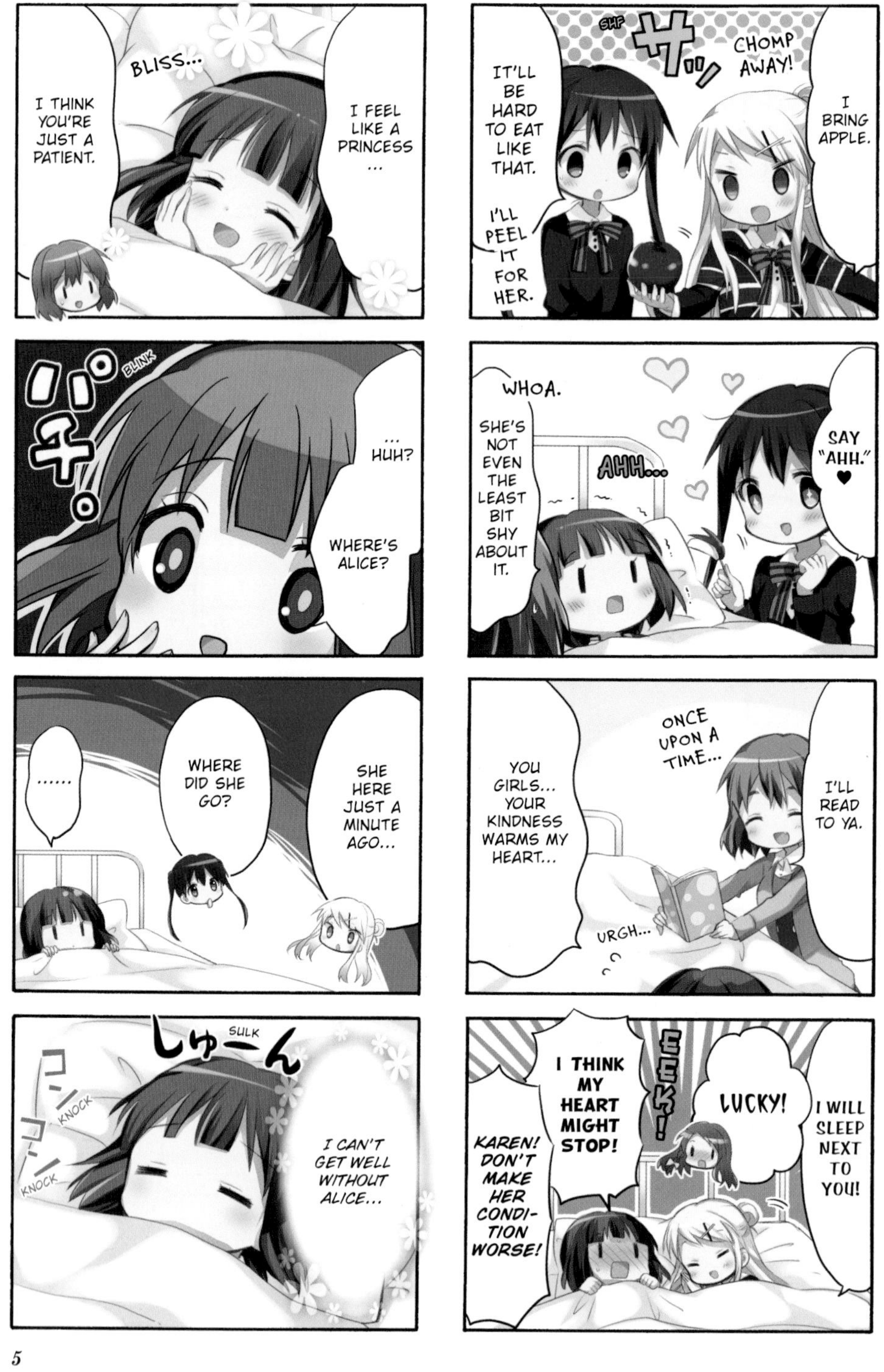
ザッ
SHF
I BRING APPLE.
CHOMP AWAY!
IT'LL BE HARD TO EAT LIKE THAT.
I'LL PEEL IT FOR HER.
SAY "AHH." ♥
AHH...
WHOA.
SHE'S NOT EVEN THE LEAST BIT SHY ABOUT IT.
I'LL READ TO YA.
ONCE UPON A TIME...
YOU GIRLS... YOUR KINDNESS WARMS MY HEART...
URGH...
I WILL SLEEP NEXT TO YOU!
LUCKY!
EEEK!
I THINK MY HEART MIGHT STOP!
KAREN! DON'T MAKE HER CONDITION WORSE!
I FEEL LIKE A PRINCESS ...
BLISS...
I THINK YOU'RE JUST A PATIENT.
... HUH?
WHERE'S ALICE?
パチ
BLINK
SHE HERE JUST A MINUTE AGO...
WHERE DID SHE GO?
......
しゅーん
SULK
I CAN'T GET WELL WITHOUT ALICE...
KNOCK
KNOCK

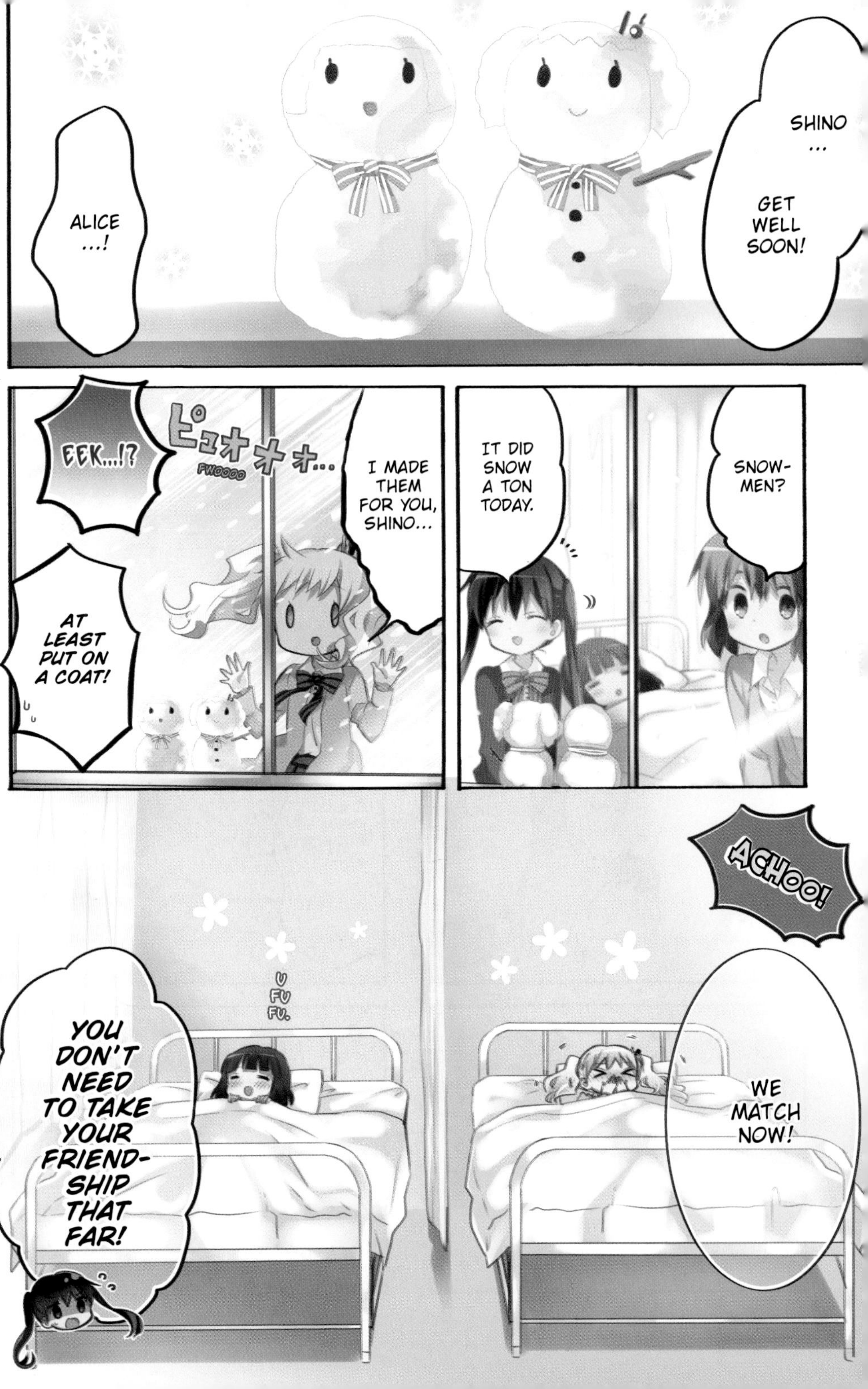
SHINO... GET WELL SOON!
ALICE...!
SNOW-MEN?
IT DID SNOW A TON TODAY.
I MADE THEM FOR YOU, SHINO...
ピュオオオ...
FWOOOO
EEK...!?
AT LEAST PUT ON A COAT!
ACHOO!
WE MATCH NOW!
UFUFU.
YOU DON'T NEED TO TAKE YOUR FRIENDSHIP THAT FAR!

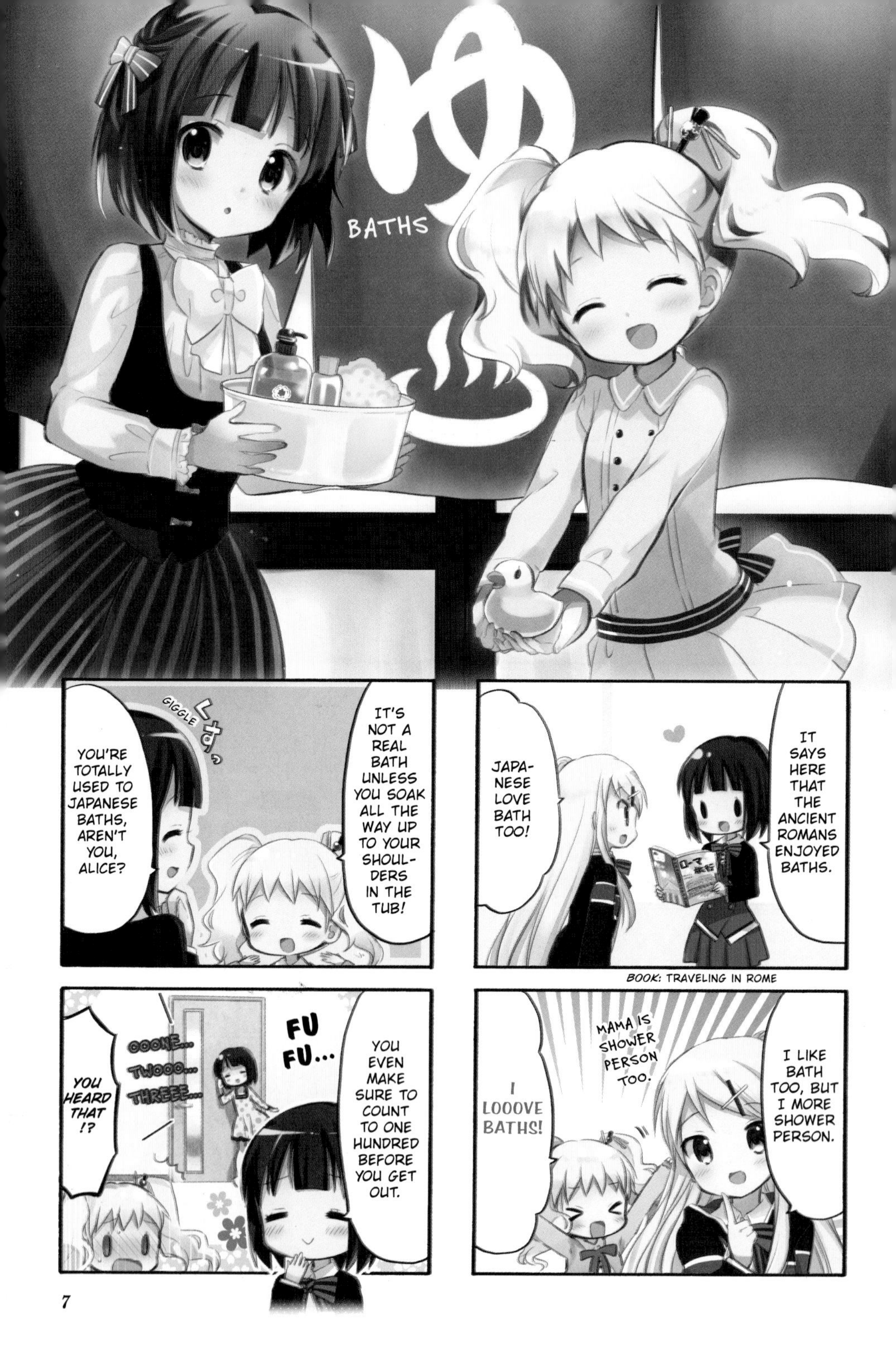
ゆ
BATHS
IT SAYS HERE THAT THE ANCIENT ROMANS ENJOYED BATHS.
JAPA-NESE LOVE BATH TOO!
BOOK: TRAVELING IN ROME
IT'S NOT A REAL BATH UNLESS YOU SOAK ALL THE WAY UP TO YOUR SHOUL-DERS IN THE TUB!
くすっ GIGGLE
YOU'RE TOTALLY USED TO JAPANESE BATHS, AREN'T YOU, ALICE?
I LIKE BATH TOO, BUT I MORE SHOWER PERSON.
MAMA IS SHOWER PERSON TOO.
I LOOOVE BATHS!
YOU EVEN MAKE SURE TO COUNT TO ONE HUNDRED BEFORE YOU GET OUT.
FU FU...
OOONE... TWOOO... THREEE...
YOU HEARD THAT!?

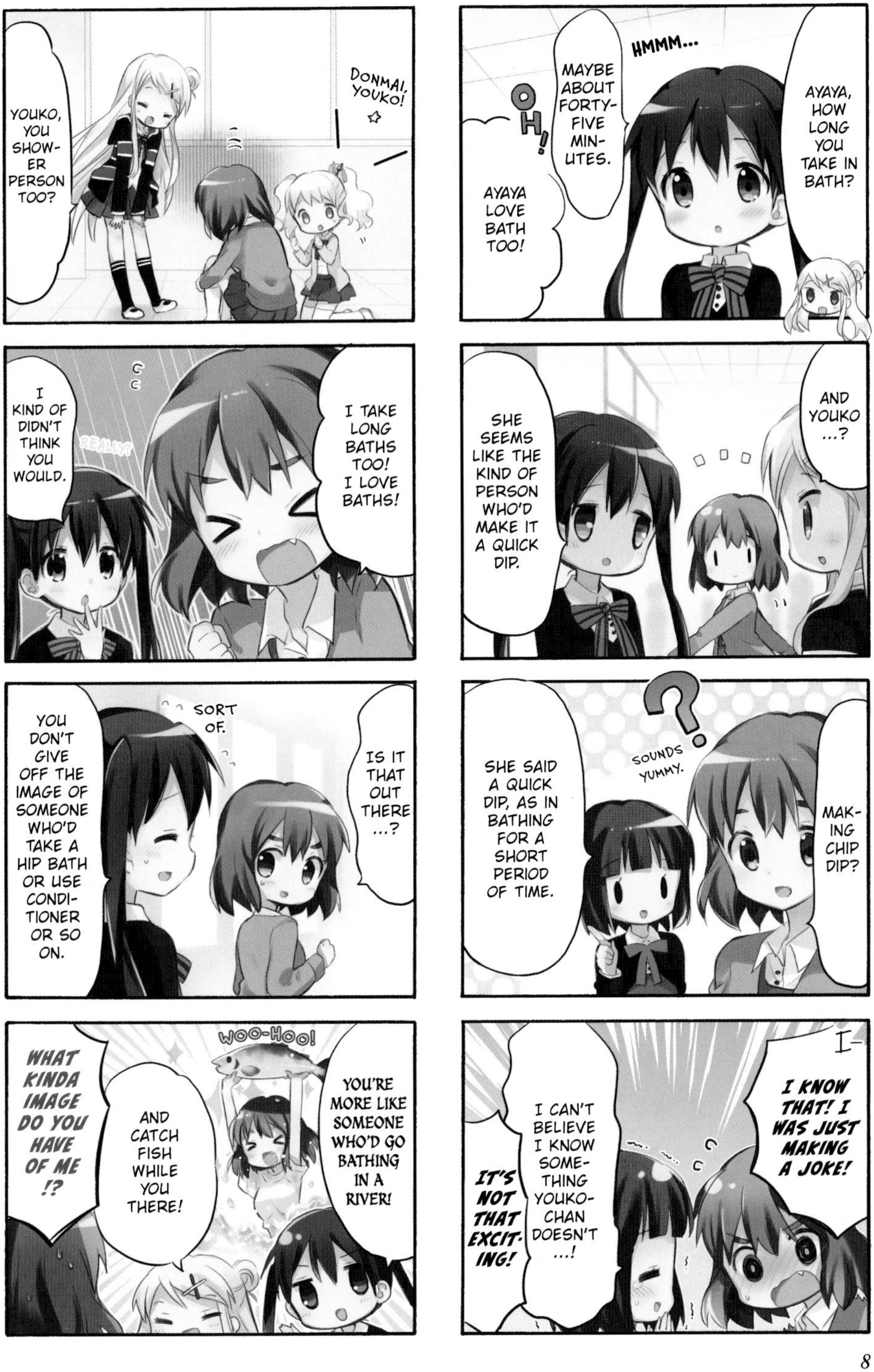
AYAYA, HOW LONG YOU TAKE IN BATH?
HMMM...
MAYBE ABOUT FORTY-FIVE MINUTES.
OH!
AYAYA LOVE BATH TOO!
AND YOUKO ...?
SHE SEEMS LIKE THE KIND OF PERSON WHO'D MAKE IT A QUICK DIP.
MAKING CHIP DIP?
SOUNDS YUMMY.
SHE SAID A QUICK DIP, AS IN BATHING FOR A SHORT PERIOD OF TIME.
I—
I KNOW THAT! I WAS JUST MAKING A JOKE!
I CAN'T BELIEVE I KNOW SOMETHING YOUKO-CHAN DOESN'T ...!
IT'S NOT THAT EXCITING!
DONMAI, YOUKO!
YOUKO, YOU SHOWER PERSON TOO?
I TAKE LONG BATHS TOO! I LOVE BATHS!
REALLY!?
I KIND OF DIDN'T THINK YOU WOULD.
IS IT THAT OUT THERE ...?
SORT OF.
YOU DON'T GIVE OFF THE IMAGE OF SOMEONE WHO'D TAKE A HIP BATH OR USE CONDITIONER OR SO ON.
WOO-HOO!
YOU'RE MORE LIKE SOMEONE WHO'D GO BATHING IN A RIVER!
AND CATCH FISH WHILE YOU THERE!
WHAT KINDA IMAGE DO YOU HAVE OF ME !?

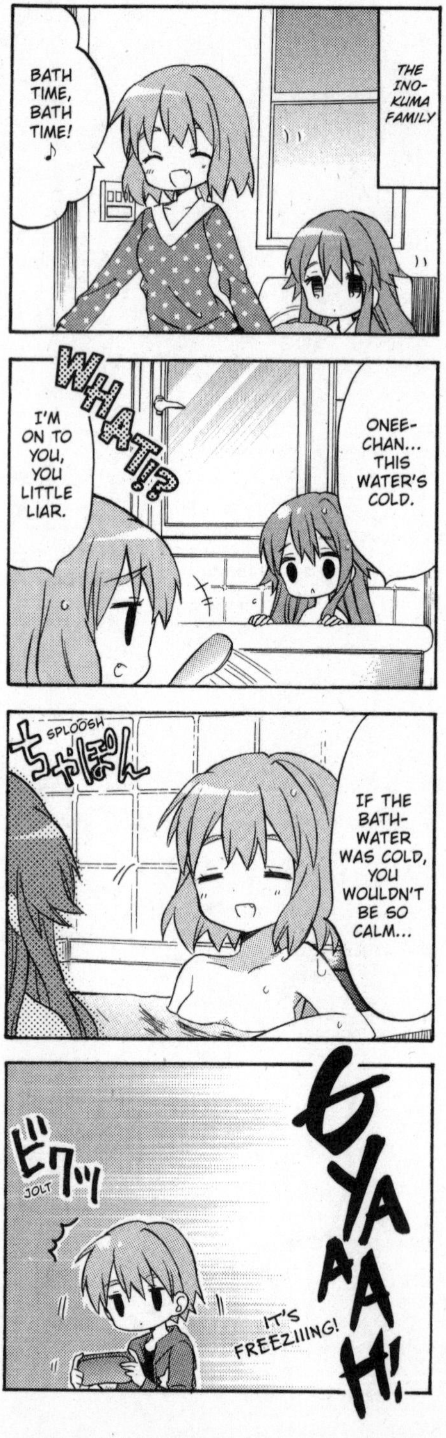
THE INO-KUMA FAMILY
BATH TIME, BATH TIME! ♪
ONEE-CHAN... THIS WATER'S COLD.
I'M ON TO YOU, YOU LITTLE LIAR.
WHAT!?
IF THE BATH-WATER WAS COLD, YOU WOULDN'T BE SO CALM...
ちゃぽん
SPLOOSH
GYAAAH!
IT'S FREEZIIING!
ビクッ
JOLT

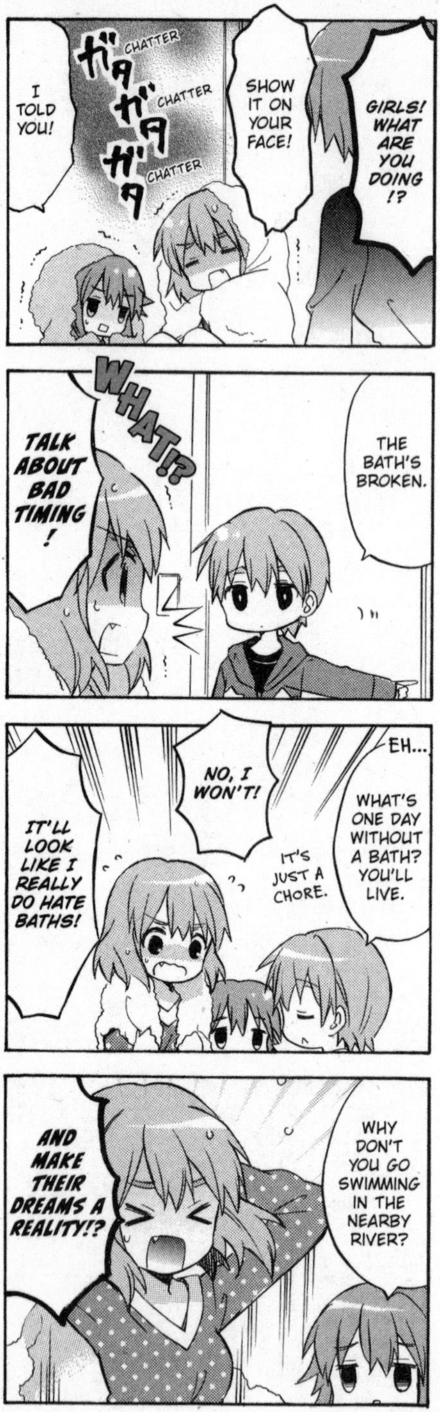
GIRLS! WHAT ARE YOU DOING!?
SHOW IT ON YOUR FACE!
ガタガタガタ
CHATTER
CHATTER
CHATTER
I TOLD YOU!
THE BATH'S BROKEN.
WHAT!?
TALK ABOUT BAD TIMING!
EH... WHAT'S ONE DAY WITHOUT A BATH? YOU'LL LIVE.
IT'S JUST A CHORE.
NO, I WON'T!
IT'LL LOOK LIKE I REALLY DO HATE BATHS!
WHY DON'T YOU GO SWIMMING IN THE NEARBY RIVER?
AND MAKE THEIR DREAMS A REALITY!?

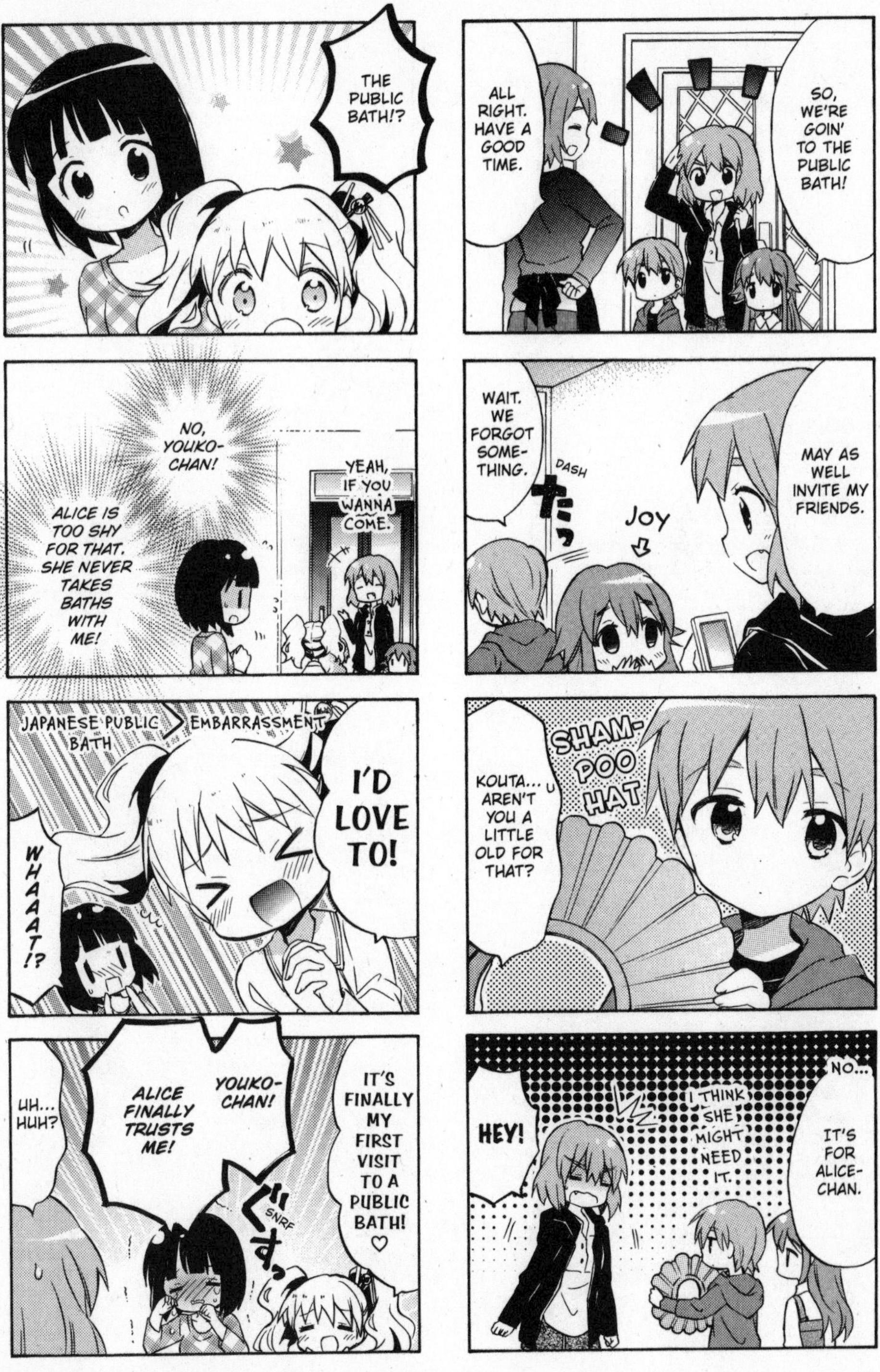
SO, WE'RE GOIN' TO THE PUBLIC BATH!
ALL RIGHT. HAVE A GOOD TIME.
MAY AS WELL INVITE MY FRIENDS.
JOY
WAIT. WE FORGOT SOME-THING.
DASH
SHAM-POO HAT
KOUTA... AREN'T YOU A LITTLE OLD FOR THAT?
NO... IT'S FOR ALICE-CHAN.
I THINK SHE MIGHT NEED IT.
HEY!
THE PUBLIC BATH!?
YEAH, IF YOU WANNA COME.
NO, YOUKO-CHAN!
ALICE IS TOO SHY FOR THAT. SHE NEVER TAKES BATHS WITH ME!
I'D LOVE TO!
JAPANESE PUBLIC BATH > EMBARRASSMENT
WHAAAAT!?
IT'S FINALLY MY FIRST VISIT TO A PUBLIC BATH! ♡
YOUKO-CHAN!
ALICE FINALLY TRUSTS ME!
SNRF
UH... HUH?

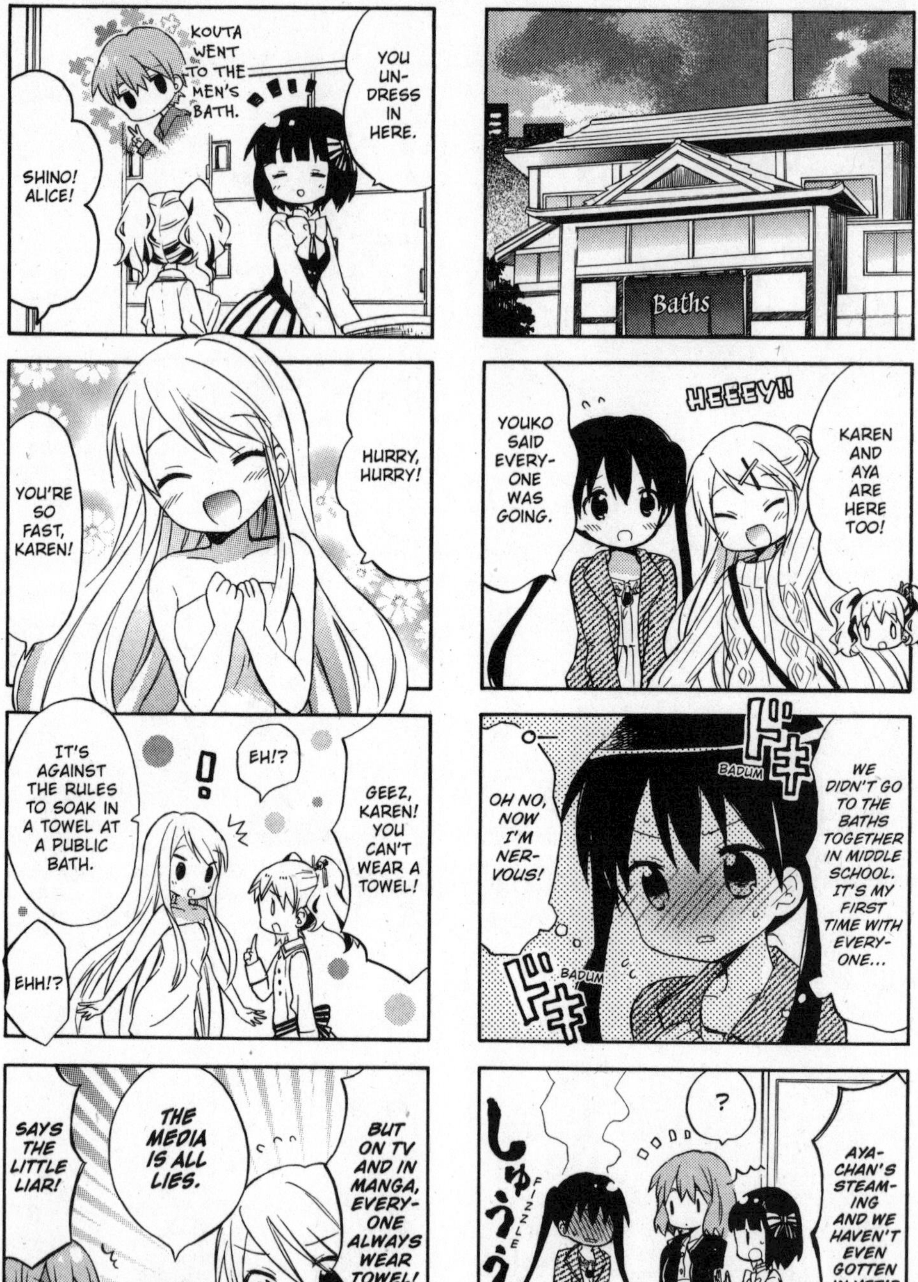
Baths
HEEEY!!
KAREN AND AYA ARE HERE TOO!
YOUKO SAID EVERY-ONE WAS GOING.
WE DIDN'T GO TO THE BATHS TOGETHER IN MIDDLE SCHOOL. IT'S MY FIRST TIME WITH EVERY-ONE...
BADUM
OH NO, NOW I'M NER-VOUS!
BADUM
?
AYA-CHAN'S STEAM-ING AND WE HAVEN'T EVEN GOTTEN IN YET!?
FIZZLE
YOU UN-DRESS IN HERE.
KOUTA WENT TO THE MEN'S BATH.
SHINO! ALICE!
HURRY, HURRY!
YOU'RE SO FAST, KAREN!
GEEZ, KAREN! YOU CAN'T WEAR A TOWEL!
EH!?
!
IT'S AGAINST THE RULES TO SOAK IN A TOWEL AT A PUBLIC BATH.
EHH!?
BUT ON TV AND IN MANGA, EVERY-ONE ALWAYS WEAR TOWEL!
THE MEDIA IS ALL LIES.
SAYS THE LITTLE LIAR!

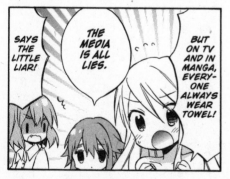

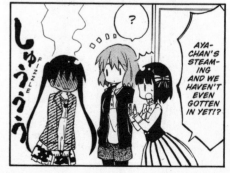

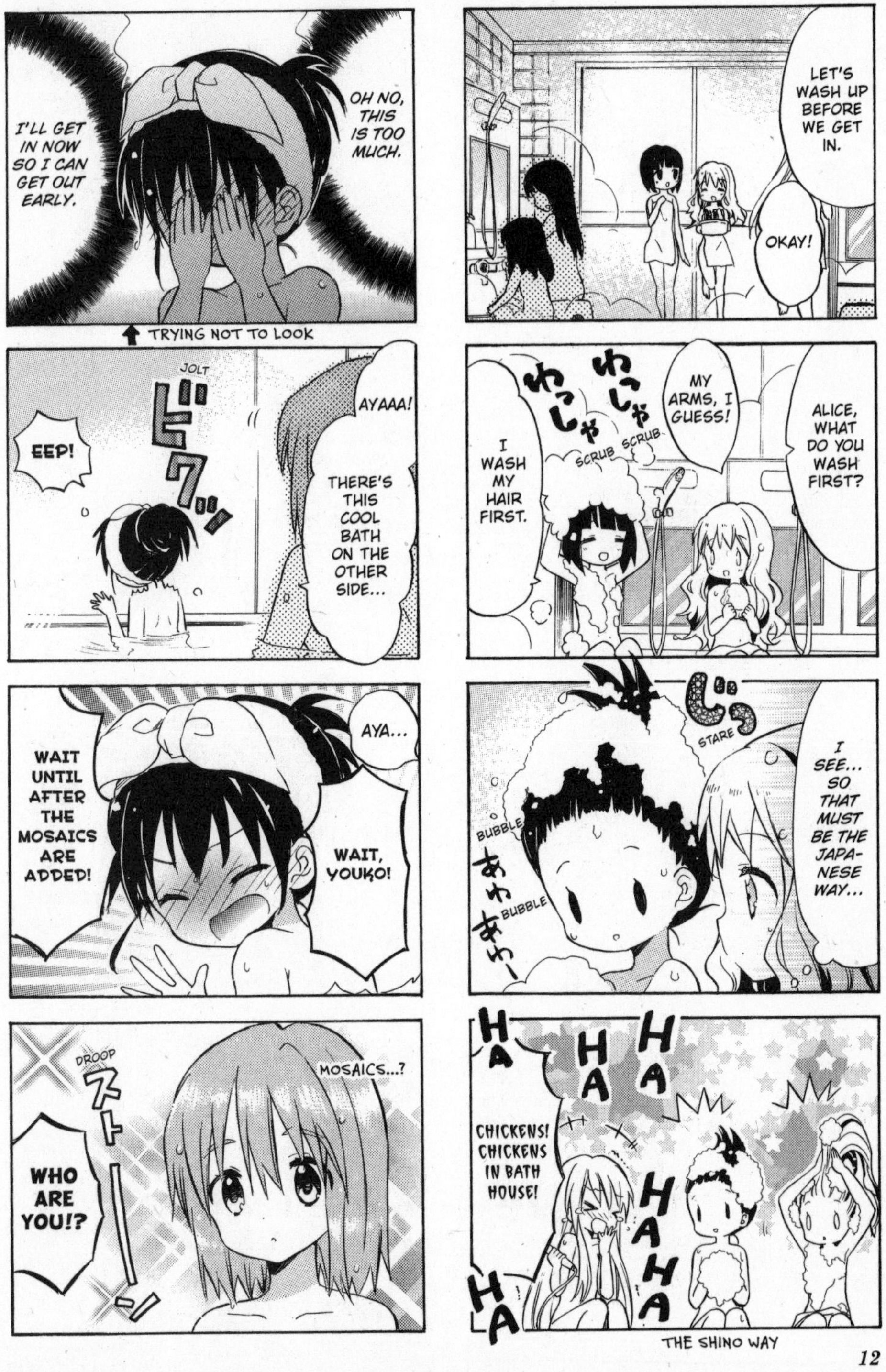
LET'S WASH UP BEFORE WE GET IN.
OKAY!
ALICE, WHAT DO YOU WASH FIRST?
MY ARMS, I GUESS!
I WASH MY HAIR FIRST.
SCRUB SCRUB
I SEE... SO THAT MUST BE THE JAPA-NESE WAY...
STARE
BUBBLE
BUBBLE
HA HA HA HA HA HA HA HA HA
CHICKENS! CHICKENS IN BATH HOUSE!
I'LL GET IN NOW SO I CAN GET OUT EARLY.
OH NO, THIS IS TOO MUCH.
AYAAA!
THERE'S THIS COOL BATH ON THE OTHER SIDE...
JOLT
EEP!
AYA...
WAIT, YOUKO!
WAIT UNTIL AFTER THE MOSAICS ARE ADDED!
MOSAICS...?
DROOP
WHO ARE YOU!?

THE SHINO WAY

↑ TRYING NOT TO LOOK

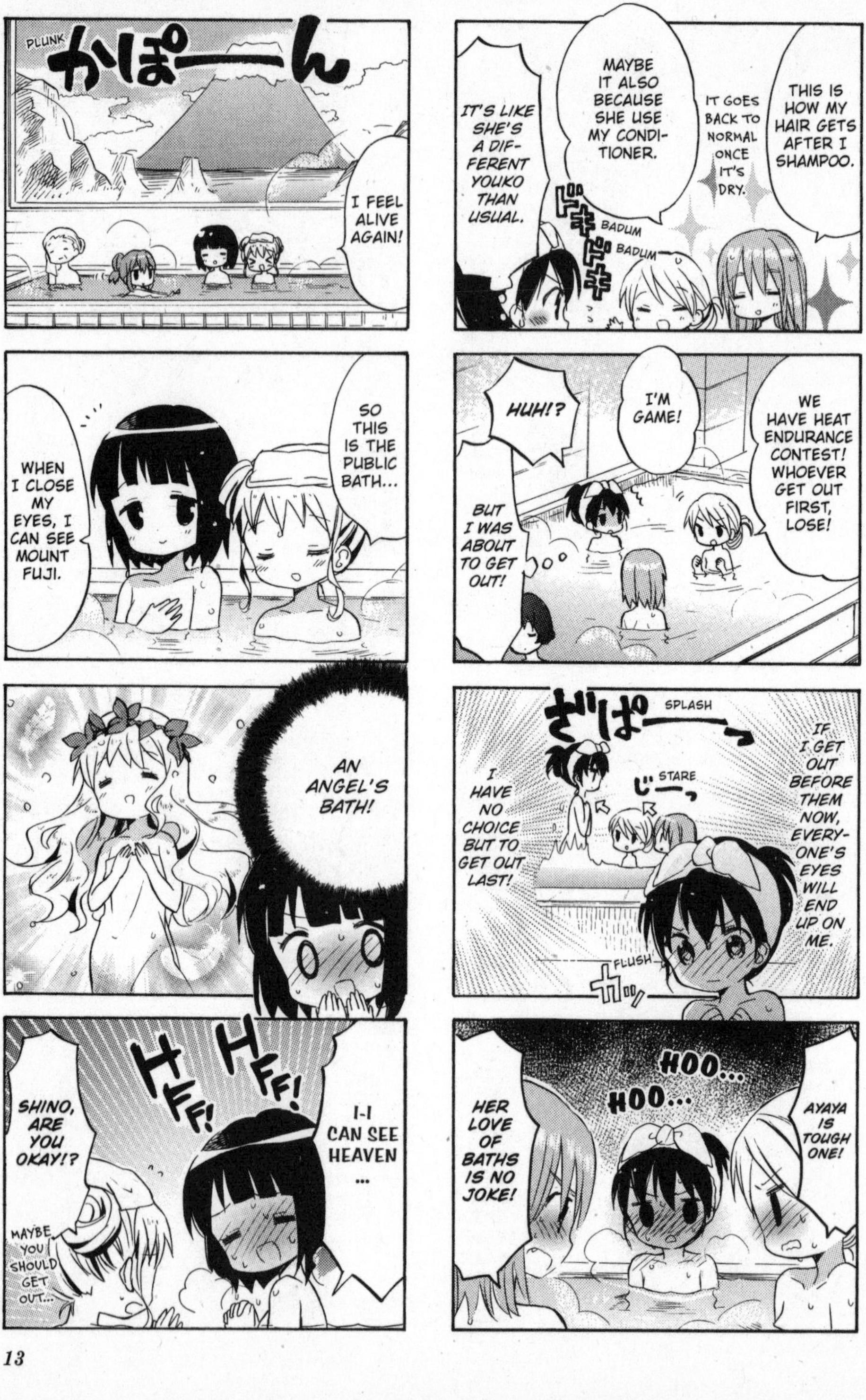
THIS IS HOW MY HAIR GETS AFTER I SHAMPOO.
IT GOES BACK TO NORMAL ONCE IT'S DRY.
MAYBE IT ALSO BECAUSE SHE USE MY CONDITIONER.
IT'S LIKE SHE'S A DIFFERENT YOUKO THAN USUAL.
ドキドキ
BADUM BADUM
WE HAVE HEAT ENDURANCE CONTEST! WHOEVER GET OUT FIRST, LOSE!
I'M GAME!
HUH!?
BUT I WAS ABOUT TO GET OUT!
ざぱーっ
SPLASH
IF I GET OUT BEFORE THEM NOW, EVERYONE'S EYES WILL END UP ON ME.
じーっ
STARE
I HAVE NO CHOICE BUT TO GET OUT LAST!
FLUSH
カッ
AYAYA IS TOUGH ONE!
HOO... HOO...
HER LOVE OF BATHS IS NO JOKE!
かぽーん
PLUNK
I FEEL ALIVE AGAIN!
SO THIS IS THE PUBLIC BATH...
WHEN I CLOSE MY EYES, I CAN SEE MOUNT FUJI.
AN ANGEL'S BATH!
HFF! HFF!
I-I CAN SEE HEAVEN ...
SHINO, ARE YOU OKAY!?
MAYBE YOU SHOULD GET OUT...

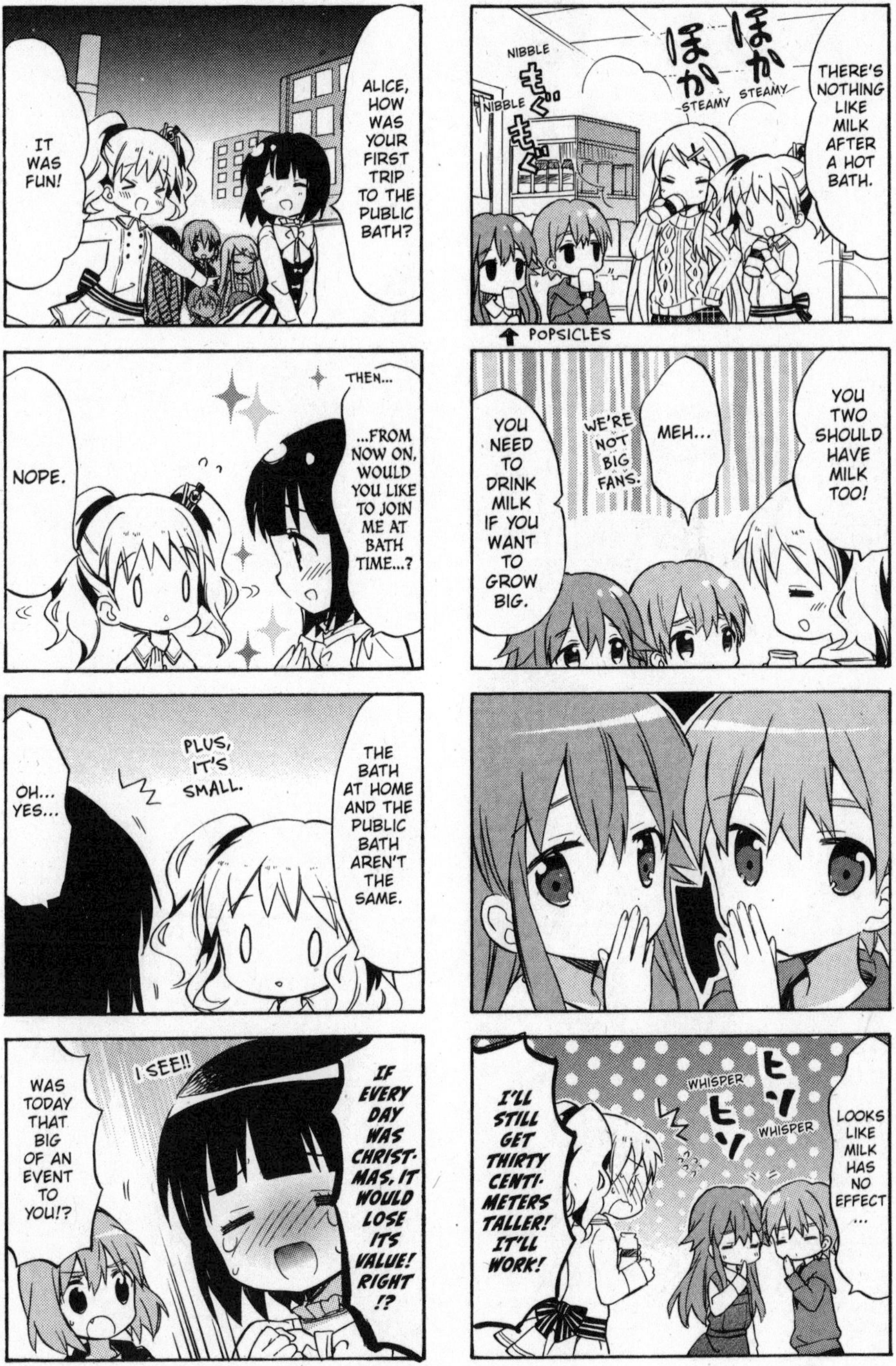
THERE'S NOTHING LIKE MILK AFTER A HOT BATH.
ほかほか
STEAMY STEAMY
もぐもぐ
NIBBLE NIBBLE
POPSICLES
YOU TWO SHOULD HAVE MILK TOO!
MEH...
WE'RE NOT BIG FANS.
YOU NEED TO DRINK MILK IF YOU WANT TO GROW BIG.
LOOKS LIKE MILK HAS NO EFFECT...
ヒソヒソ
WHISPER WHISPER
I'LL STILL GET THIRTY CENTIMETERS TALLER! IT'LL WORK!
ALICE, HOW WAS YOUR FIRST TRIP TO THE PUBLIC BATH?
IT WAS FUN!
THEN...
...FROM NOW ON, WOULD YOU LIKE TO JOIN ME AT BATH TIME...?
NOPE.
THE BATH AT HOME AND THE PUBLIC BATH AREN'T THE SAME.
PLUS, IT'S SMALL.
OH... YES...
IF EVERY DAY WAS CHRISTMAS, IT WOULD LOSE ITS VALUE! RIGHT!?
I SEE!!
WAS TODAY THAT BIG OF AN EVENT TO YOU!?

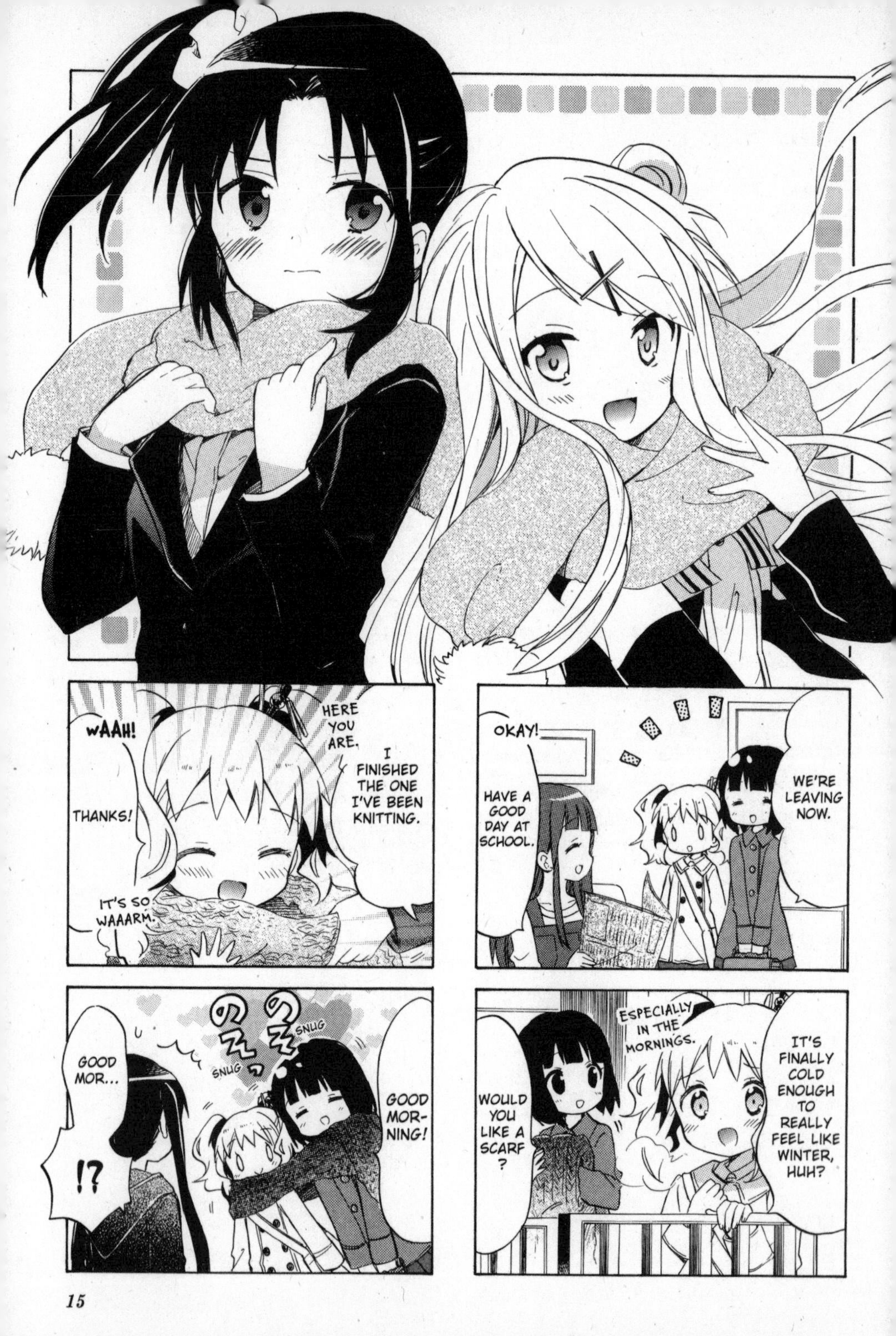

WE'RE LEAVING NOW.
OKAY!
HAVE A GOOD DAY AT SCHOOL.
HERE YOU ARE.
I FINISHED THE ONE I'VE BEEN KNITTING.
WAAH!
THANKS!
IT'S SO WAAARM.
IT'S FINALLY COLD ENOUGH TO REALLY FEEL LIKE WINTER, HUH?
ESPECIALLY IN THE MORNINGS.
WOULD YOU LIKE A SCARF?
GOOD MORNING!
SNUG
SNUG
GOOD MOR...
!?

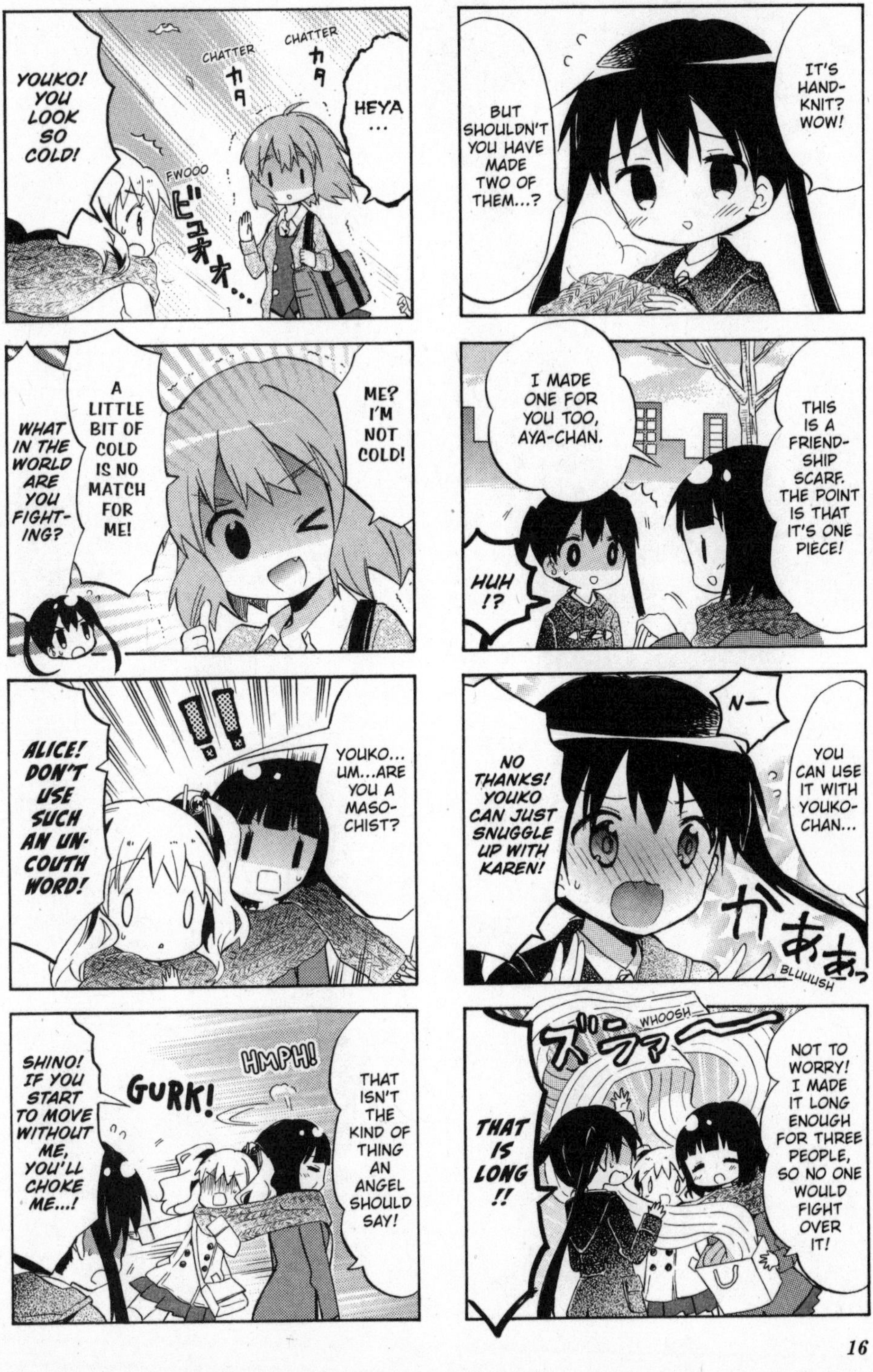
IT'S HAND-KNIT? WOW!
BUT SHOULDN'T YOU HAVE MADE TWO OF THEM...?
THIS IS A FRIEND-SHIP SCARF. THE POINT IS THAT IT'S ONE PIECE!
I MADE ONE FOR YOU TOO, AYA-CHAN.
HUH !?
N—
YOU CAN USE IT WITH YOUKO-CHAN...
NO THANKS! YOUKO CAN JUST SNUGGLE UP WITH KAREN!
かあぁっ
BLUUUSH
NOT TO WORRY! I MADE IT LONG ENOUGH FOR THREE PEOPLE, SO NO ONE WOULD FIGHT OVER IT!
WHOOSH
ズファ〜〜
THAT IS LONG !!
HEYA ...
CHATTER
カタ
CHATTER
カタ
FWOOO
ビュオオオ...
YOUKO! YOU LOOK SO COLD!
ME? I'M NOT COLD!
A LITTLE BIT OF COLD IS NO MATCH FOR ME!
WHAT IN THE WORLD ARE YOU FIGHT-ING?
YOUKO... UM...ARE YOU A MASO-CHIST?
ALICE! DON'T USE SUCH AN UN-COUTH WORD!
THAT ISN'T THE KIND OF THING AN ANGEL SHOULD SAY!
HMPH!
GURK!
SHINO! IF YOU START TO MOVE WITHOUT ME, YOU'LL CHOKE ME...!

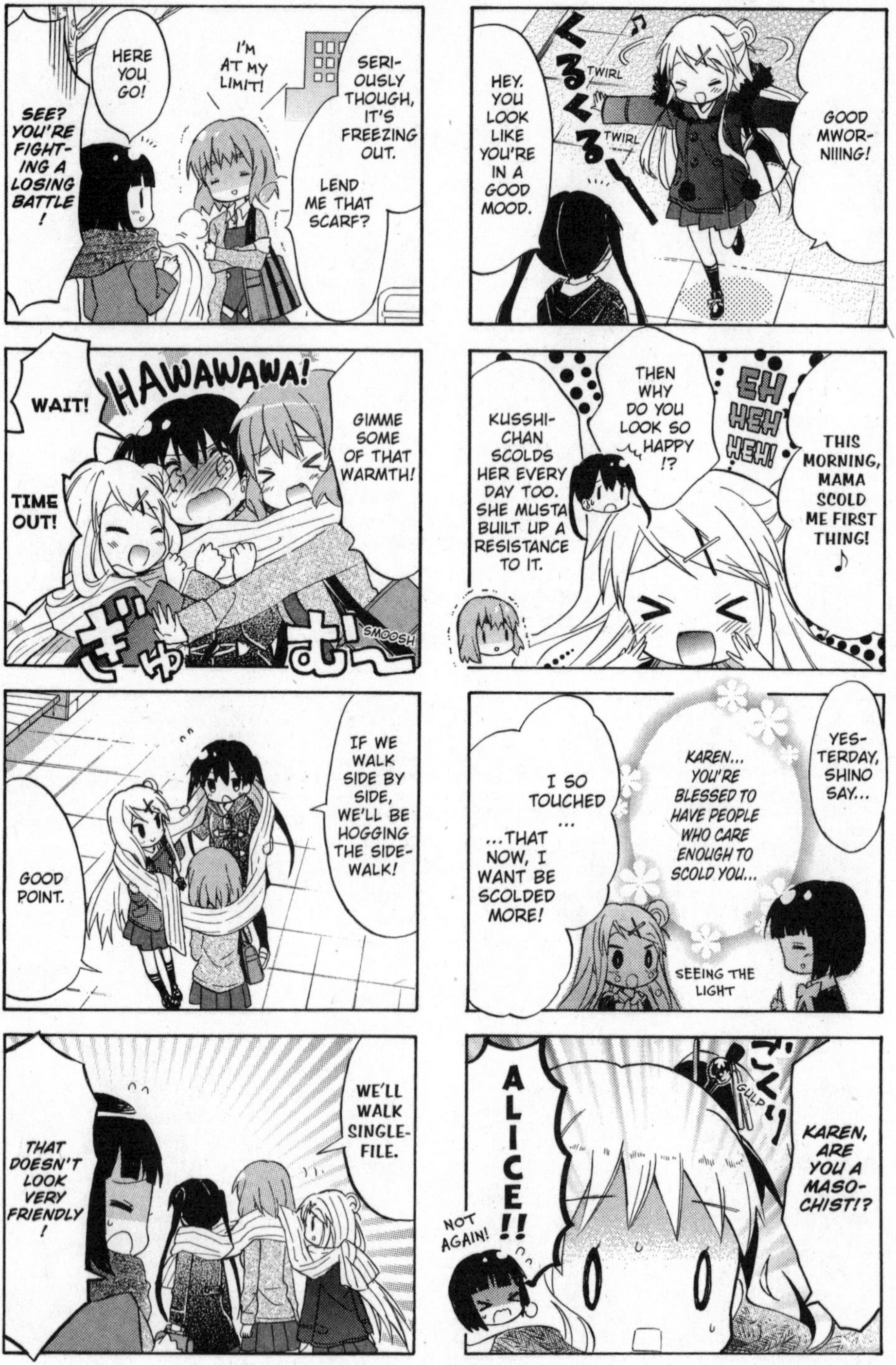
GOOD MWORNIIING!
くるくる
TWIRL
TWIRL
HEY. YOU LOOK LIKE YOU'RE IN A GOOD MOOD.
THIS MORNING, MAMA SCOLD ME FIRST THING! ♪
EH HEH HEH!
THEN WHY DO YOU LOOK SO HAPPY!?
KUSSHI-CHAN SCOLDS HER EVERY DAY TOO. SHE MUSTA BUILT UP A RESISTANCE TO IT.
YESTERDAY, SHINO SAY...
KAREN... YOU'RE BLESSED TO HAVE PEOPLE WHO CARE ENOUGH TO SCOLD YOU...
I SO TOUCHED ...
...THAT NOW, I WANT BE SCOLDED MORE!
SEEING THE LIGHT
KAREN, ARE YOU A MASOCHIST!?
ごくり
GULP
ALICE!!
NOT AGAIN!
SERI-OUSLY THOUGH, IT'S FREEZING OUT.
LEND ME THAT SCARF?
I'M AT MY LIMIT!
HERE YOU GO!
SEE? YOU'RE FIGHT-ING A LOSING BATTLE!
GIMME SOME OF THAT WARMTH!
HAWAWAWA!
WAIT!
TIME OUT!
ぎゅむ〜
SMOOSH
IF WE WALK SIDE BY SIDE, WE'LL BE HOGGING THE SIDE-WALK!
GOOD POINT.
WE'LL WALK SINGLE-FILE.
THAT DOESN'T LOOK VERY FRIENDLY!

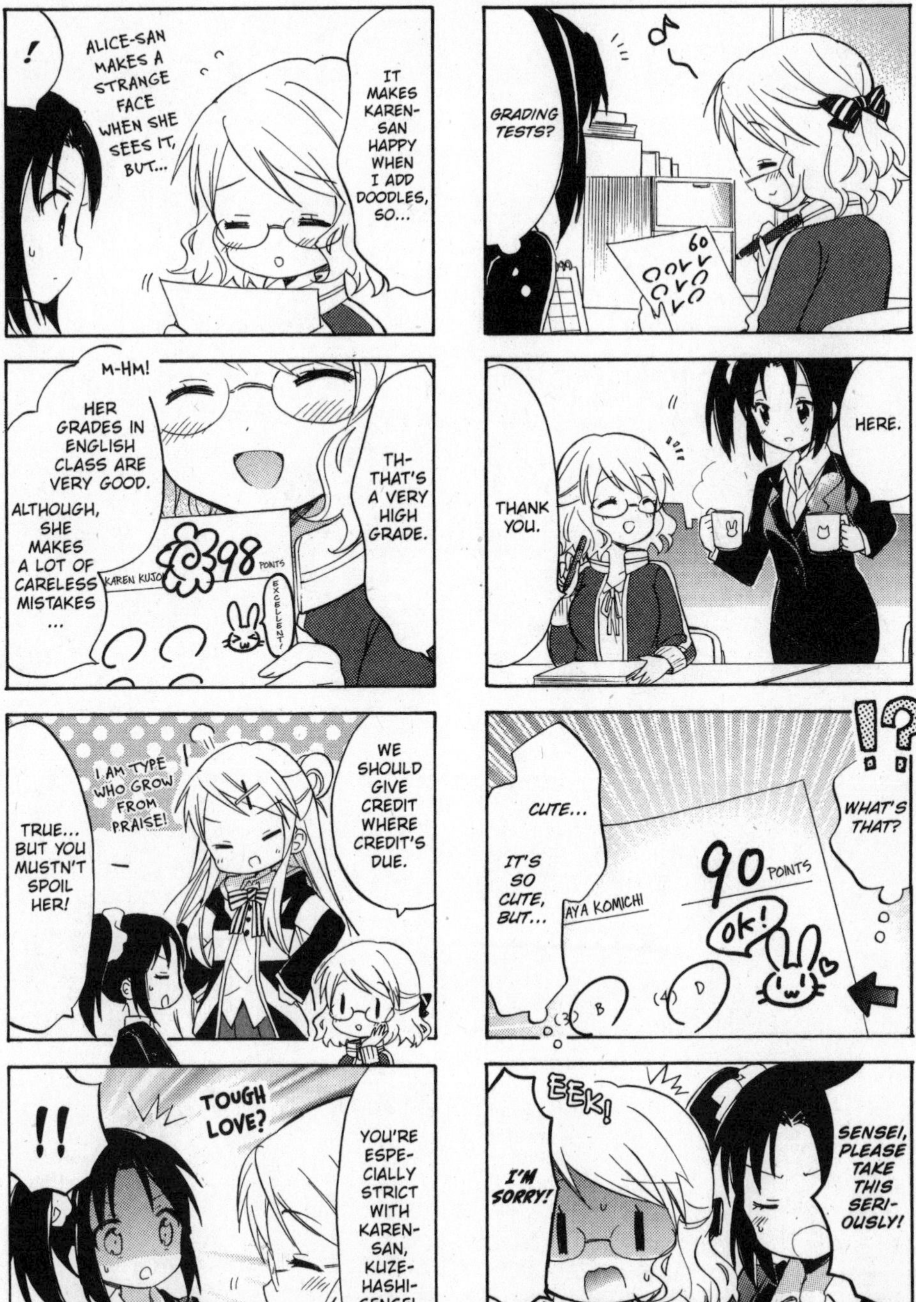
GRADING TESTS?
60
HERE.
THANK YOU.
!?
WHAT'S THAT?
CUTE...
IT'S SO CUTE, BUT...
90 POINTS
AYA KOMICHI
OK!
(3) B
(4) D
SENSEI, PLEASE TAKE THIS SERI-OUSLY!
EEK!
I'M SORRY!
IT MAKES KAREN-SAN HAPPY WHEN I ADD DOODLES, SO...
!
ALICE-SAN MAKES A STRANGE FACE WHEN SHE SEES IT, BUT...
TH-THAT'S A VERY HIGH GRADE.
M-HM!
HER GRADES IN ENGLISH CLASS ARE VERY GOOD.
ALTHOUGH, SHE MAKES A LOT OF CARELESS MISTAKES...
98 POINTS
KAREN KUJO
EXCELLENT!
WE SHOULD GIVE CREDIT WHERE CREDIT'S DUE.
I AM TYPE WHO GROW FROM PRAISE!
TRUE... BUT YOU MUSTN'T SPOIL HER!
YOU'RE ESPE-CIALLY STRICT WITH KAREN-SAN, KUZE-HASHI-SENSEI.
TOUGH LOVE?
!!

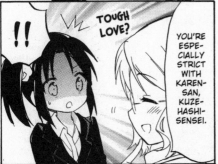

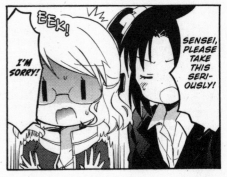

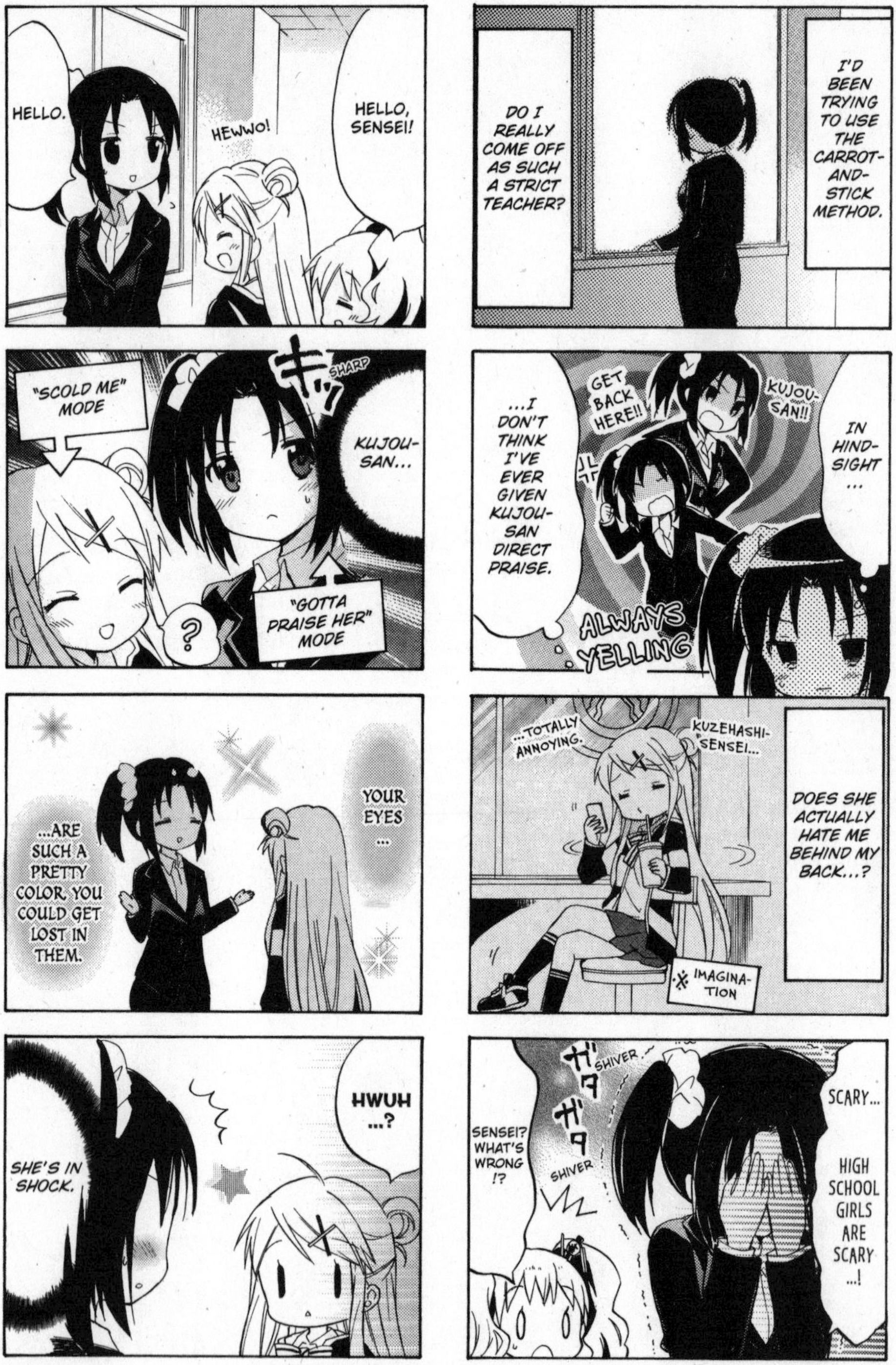

I'D BEEN TRYING TO USE THE CARROT-AND-STICK METHOD.
DO I REALLY COME OFF AS SUCH A STRICT TEACHER?
IN HINDSIGHT...
KUJOU-SAN!!
GET BACK HERE!!
...I DON'T THINK I'VE EVER GIVEN KUJOU-SAN DIRECT PRAISE.
ALWAYS YELLING
DOES SHE ACTUALLY HATE ME BEHIND MY BACK...?
KUZEHASHI-SENSEI...
...TOTALLY ANNOYING.
※ IMAGINATION
SCARY...
HIGH SCHOOL GIRLS ARE SCARY...!
ガタ SHIVER
ガタ SHIVER
SENSEI!? WHAT'S WRONG!?
HELLO, SENSEI!
HEWWO!
HELLO.
KUJOU-SAN...
キッ SHARP
"SCOLD ME" MODE
"GOTTA PRAISE HER" MODE
?
YOUR EYES...
...ARE SUCH A PRETTY COLOR YOU COULD GET LOST IN THEM.
HWUH...?
SHE'S IN SHOCK.

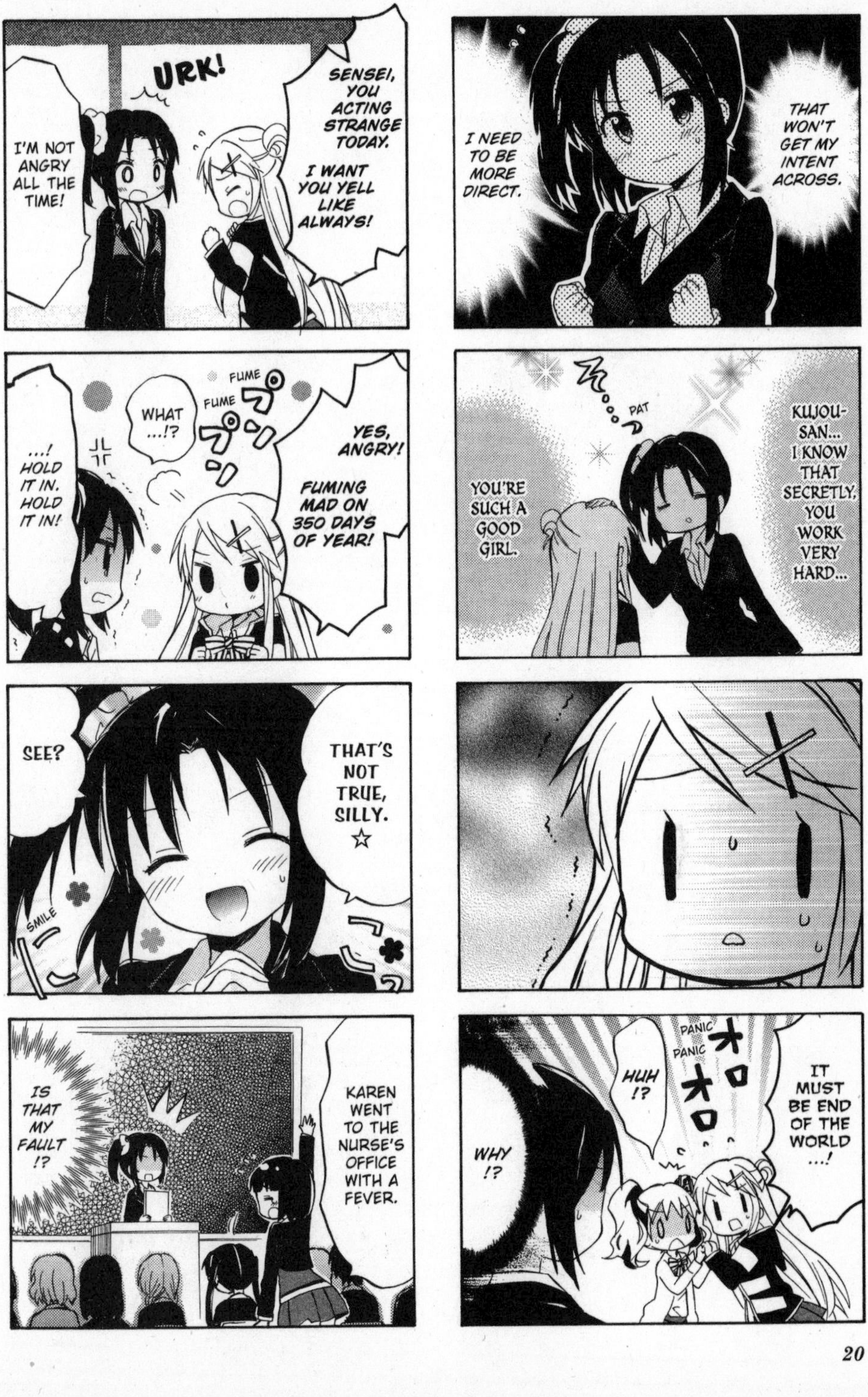
THAT WON'T GET MY INTENT ACROSS.
I NEED TO BE MORE DIRECT.
KUJOU-SAN... I KNOW THAT SECRETLY, YOU WORK VERY HARD...
PAT
YOU'RE SUCH A GOOD GIRL.
IT MUST BE END OF THE WORLD ...!
PANIC
PANIC
HUH !?
WHY !?
SENSEI, YOU ACTING STRANGE TODAY.
I WANT YOU YELL LIKE ALWAYS!
URK!
I'M NOT ANGRY ALL THE TIME!
YES, ANGRY!
FUMING MAD ON 350 DAYS OF YEAR!
FUME
FUME
WHAT ...!?
...! HOLD IT IN. HOLD IT IN!
THAT'S NOT TRUE, SILLY. ☆
SEE?
SMILE
KAREN WENT TO THE NURSE'S OFFICE WITH A FEVER.
IS THAT MY FAULT !?

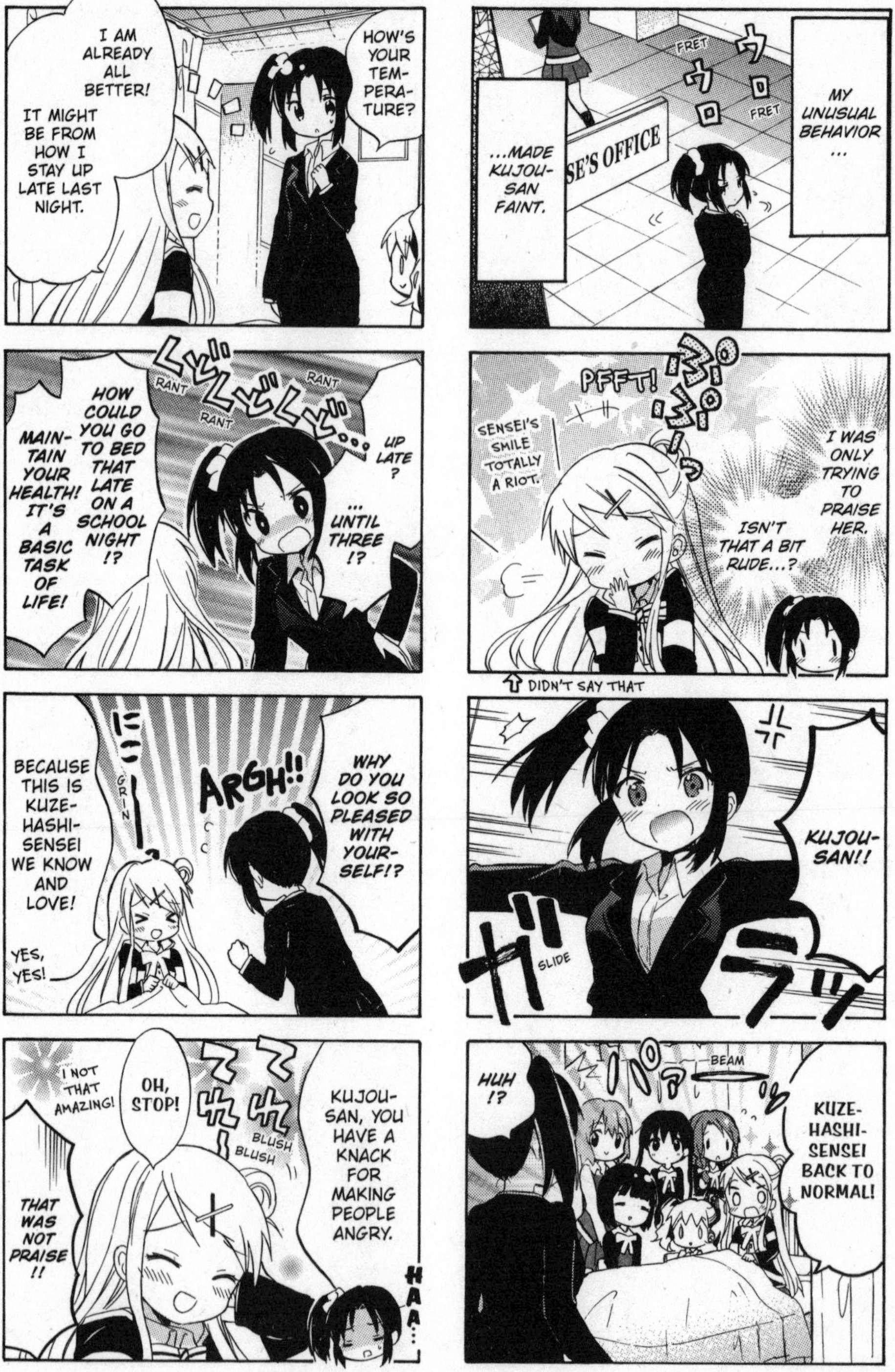
MY UNUSUAL BEHAVIOR ...
FRET
FRET
...MADE KUJOU-SAN FAINT.
SE'S OFFICE
PFFT!
I WAS ONLY TRYING TO PRAISE HER.
ISN'T THAT A BIT RUDE...?
SENSEI'S SMILE TOTALLY A RIOT.
⇧ DIDN'T SAY THAT
KUJOU-SAN!!
SLIDE
KUZE-HASHI-SENSEI BACK TO NORMAL!
BEAM
HUH !?
HOW'S YOUR TEMPERATURE?
I AM ALREADY ALL BETTER!
IT MIGHT BE FROM HOW I STAY UP LATE LAST NIGHT.
UP LATE? ...UNTIL THREE!?
RANT
RANT
RANT
HOW COULD YOU GO TO BED THAT LATE ON A SCHOOL NIGHT!?
MAINTAIN YOUR HEALTH! IT'S A BASIC TASK OF LIFE!
WHY DO YOU LOOK SO PLEASED WITH YOURSELF!?
ARGH!!
GRIN
BECAUSE THIS IS KUZE-HASHI-SENSEI WE KNOW AND LOVE!
YES, YES!
KUJOU-SAN, YOU HAVE A KNACK FOR MAKING PEOPLE ANGRY.
BLUSH
BLUSH
OH, STOP!
I NOT THAT AMAZING!
THAT WAS NOT PRAISE!!
HAA...

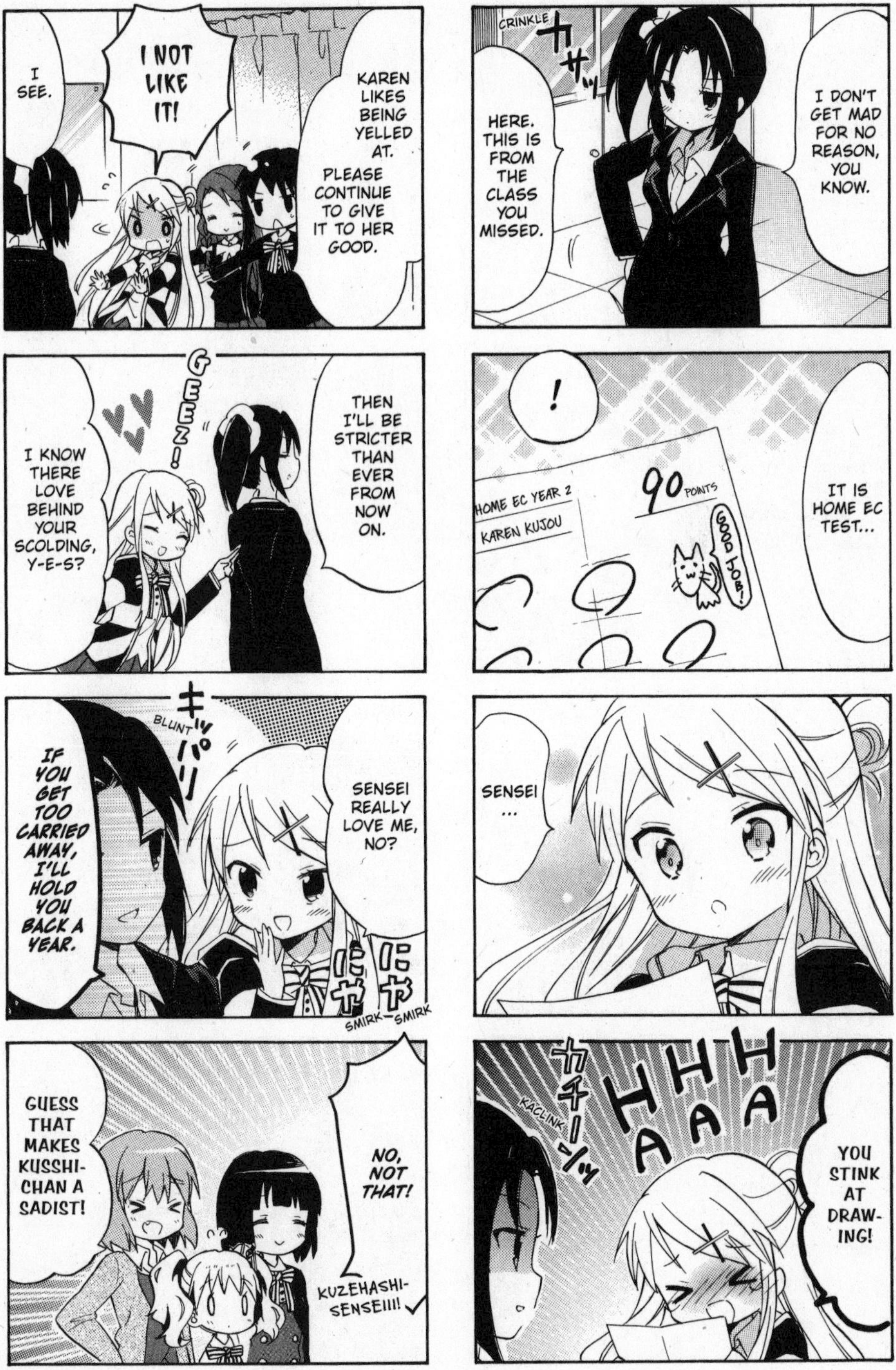
I DON'T GET MAD FOR NO REASON, YOU KNOW.
カサッ
CRINKLE
HERE. THIS IS FROM THE CLASS YOU MISSED.
IT IS HOME EC TEST...
!
90 POINTS
HOME EC YEAR 2
KAREN KUJOU
GOOD JOB!
SENSEI ...
YOU STINK AT DRAWING!
HAHAHA
カチーンッ
KACLINK
KAREN LIKES BEING YELLED AT. PLEASE CONTINUE TO GIVE IT TO HER GOOD.
I NOT LIKE IT!
I SEE.
THEN I'LL BE STRICTER THAN EVER FROM NOW ON.
GEEZ!
I KNOW THERE LOVE BEHIND YOUR SCOLDING, Y-E-S?
SENSEI REALLY LOVE ME, NO?
にやにや
SMIRK-SMIRK
キッパリ
BLUNT
IF YOU GET TOO CARRIED AWAY, I'LL HOLD YOU BACK A YEAR.
NO, NOT THAT!
KUZEHASHI-SENSEIII!
GUESS THAT MAKES KUSSHI-CHAN A SADIST!

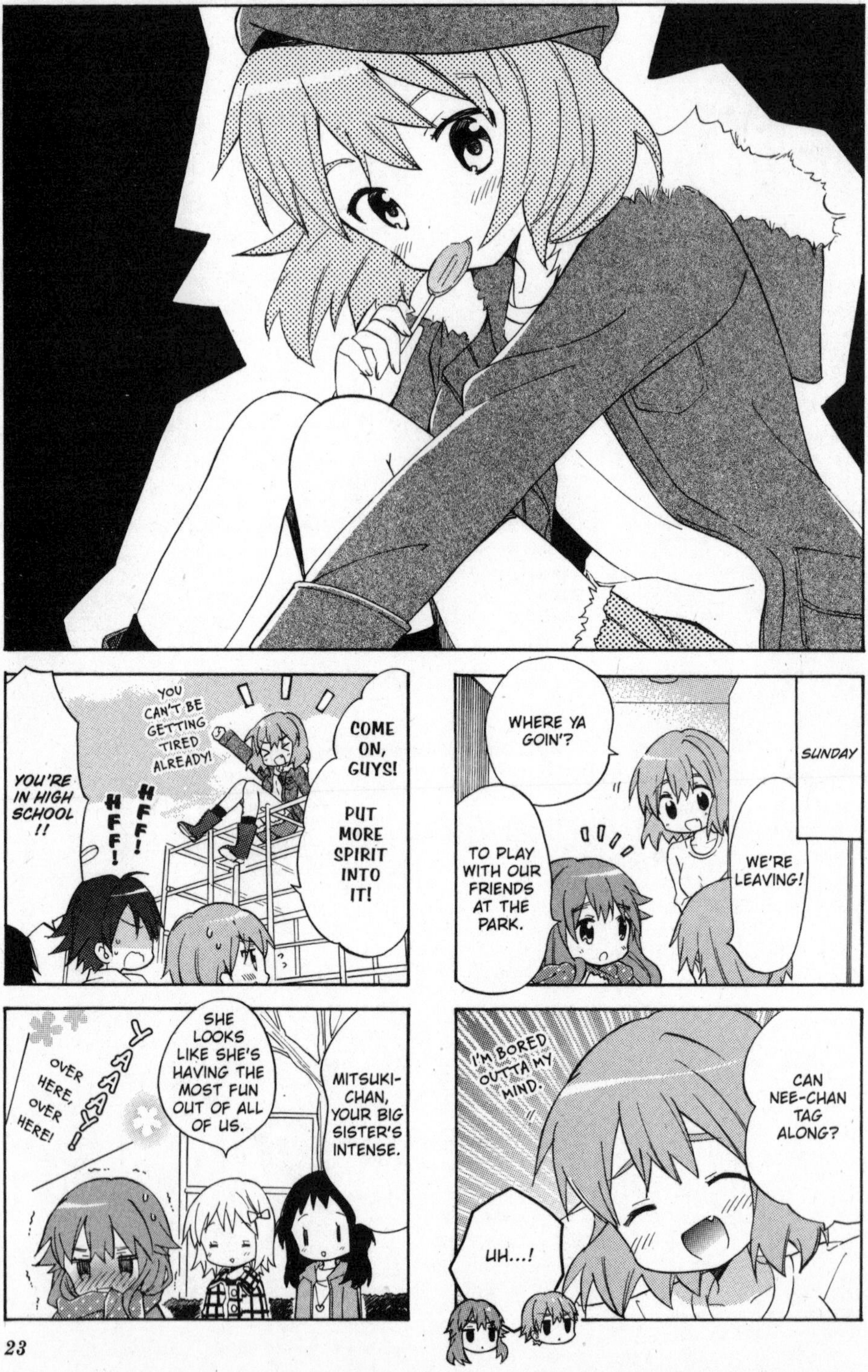
SUNDAY
WE'RE LEAVING!
WHERE YA GOIN'?
TO PLAY WITH OUR FRIENDS AT THE PARK.
COME ON, GUYS!
PUT MORE SPIRIT INTO IT!
YOU CAN'T BE GETTING TIRED ALREADY!
HFF!
HFF!
YOU'RE IN HIGH SCHOOL!!
CAN NEE-CHAN TAG ALONG?
I'M BORED OUTTA MY MIND.
UH...!
MITSUKI-CHAN, YOUR BIG SISTER'S INTENSE.
SHE LOOKS LIKE SHE'S HAVING THE MOST FUN OUT OF ALL OF US.
YAAAY!
OVER HERE, OVER HERE!

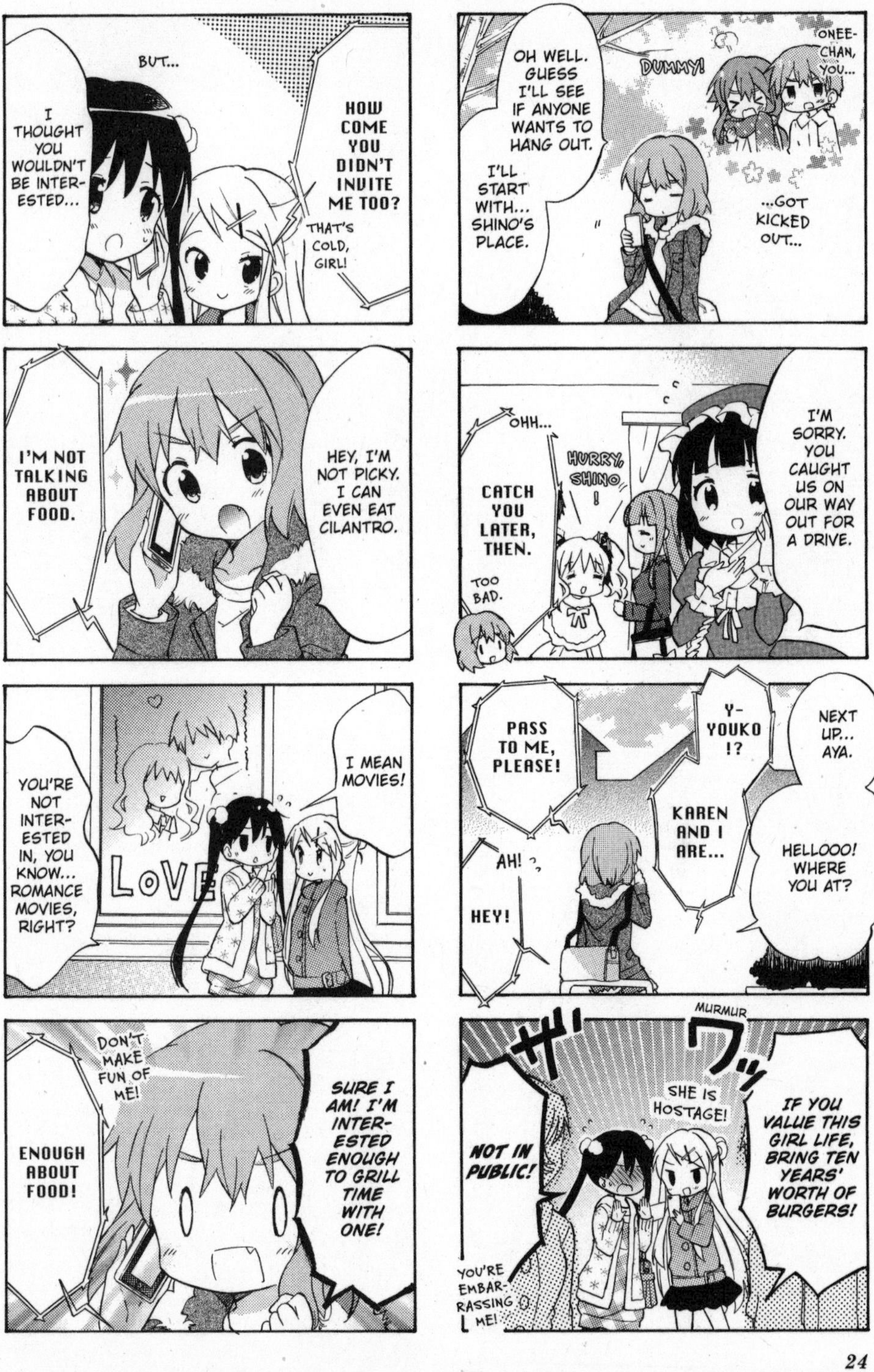
ONEE-CHAN, YOU...
...GOT KICKED OUT...
DUMMY!
OH WELL. GUESS I'LL SEE IF ANYONE WANTS TO HANG OUT.
I'LL START WITH... SHINO'S PLACE.
I'M SORRY. YOU CAUGHT US ON OUR WAY OUT FOR A DRIVE.
HURRY, SHINO!
OHH...
CATCH YOU LATER, THEN.
TOO BAD.
NEXT UP... AYA.
HELLOOO! WHERE YOU AT?
Y-YOUKO!?
KAREN AND I ARE...
PASS TO ME, PLEASE!
AH!
HEY!
MURMUR
ザワッ
IF YOU VALUE THIS GIRL LIFE, BRING TEN YEARS' WORTH OF BURGERS!
SHE IS HOSTAGE!
NOT IN PUBLIC!
YOU'RE EMBARRASSING ME!
HOW COME YOU DIDN'T INVITE ME TOO?
THAT'S COLD, GIRL!
BUT...
I THOUGHT YOU WOULDN'T BE INTERESTED...
HEY, I'M NOT PICKY. I CAN EVEN EAT CILANTRO.
I'M NOT TALKING ABOUT FOOD.
I MEAN MOVIES!
YOU'RE NOT INTERESTED IN, YOU KNOW... ROMANCE MOVIES, RIGHT?
LOVE
SURE I AM! I'M INTERESTED ENOUGH TO GRILL TIME WITH ONE!
DON'T MAKE FUN OF ME!
ENOUGH ABOUT FOOD!

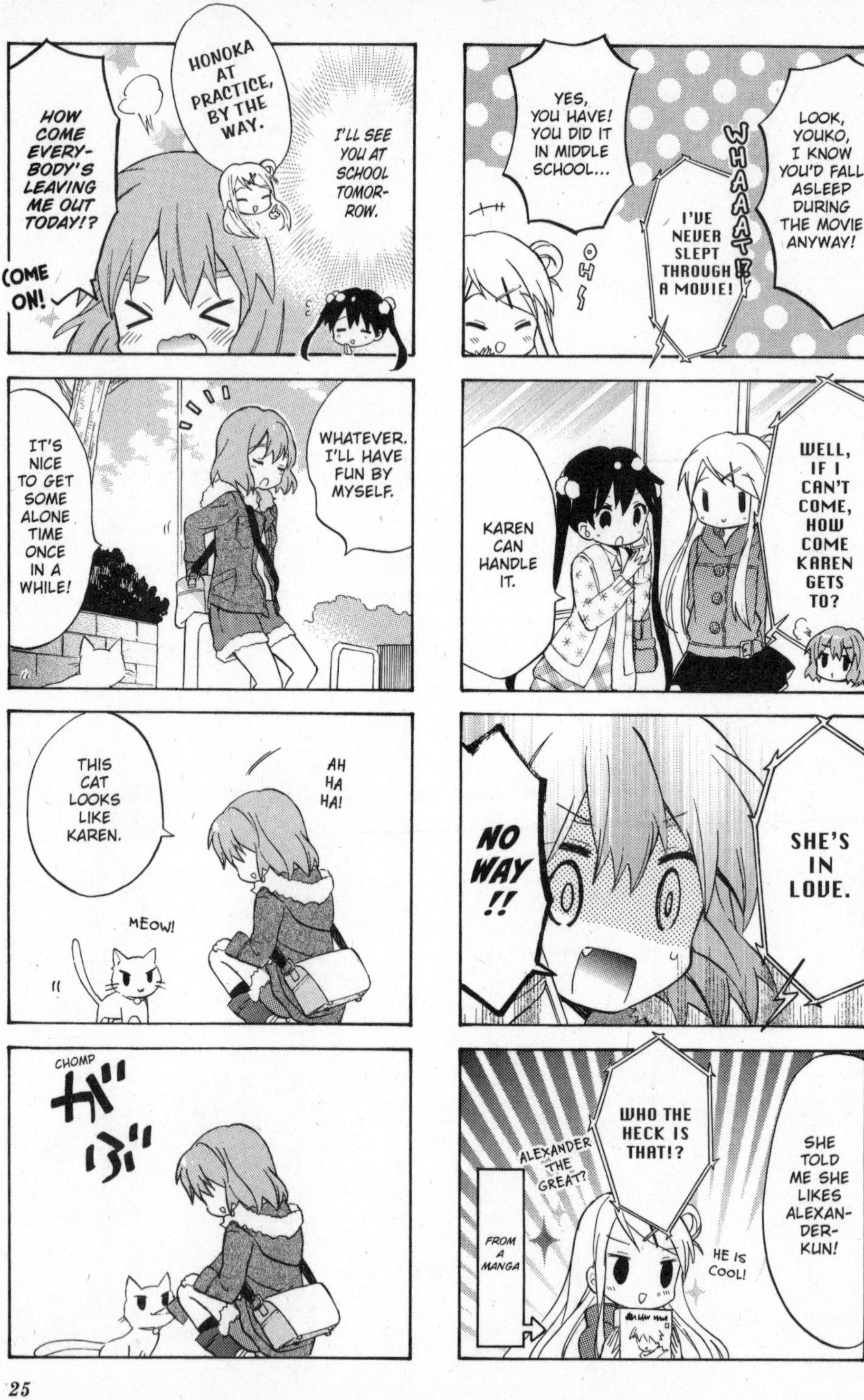

LOOK, YOUKO, I KNOW YOU'D FALL ASLEEP DURING THE MOVIE ANYWAY!
WHAAAAT!?
I'VE NEVER SLEPT THROUGH A MOVIE!
YES, YOU HAVE! YOU DID IT IN MIDDLE SCHOOL...
OH!
WELL, IF I CAN'T COME, HOW COME KAREN GETS TO?
KAREN CAN HANDLE IT.
SHE'S IN LOVE.
NO WAY!!
SHE TOLD ME SHE LIKES ALEXANDER-KUN!
HE IS COOL!
WHO THE HECK IS THAT!?
ALEXANDER THE GREAT?
FROM A MANGA
I'LL SEE YOU AT SCHOOL TOMORROW.
HONOKA AT PRACTICE, BY THE WAY.
HOW COME EVERYBODY'S LEAVING ME OUT TODAY!?
COME ON!
WHATEVER. I'LL HAVE FUN BY MYSELF.
IT'S NICE TO GET SOME ALONE TIME ONCE IN A WHILE!
AH HA HA!
THIS CAT LOOKS LIKE KAREN.
MEOW!
CHOMP

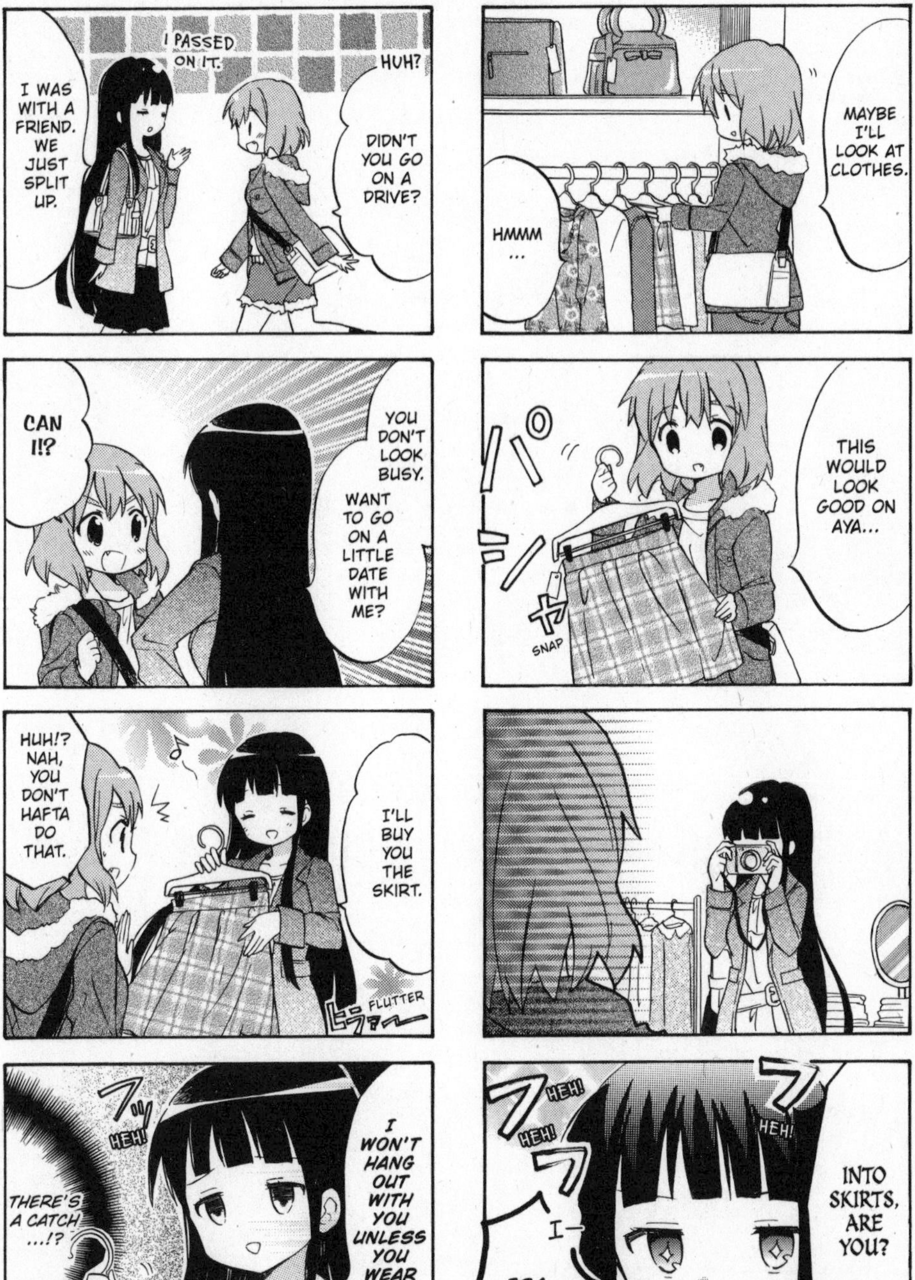
MAYBE I'LL LOOK AT CLOTHES.
HMMM ...
THIS WOULD LOOK GOOD ON AYA...
SNAP
INTO SKIRTS, ARE YOU?
HEH!
HEH!
HEH!
I—
ISA-NEE!?
HEH!
HUH? DIDN'T YOU GO ON A DRIVE?
I PASSED ON IT.
I WAS WITH A FRIEND. WE JUST SPLIT UP.
YOU DON'T LOOK BUSY. WANT TO GO ON A LITTLE DATE WITH ME?
CAN I!?
I'LL BUY YOU THE SKIRT.
HUH!? NAH, YOU DON'T HAFTA DO THAT.
FLUTTER
I WON'T HANG OUT WITH YOU UNLESS YOU WEAR THIS.
HEH!
THERE'S A CATCH ...!?

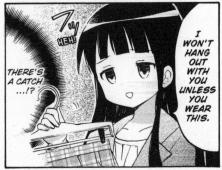

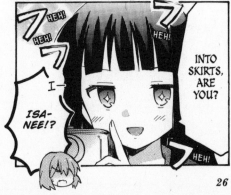

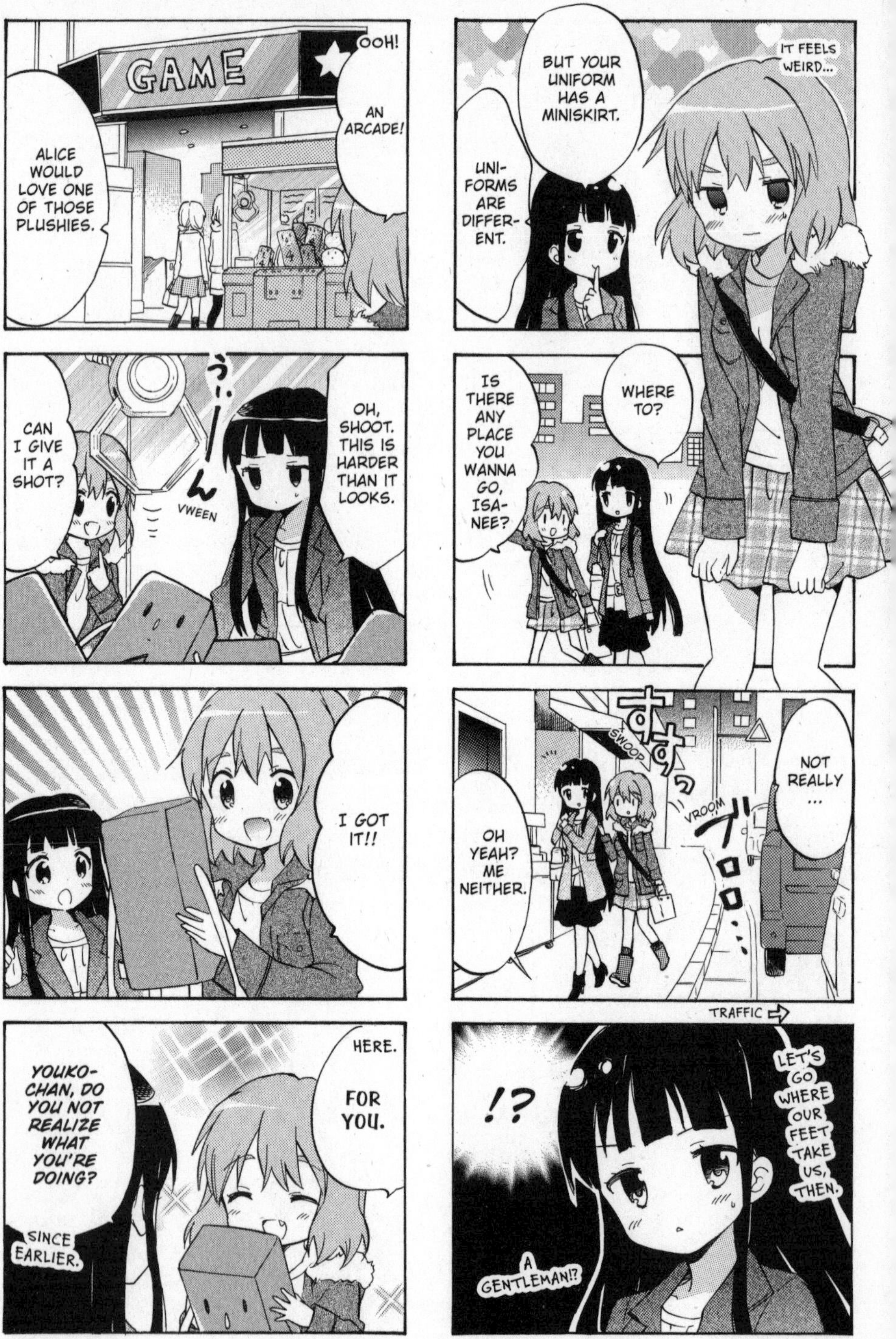
IT FEELS WEIRD...
BUT YOUR UNIFORM HAS A MINISKIRT.
UNI-FORMS ARE DIFFER-ENT.
WHERE TO?
IS THERE ANY PLACE YOU WANNA GO, ISA-NEE?
NOT REALLY ...
SWOOP
VROOM
OH YEAH? ME NEITHER.
TRAFFIC ⇨
LET'S GO WHERE OUR FEET TAKE US, THEN.
!?
A GENTLEMAN!?
OOH!
AN ARCADE!
GAME
ALICE WOULD LOVE ONE OF THOSE PLUSHIES.
OH, SHOOT. THIS IS HARDER THAN IT LOOKS.
VWEEN
CAN I GIVE IT A SHOT?
I GOT IT!!
HERE.
FOR YOU.
YOUKO-CHAN, DO YOU NOT REALIZE WHAT YOU'RE DOING?
SINCE EARLIER.

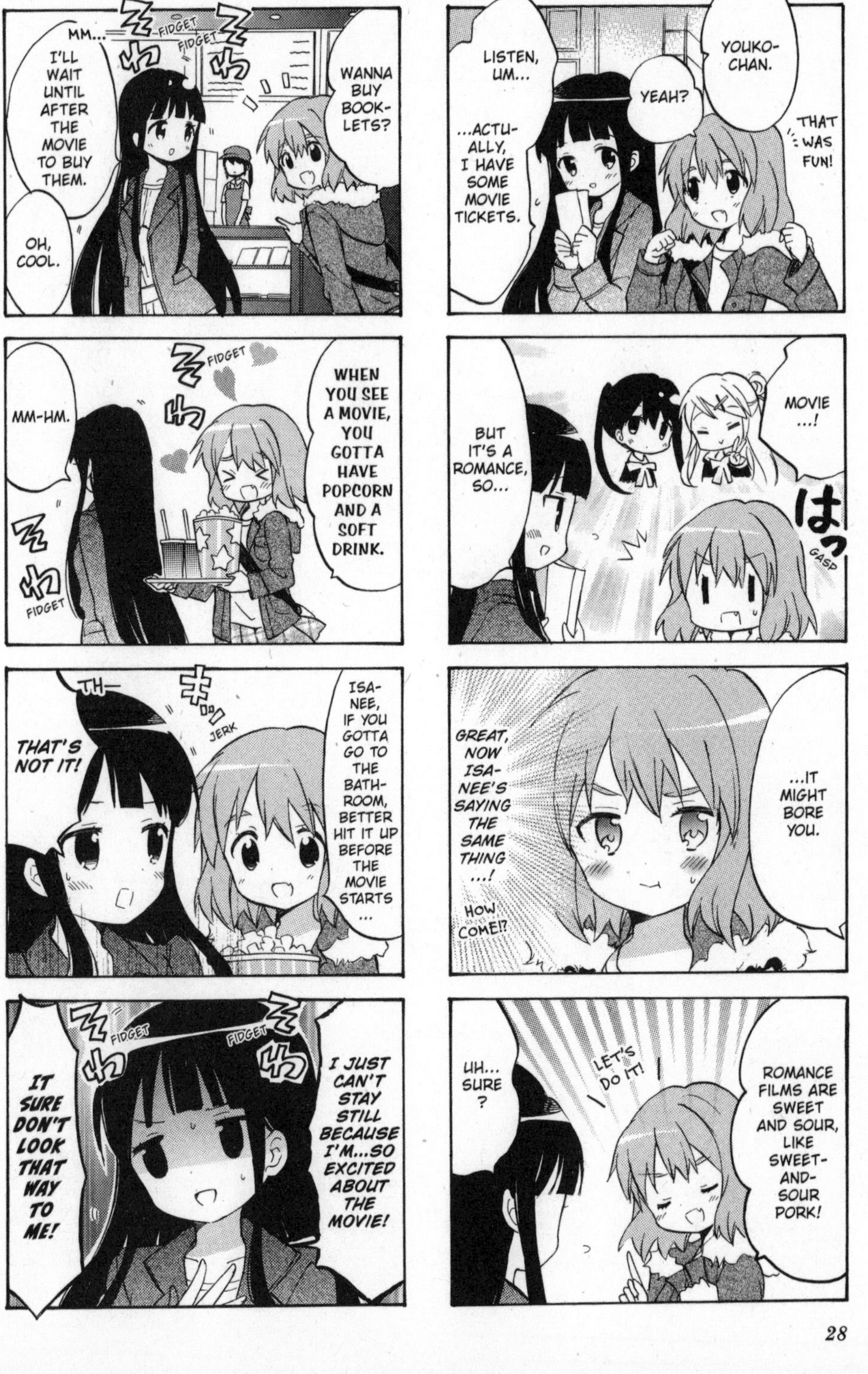
YOUKO-CHAN.
THAT WAS FUN!
YEAH?
LISTEN, UM...
...ACTUALLY, I HAVE SOME MOVIE TICKETS.
MOVIE ...!
はっ
GASP
BUT IT'S A ROMANCE, SO...
...IT MIGHT BORE YOU.
GREAT, NOW ISA-NEE'S SAYING THE SAME THING ...!
HOW COME!?
ROMANCE FILMS ARE SWEET AND SOUR, LIKE SWEET-AND-SOUR PORK!
LET'S DO IT!
UH... SURE ?
WANNA BUY BOOKLETS?
そわ
FIDGET
そわ
FIDGET
MM... I'LL WAIT UNTIL AFTER THE MOVIE TO BUY THEM.
OH, COOL.
WHEN YOU SEE A MOVIE, YOU GOTTA HAVE POPCORN AND A SOFT DRINK.
そわ
FIDGET
MM-HM.
そわ
FIDGET
ISA-NEE, IF YOU GOTTA GO TO THE BATHROOM, BETTER HIT IT UP BEFORE THE MOVIE STARTS ...
JERK
TH—
THAT'S NOT IT!
I JUST CAN'T STAY STILL BECAUSE I'M...SO EXCITED ABOUT THE MOVIE!
そわ
FIDGET
そわ
FIDGET
IT SURE DON'T LOOK THAT WAY TO ME!

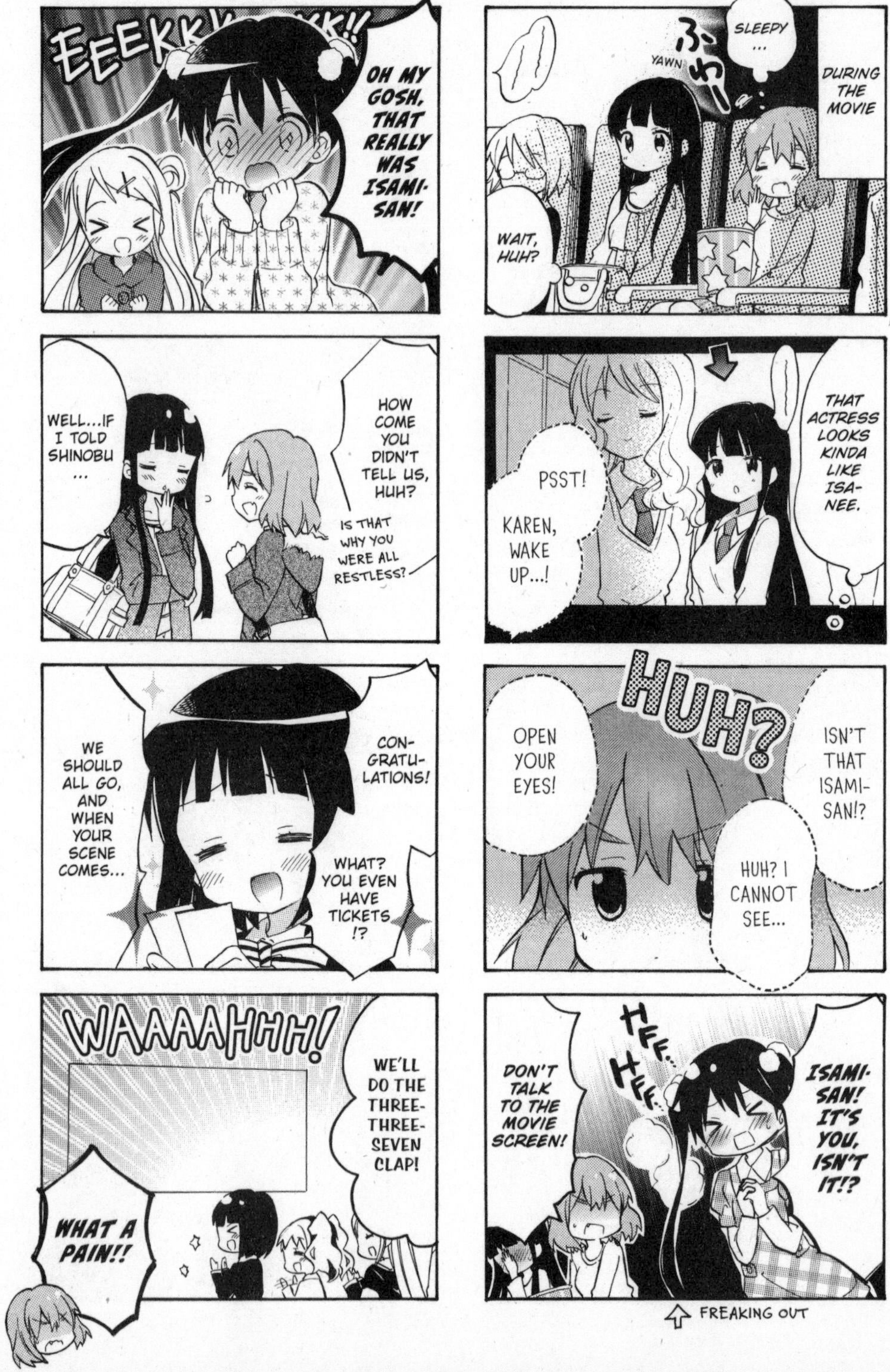
DURING THE MOVIE
SLEEPY ...
ふわ～
YAWN
WAIT, HUH?
THAT ACTRESS LOOKS KINDA LIKE ISA-NEE.
PSST!
KAREN, WAKE UP...!
HUH?
ISN'T THAT ISAMI-SAN!?
HUH? I CANNOT SEE...
OPEN YOUR EYES!
ISAMI-SAN! IT'S YOU, ISN'T IT!?
HFF... HFF...
DON'T TALK TO THE MOVIE SCREEN!
FREAKING OUT
EEEKK... KK!!
OH MY GOSH, THAT REALLY WAS ISAMI-SAN!
HOW COME YOU DIDN'T TELL US, HUH?
IS THAT WHY YOU WERE ALL RESTLESS?
WELL...IF I TOLD SHINOBU ...
CONGRATULATIONS!
WHAT? YOU EVEN HAVE TICKETS !?
WE SHOULD ALL GO, AND WHEN YOUR SCENE COMES...
WE'LL DO THE THREE-THREE-SEVEN CLAP!
WAAAAHHH!
WHAT A PAIN!!

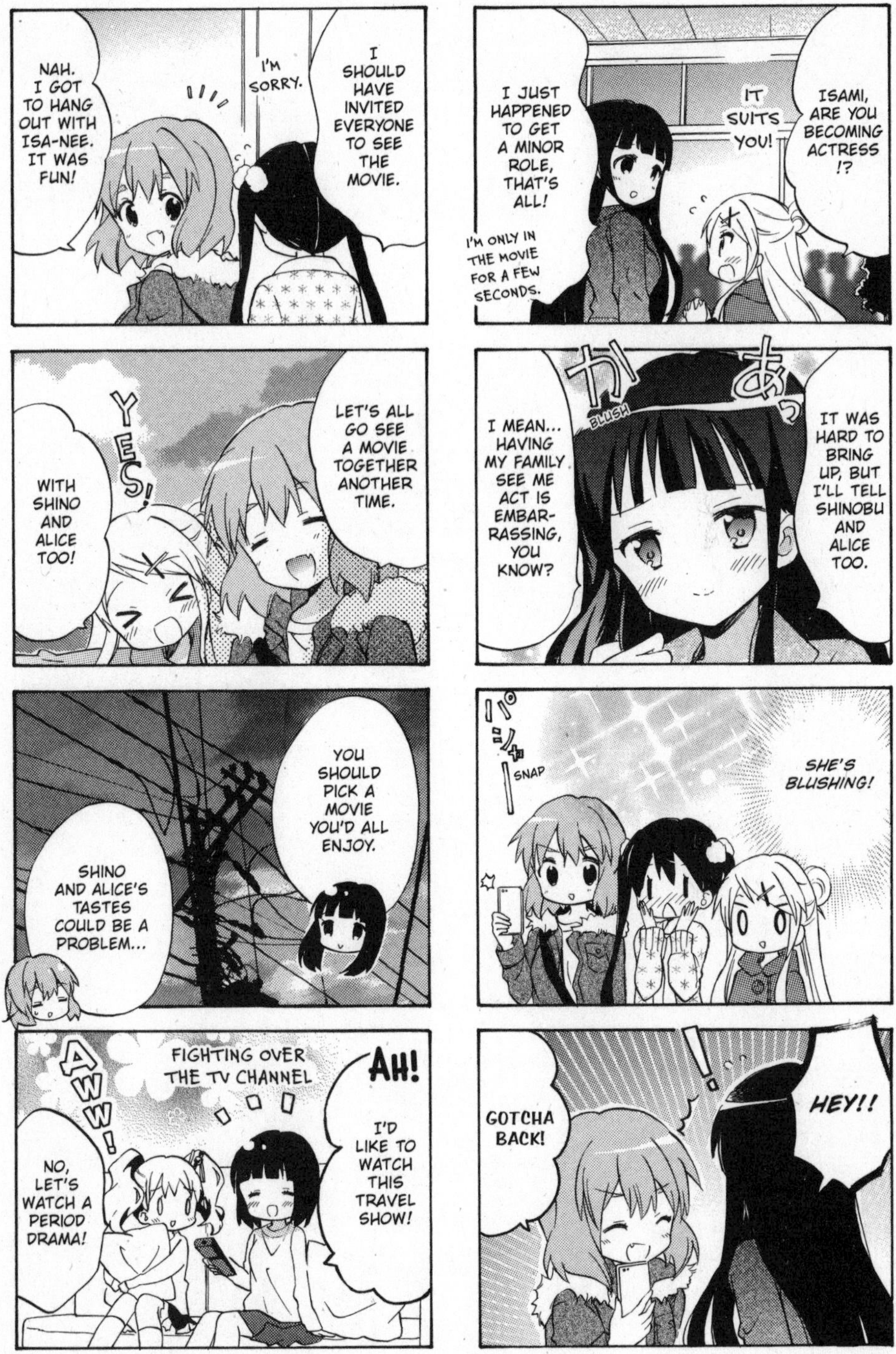
ISAMI, ARE YOU BECOMING ACTRESS !?
IT SUITS YOU!
I JUST HAPPENED TO GET A MINOR ROLE, THAT'S ALL!
I'M ONLY IN THE MOVIE FOR A FEW SECONDS.
IT WAS HARD TO BRING UP, BUT I'LL TELL SHINOBU AND ALICE TOO.
かあっ
BLUSH
I MEAN... HAVING MY FAMILY SEE ME ACT IS EMBARRASSING, YOU KNOW?
SHE'S BLUSHING!
パシャ
SNAP
HEY!!
!
GOTCHA BACK!
I SHOULD HAVE INVITED EVERYONE TO SEE THE MOVIE.
I'M SORRY.
NAH. I GOT TO HANG OUT WITH ISA-NEE. IT WAS FUN!
LET'S ALL GO SEE A MOVIE TOGETHER ANOTHER TIME.
YES!
WITH SHINO AND ALICE TOO!
YOU SHOULD PICK A MOVIE YOU'D ALL ENJOY.
SHINO AND ALICE'S TASTES COULD BE A PROBLEM...
AH!
I'D LIKE TO WATCH THIS TRAVEL SHOW!
FIGHTING OVER THE TV CHANNEL
AWW!
NO, LET'S WATCH A PERIOD DRAMA!

Q. WHAT MOVIE WOULD YOU LIKE TO SEE?

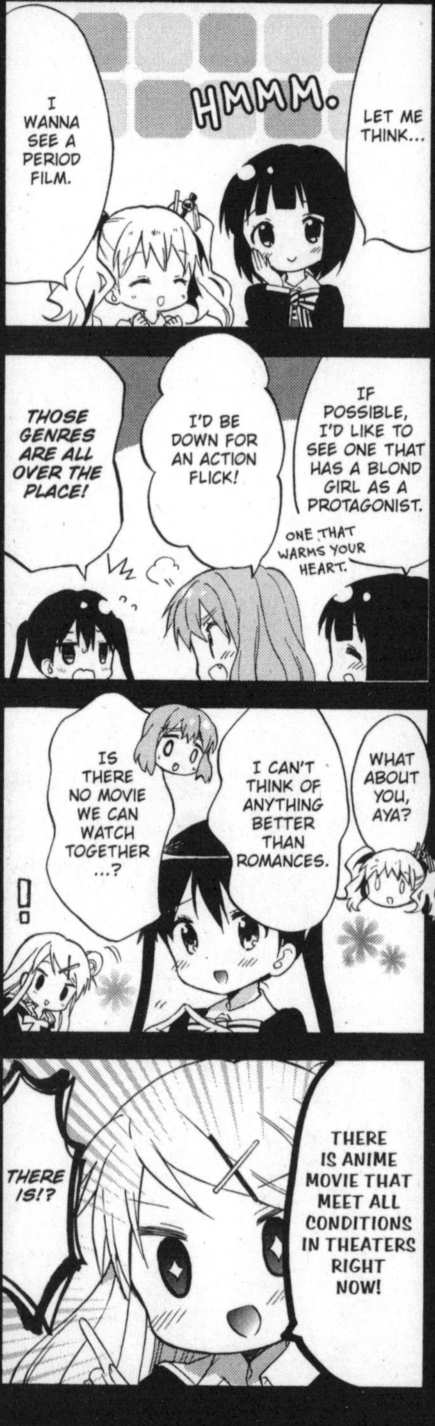

LET ME THINK...
HMMM.
I WANNA SEE A PERIOD FILM.
IF POSSIBLE, I'D LIKE TO SEE ONE THAT HAS A BLOND GIRL AS A PROTAGONIST.
ONE THAT WARMS YOUR HEART.
I'D BE DOWN FOR AN ACTION FLICK!
THOSE GENRES ARE ALL OVER THE PLACE!
WHAT ABOUT YOU, AYA?
I CAN'T THINK OF ANYTHING BETTER THAN ROMANCES.
IS THERE NO MOVIE WE CAN WATCH TOGETHER ...?
!
THERE IS ANIME MOVIE THAT MEET ALL CONDITIONS IN THEATERS RIGHT NOW!
THERE IS!?

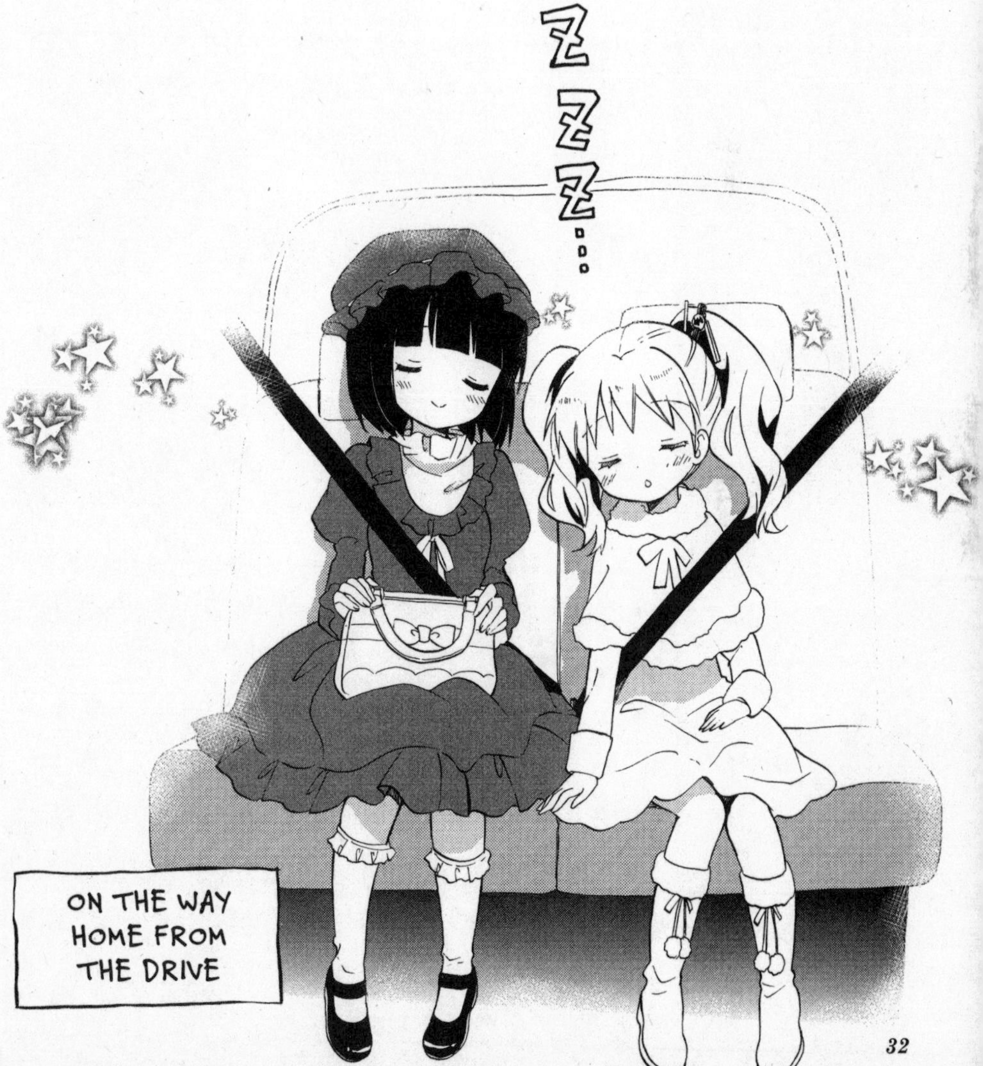
Z Z Z...
ON THE WAY HOME FROM THE DRIVE

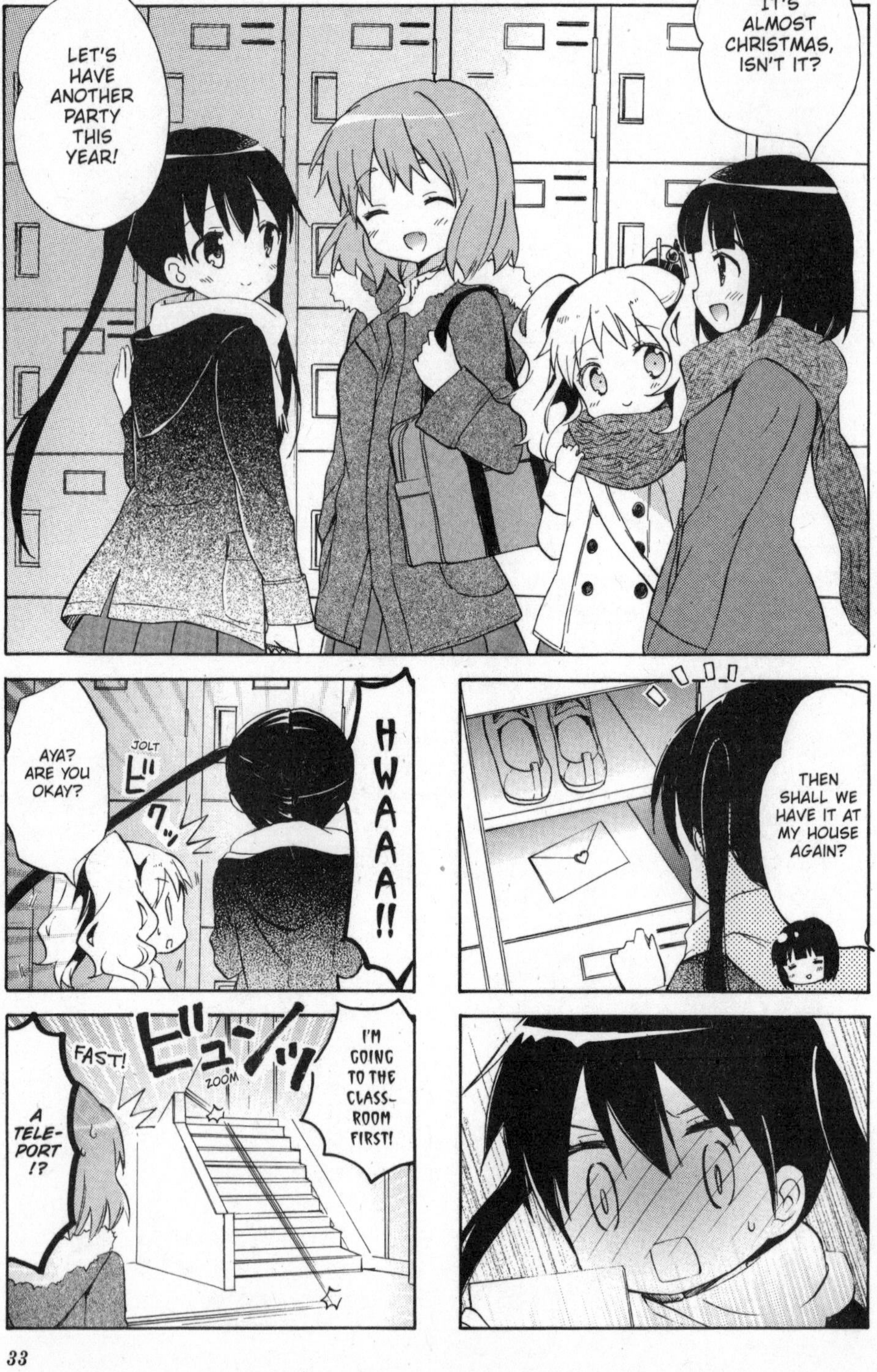
IT'S ALMOST CHRISTMAS, ISN'T IT?
LET'S HAVE ANOTHER PARTY THIS YEAR!
THEN SHALL WE HAVE IT AT MY HOUSE AGAIN?
HWAAAA!!
JOLT
ビクッ
AYA? ARE YOU OKAY?
I'M GOING TO THE CLASS-ROOM FIRST!
ビューンッ
ZOOM
FAST!
A TELE-PORT!?

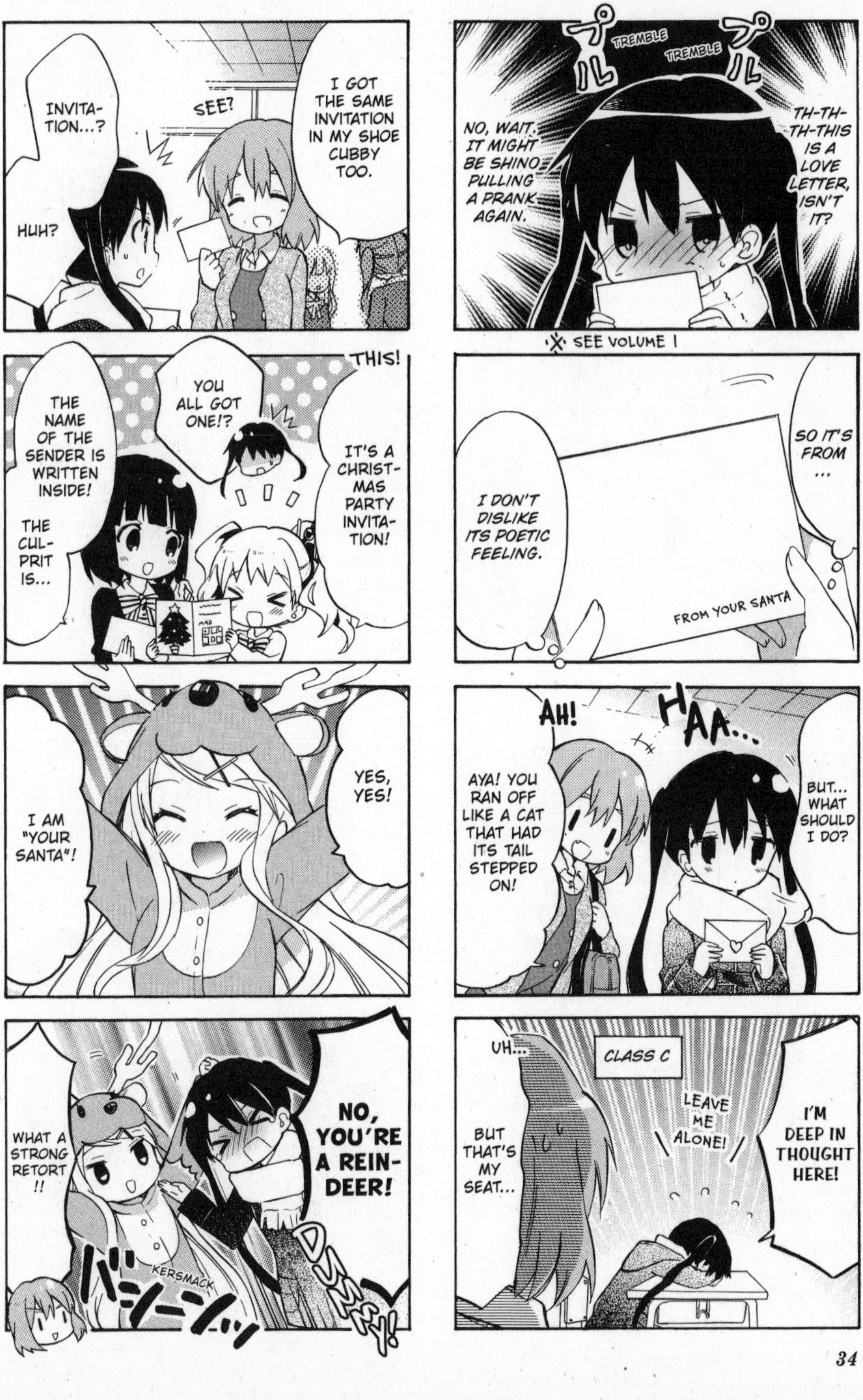
TREMBLE
TREMBLE
TH-TH-TH-THIS IS A LOVE LETTER, ISN'T IT?
NO, WAIT. IT MIGHT BE SHINO※ PULLING A PRANK AGAIN.
※ SEE VOLUME 1
SO IT'S FROM ...
I DON'T DISLIKE ITS POETIC FEELING.
FROM YOUR SANTA
HAA...
BUT... WHAT SHOULD I DO?
AH!
AYA! YOU RAN OFF LIKE A CAT THAT HAD ITS TAIL STEPPED ON!
CLASS C
I'M DEEP IN THOUGHT HERE!
LEAVE ME ALONE!
UH...
BUT THAT'S MY SEAT...
I GOT THE SAME INVITATION IN MY SHOE CUBBY TOO.
SEE?
INVITATION...?
HUH?
THIS!
IT'S A CHRISTMAS PARTY INVITATION!
YOU ALL GOT ONE!?
THE NAME OF THE SENDER IS WRITTEN INSIDE!
THE CULPRIT IS...
YES, YES!
I AM "YOUR SANTA"!
NO, YOU'RE A REINDEER!
DUMMY!
KERSMACK
WHAT A STRONG RETORT!!

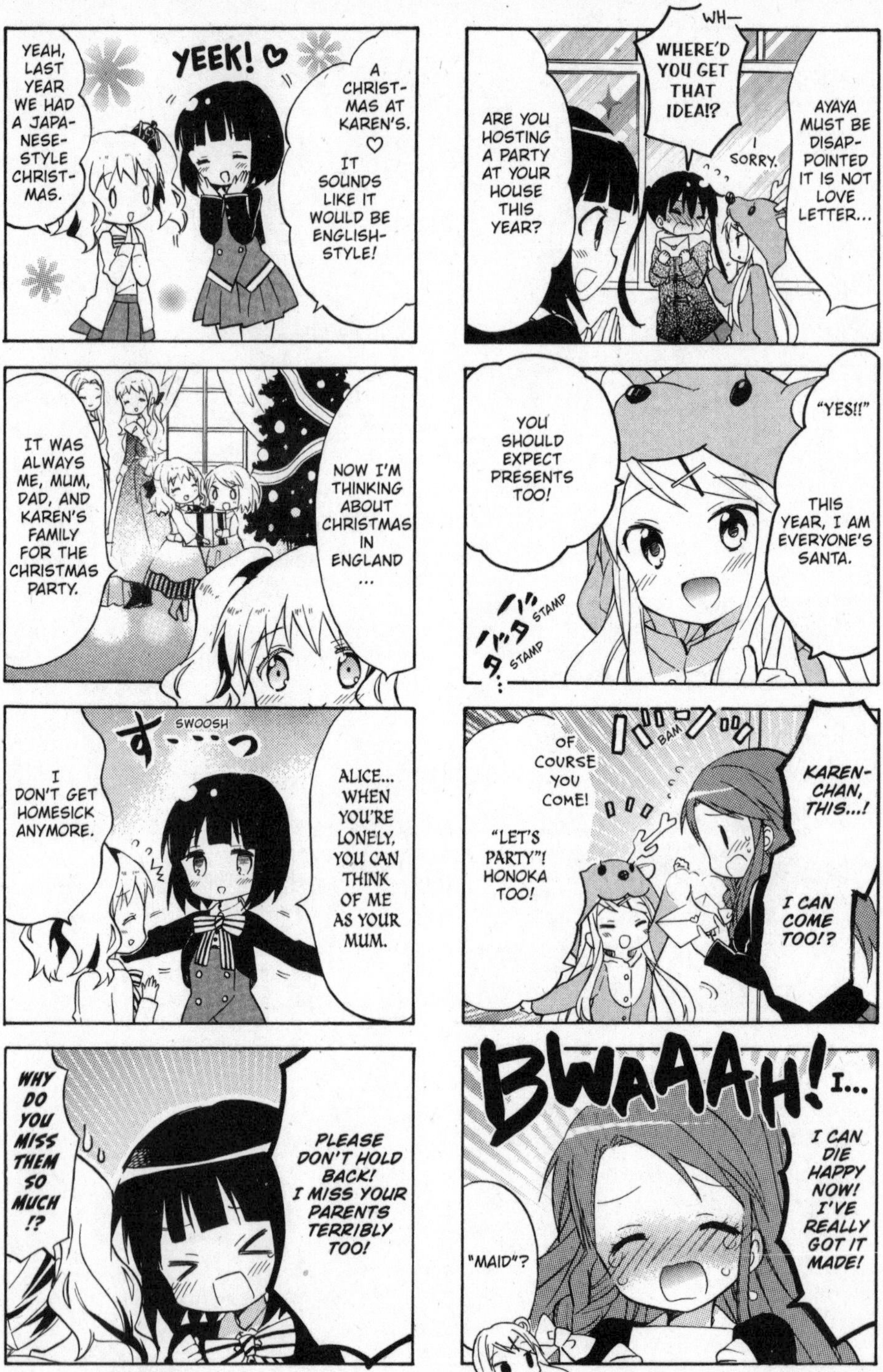
AYAYA MUST BE DISAPPOINTED IT IS NOT LOVE LETTER...
WH—
WHERE'D YOU GET THAT IDEA!?
I SORRY.
ARE YOU HOSTING A PARTY AT YOUR HOUSE THIS YEAR?
"YES!!"
THIS YEAR, I AM EVERYONE'S SANTA.
YOU SHOULD EXPECT PRESENTS TOO!
STAMP
STAMP
KAREN-CHAN, THIS...!
I CAN COME TOO!?
BAM
OF COURSE YOU COME!
"LET'S PARTY"! HONOKA TOO!
BWAAAH!
I...
I CAN DIE HAPPY NOW! I'VE REALLY GOT IT MADE!
"MAID"?
A CHRIST-MAS AT KAREN'S. ♡
IT SOUNDS LIKE IT WOULD BE ENGLISH-STYLE!
YEEK! ♡
YEAH, LAST YEAR WE HAD A JAPA-NESE-STYLE CHRIST-MAS.
NOW I'M THINKING ABOUT CHRISTMAS IN ENGLAND ...
IT WAS ALWAYS ME, MUM, DAD, AND KAREN'S FAMILY FOR THE CHRISTMAS PARTY.
SWOOSH
ALICE... WHEN YOU'RE LONELY, YOU CAN THINK OF ME AS YOUR MUM.
I DON'T GET HOMESICK ANYMORE.
PLEASE DON'T HOLD BACK! I MISS YOUR PARENTS TERRIBLY TOO!
WHY DO YOU MISS THEM SO MUCH!?

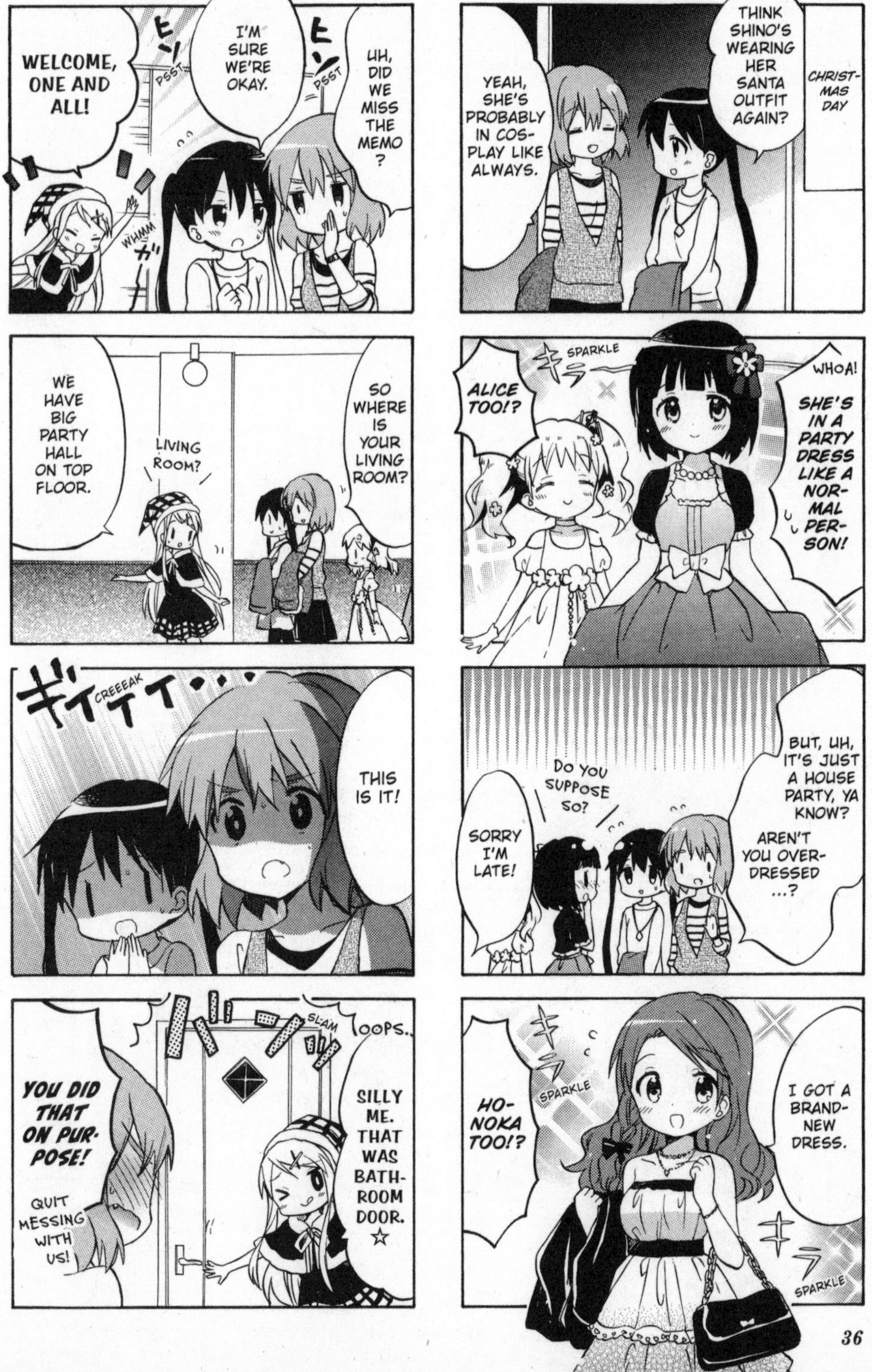
CHRIST-MAS DAY
THINK SHINO'S WEARING HER SANTA OUTFIT AGAIN?
YEAH, SHE'S PROBABLY IN COS-PLAY LIKE ALWAYS.
WHOA!
SHE'S IN A PARTY DRESS LIKE A NOR-MAL PER-SON!
SPARKLE
ALICE TOO!?
BUT, UH, IT'S JUST A HOUSE PARTY, YA KNOW?
AREN'T YOU OVER-DRESSED ...?
DO YOU SUPPOSE SO?
SORRY I'M LATE!
I GOT A BRAND-NEW DRESS.
SPARKLE
SPARKLE
HO-NOKA TOO!?
UH, DID WE MISS THE MEMO?
PSST
I'M SURE WE'RE OKAY.
PSST
WELCOME, ONE AND ALL!
WHMM
SO WHERE IS YOUR LIVING ROOM?
LIVING ROOM?
WE HAVE BIG PARTY HALL ON TOP FLOOR.
CREEEAK
THIS IS IT!
SLAM
OOPS..
SILLY ME. THAT WAS BATH-ROOM DOOR. ☆
YOU DID THAT ON PUR-POSE!
QUIT MESSING WITH US!

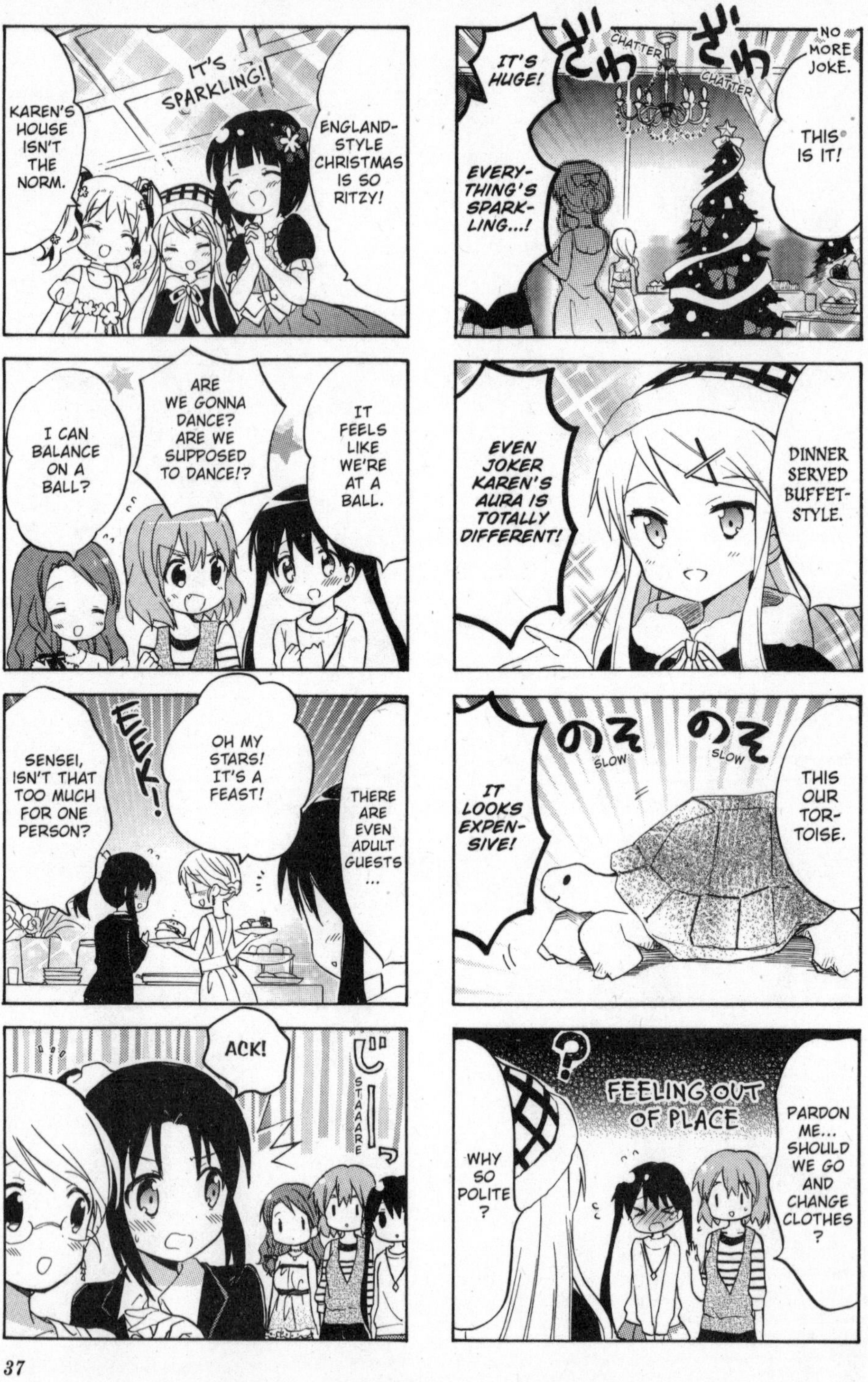
NO MORE JOKE.
THIS IS IT!
ざわ CHATTER
ざわ CHATTER
IT'S HUGE!
EVERYTHING'S SPARKLING...!
DINNER SERVED BUFFET-STYLE.
EVEN JOKER KAREN'S AURA IS TOTALLY DIFFERENT!
のそ SLOW
のそ SLOW
THIS OUR TORTOISE.
IT LOOKS EXPENSIVE!
PARDON ME... SHOULD WE GO AND CHANGE CLOTHES?
FEELING OUT OF PLACE
?
WHY SO POLITE?
ENGLAND-STYLE CHRISTMAS IS SO RITZY!
IT'S SPARKLING!
KAREN'S HOUSE ISN'T THE NORM.
IT FEELS LIKE WE'RE AT A BALL.
ARE WE GONNA DANCE? ARE WE SUPPOSED TO DANCE!?
I CAN BALANCE ON A BALL?
THERE ARE EVEN ADULT GUESTS...
OH MY STARS! IT'S A FEAST!
EEK!
SENSEI, ISN'T THAT TOO MUCH FOR ONE PERSON?
じーっ STAAARE
ACK!

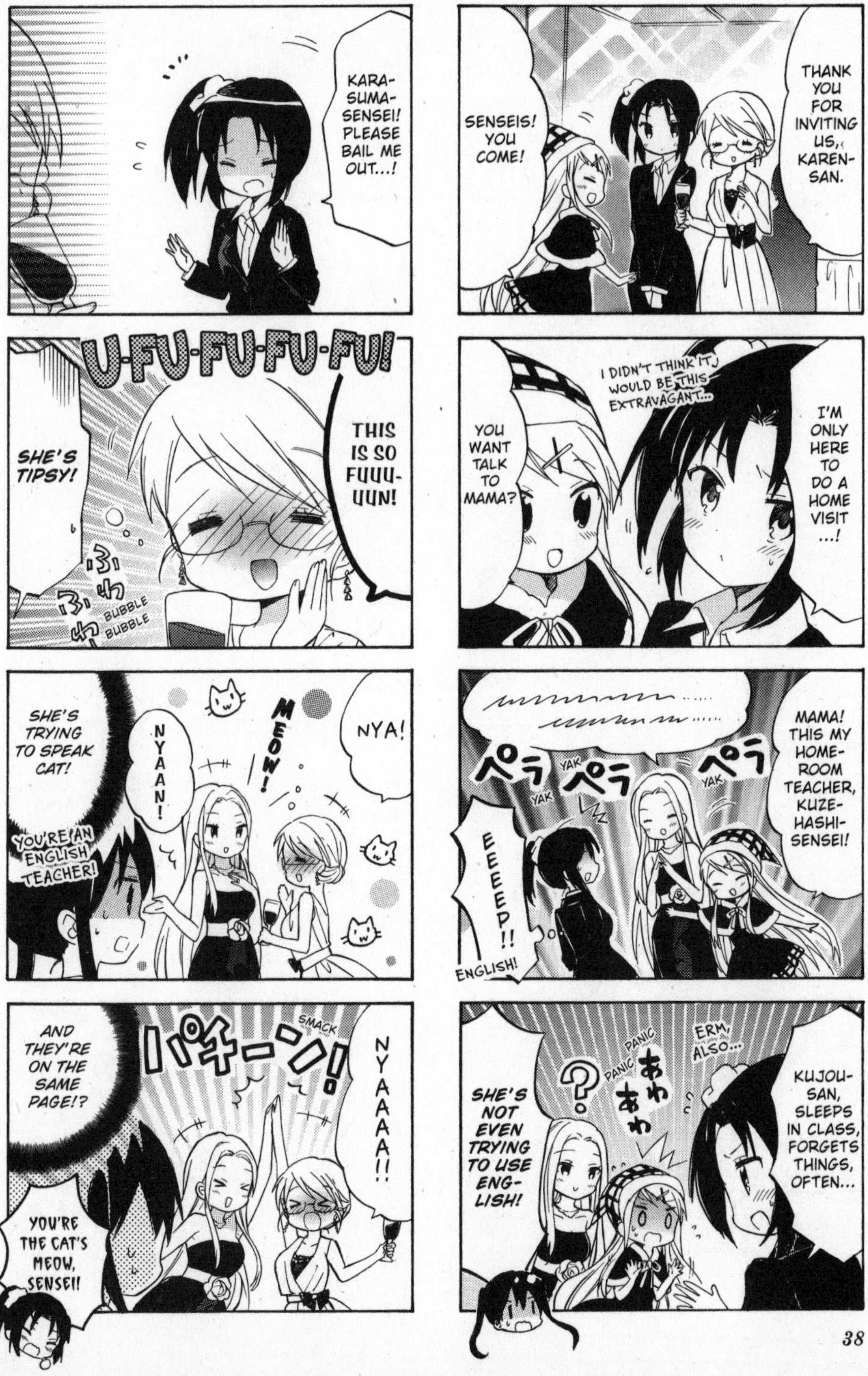
THANK YOU FOR INVITING US, KAREN-SAN.
SENSEIS! YOU COME!
KARA-SUMA-SENSEI! PLEASE BAIL ME OUT...!
I'M ONLY HERE TO DO A HOME VISIT ...!
I DIDN'T THINK IT WOULD BE THIS EXTRAVAGANT...
YOU WANT TALK TO MAMA?
THIS IS SO FUUUU-UUN!
U-FU-FU-FU-FU!
SHE'S TIPSY!
ふわ ふわ
BUBBLE BUBBLE
MAMA! THIS MY HOME-ROOM TEACHER, KUZE-HASHI-SENSEI!
ペラ YAK ペラ YAK ペラ YAK
EEEEEP!!
ENGLISH!
NYA!
MEOW!
NYAAN!
SHE'S TRYING TO SPEAK CAT!
YOU'RE AN ENGLISH TEACHER!
KUJOU-SAN, SLEEPS IN CLASS, FORGETS THINGS, OFTEN...
ERM, ALSO...
PANIC PANIC
あわ あわ
SHE'S NOT EVEN TRYING TO USE ENGLISH!
NYAAAAA!!
SMACK
パチーン!
AND THEY'RE ON THE SAME PAGE!?
YOU'RE THE CAT'S MEOW, SENSEI!

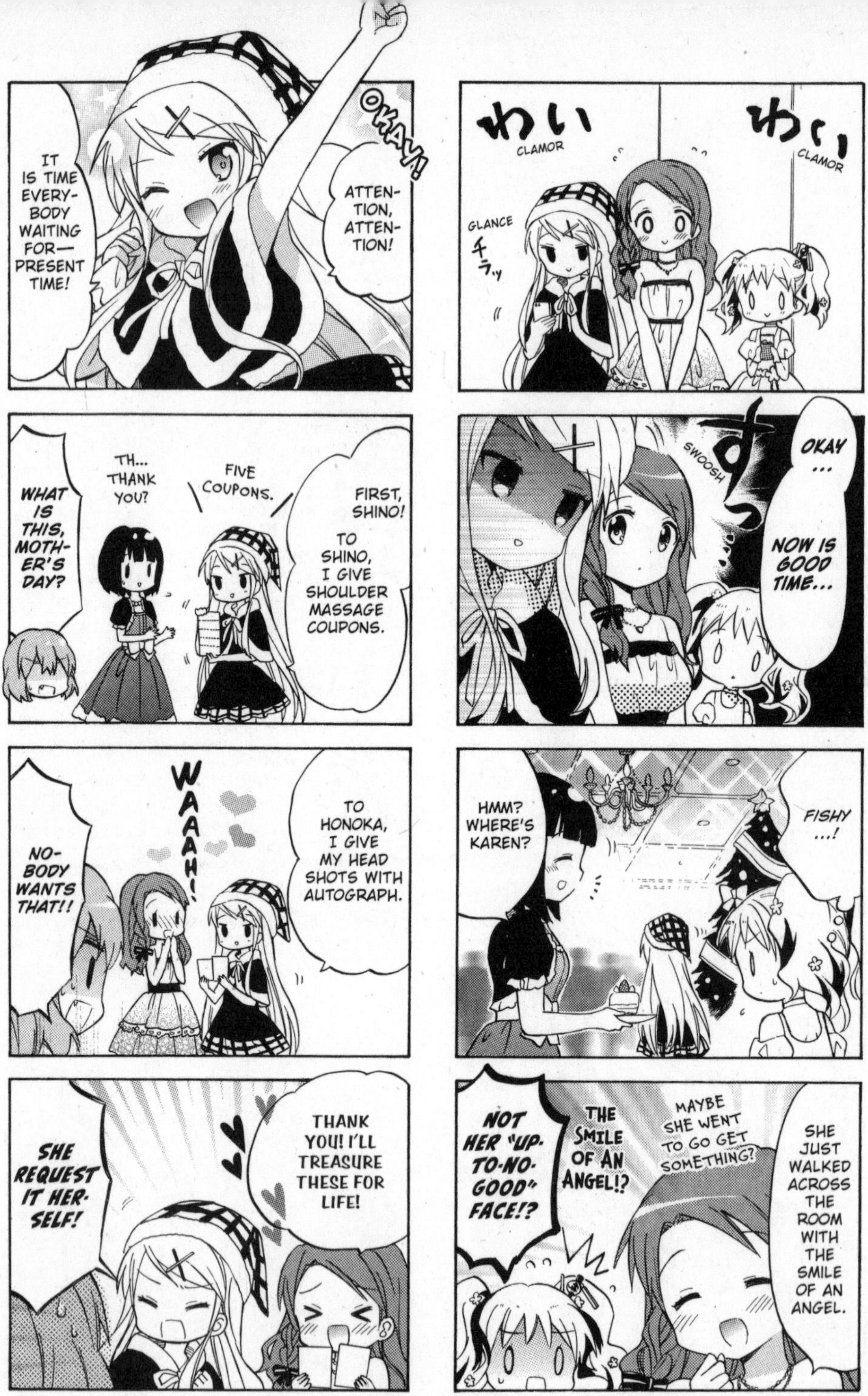
わい
CLAMOR
わい
CLAMOR
GLANCE
チラッ
すっ
SWOOSH
OKAY... NOW IS GOOD TIME...
HMM? WHERE'S KAREN?
FISHY ...!
SHE JUST WALKED ACROSS THE ROOM WITH THE SMILE OF AN ANGEL.
MAYBE SHE WENT TO GO GET SOMETHING?
THE SMILE OF AN ANGEL!?
NOT HER "UP-TO-NO-GOOD" FACE!?
ATTENTION, ATTENTION!
OKAY!
IT IS TIME EVERYBODY WAITING FOR—PRESENT TIME!
FIRST, SHINO!
TO SHINO, I GIVE SHOULDER MASSAGE COUPONS.
FIVE COUPONS.
TH... THANK YOU?
WHAT IS THIS, MOTHER'S DAY?
TO HONOKA, I GIVE MY HEAD SHOTS WITH AUTOGRAPH.
WAAAH!
NOBODY WANTS THAT!!
THANK YOU! I'LL TREASURE THESE FOR LIFE!
SHE REQUEST IT HERSELF!

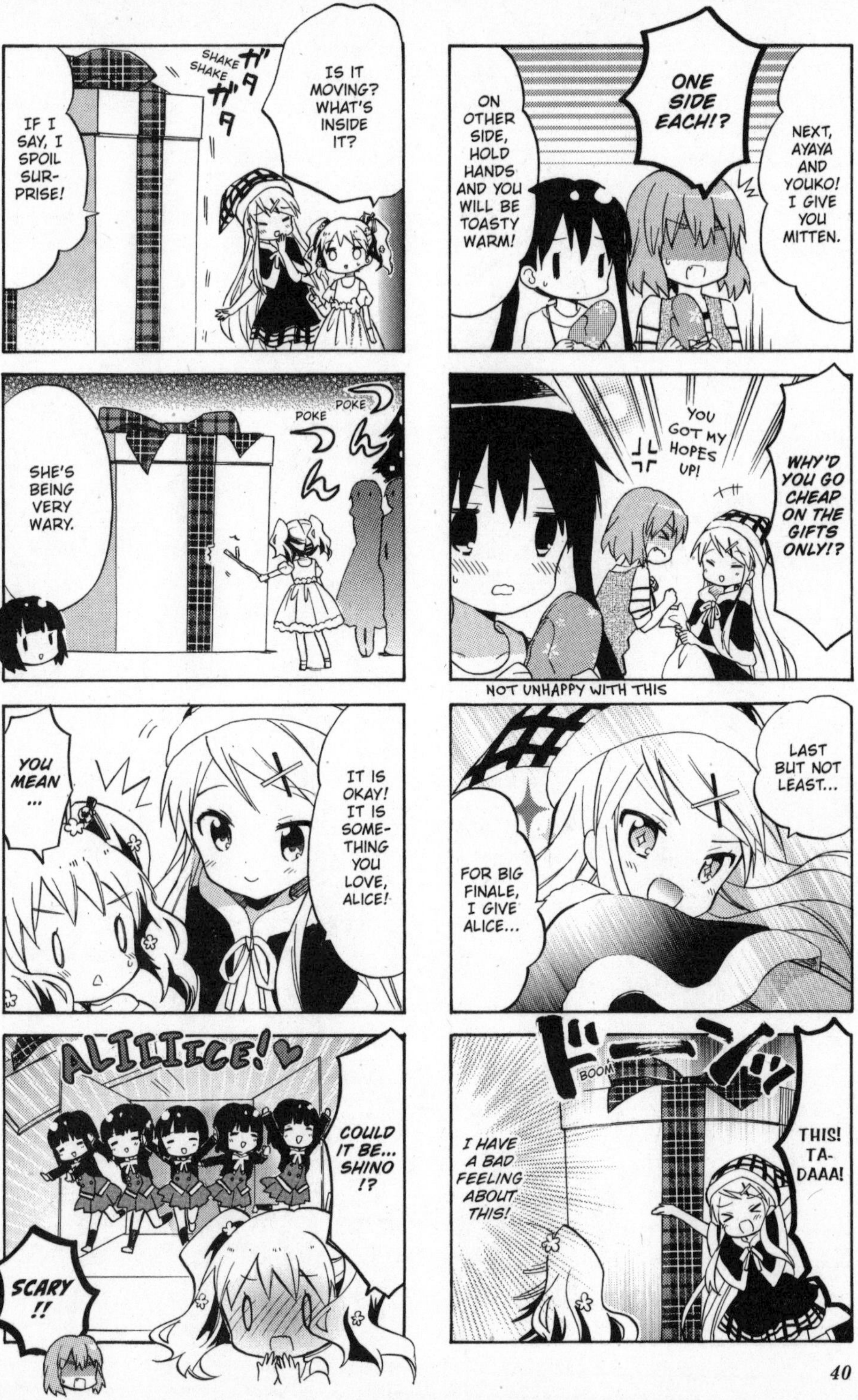
NEXT, AYAYA AND YOUKO! I GIVE YOU MITTEN.
ONE SIDE EACH!?
ON OTHER SIDE, HOLD HANDS AND YOU WILL BE TOASTY WARM!
WHY'D YOU GO CHEAP ON THE GIFTS ONLY!?
YOU GOT MY HOPES UP!
NOT UNHAPPY WITH THIS
LAST BUT NOT LEAST...
FOR BIG FINALE, I GIVE ALICE...
BOOM
THIS! TA-DAAA!
I HAVE A BAD FEELING ABOUT THIS!
IS IT MOVING? WHAT'S INSIDE IT?
SHAKE SHAKE
IF I SAY, I SPOIL SUR-PRISE!
POKE POKE
SHE'S BEING VERY WARY.
IT IS OKAY! IT IS SOME-THING YOU LOVE, ALICE!
YOU MEAN...
ALIIIICE!♥
COULD IT BE... SHINO!?
SCARY!!

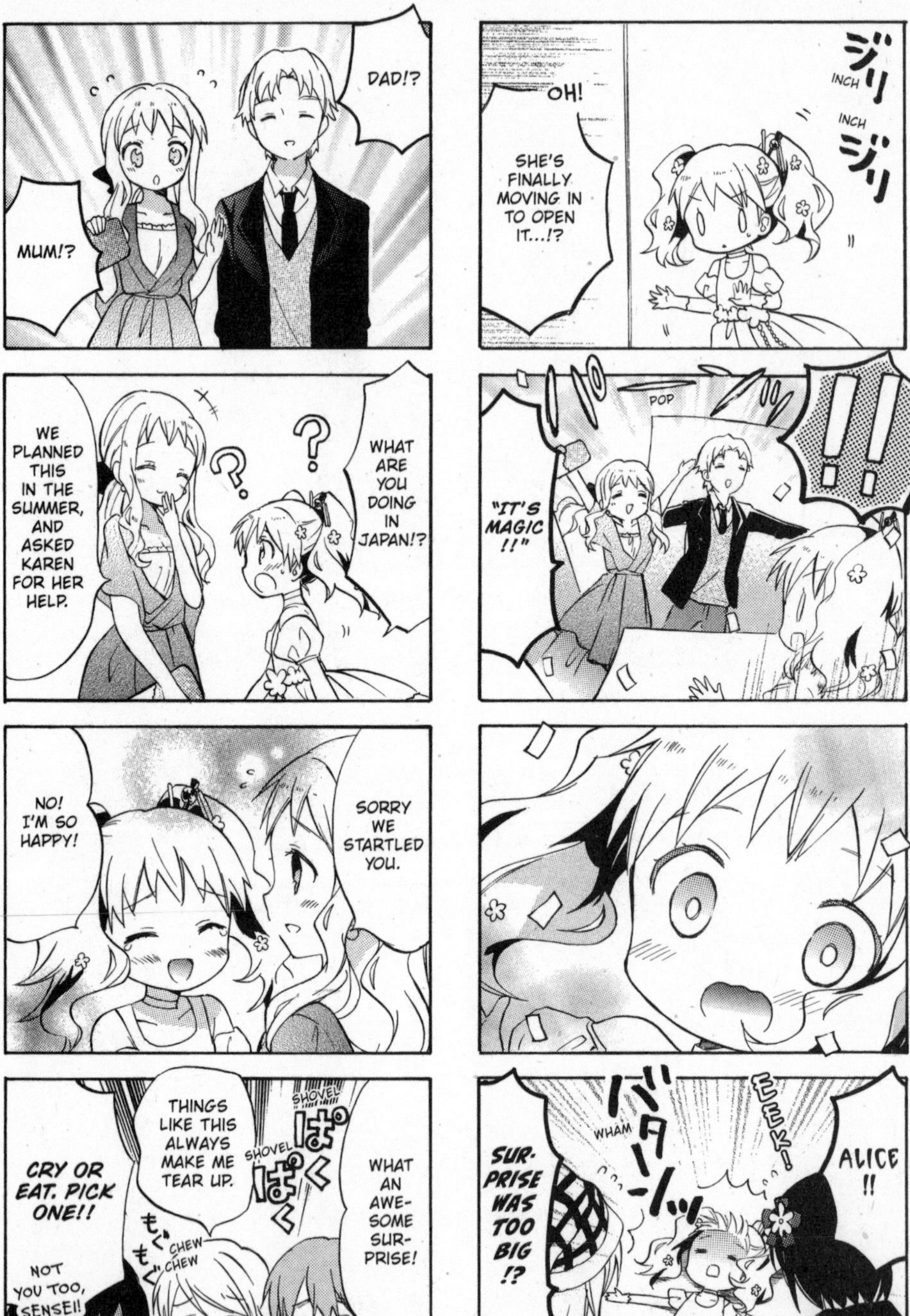
ジリ INCH ジリ INCH
OH!
SHE'S FINALLY MOVING IN TO OPEN IT...!?
!!
パッ POP
"IT'S MAGIC!!"
ALICE!!
バターンッ WHAM
SUR-PRISE WAS TOO BIG!?
DAD!?
MUM!?
WHAT ARE YOU DOING IN JAPAN!?
WE PLANNED THIS IN THE SUMMER, AND ASKED KAREN FOR HER HELP.
SORRY WE STARTLED YOU.
NO! I'M SO HAPPY!
WHAT AN AWE-SOME SUR-PRISE!
ぱくぱく SHOVEL SHOVEL
THINGS LIKE THIS ALWAYS MAKE ME TEAR UP.
もぐもぐ CHEW CHEW
CRY OR EAT. PICK ONE!!
NOT YOU TOO, SENSEI!!

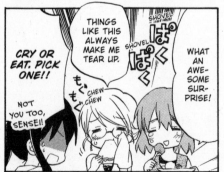

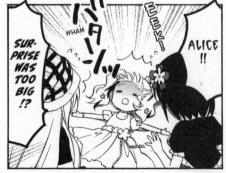

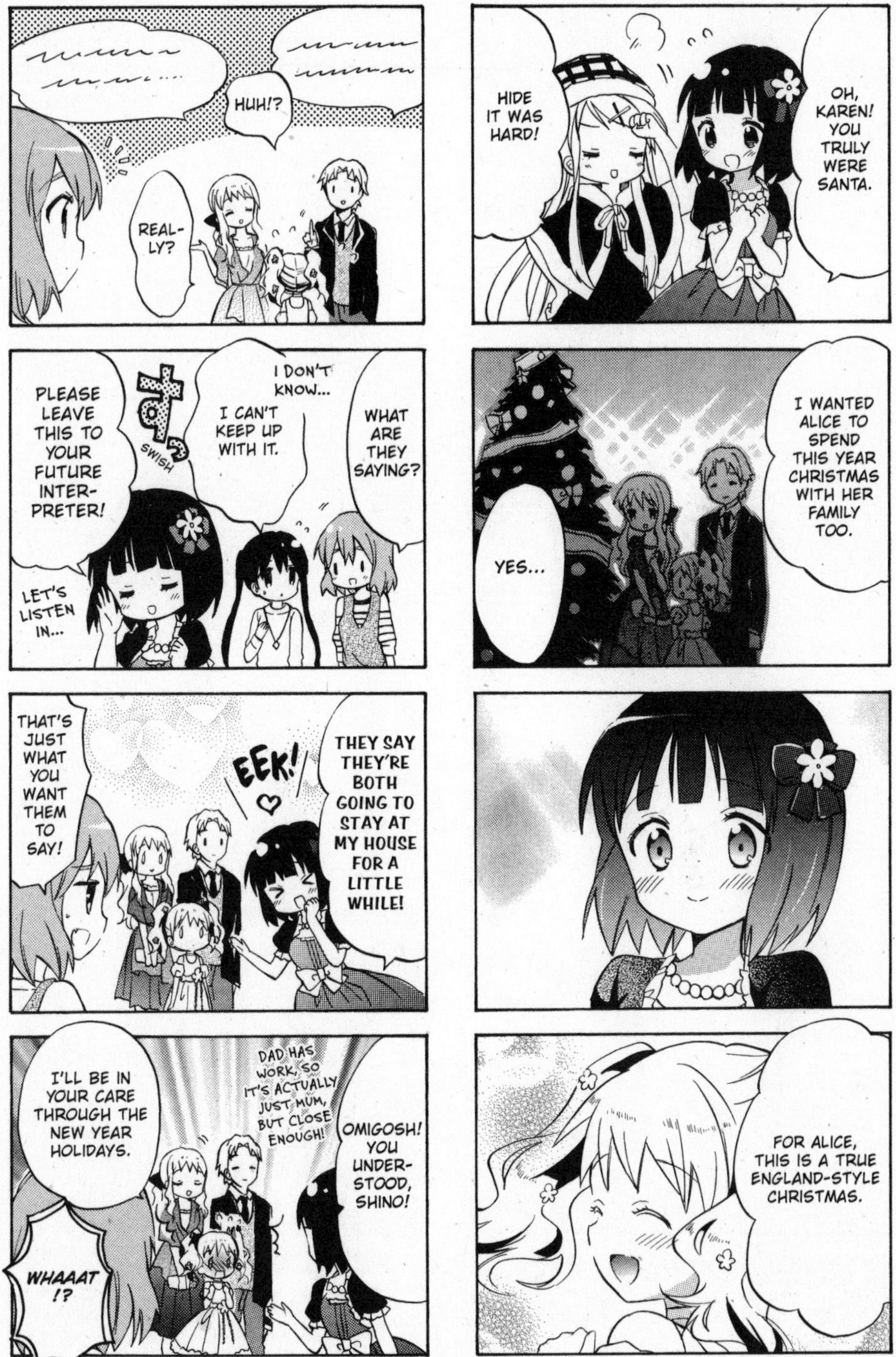
OH, KAREN! YOU TRULY WERE SANTA.
HIDE IT WAS HARD!
HUH!?
REALLY?
I WANTED ALICE TO SPEND THIS YEAR CHRISTMAS WITH HER FAMILY TOO.
YES...
WHAT ARE THEY SAYING?
I DON'T KNOW...
I CAN'T KEEP UP WITH IT.
す
SWISH
PLEASE LEAVE THIS TO YOUR FUTURE INTERPRETER!
LET'S LISTEN IN...
THEY SAY THEY'RE BOTH GOING TO STAY AT MY HOUSE FOR A LITTLE WHILE!
EEK!
THAT'S JUST WHAT YOU WANT THEM TO SAY!
FOR ALICE, THIS IS A TRUE ENGLAND-STYLE CHRISTMAS.
OMIGOSH! YOU UNDERSTOOD, SHINO!
DAD HAS WORK, SO IT'S ACTUALLY JUST MUM, BUT CLOSE ENOUGH!
I'LL BE IN YOUR CARE THROUGH THE NEW YEAR HOLIDAYS.
WHAAAT !?

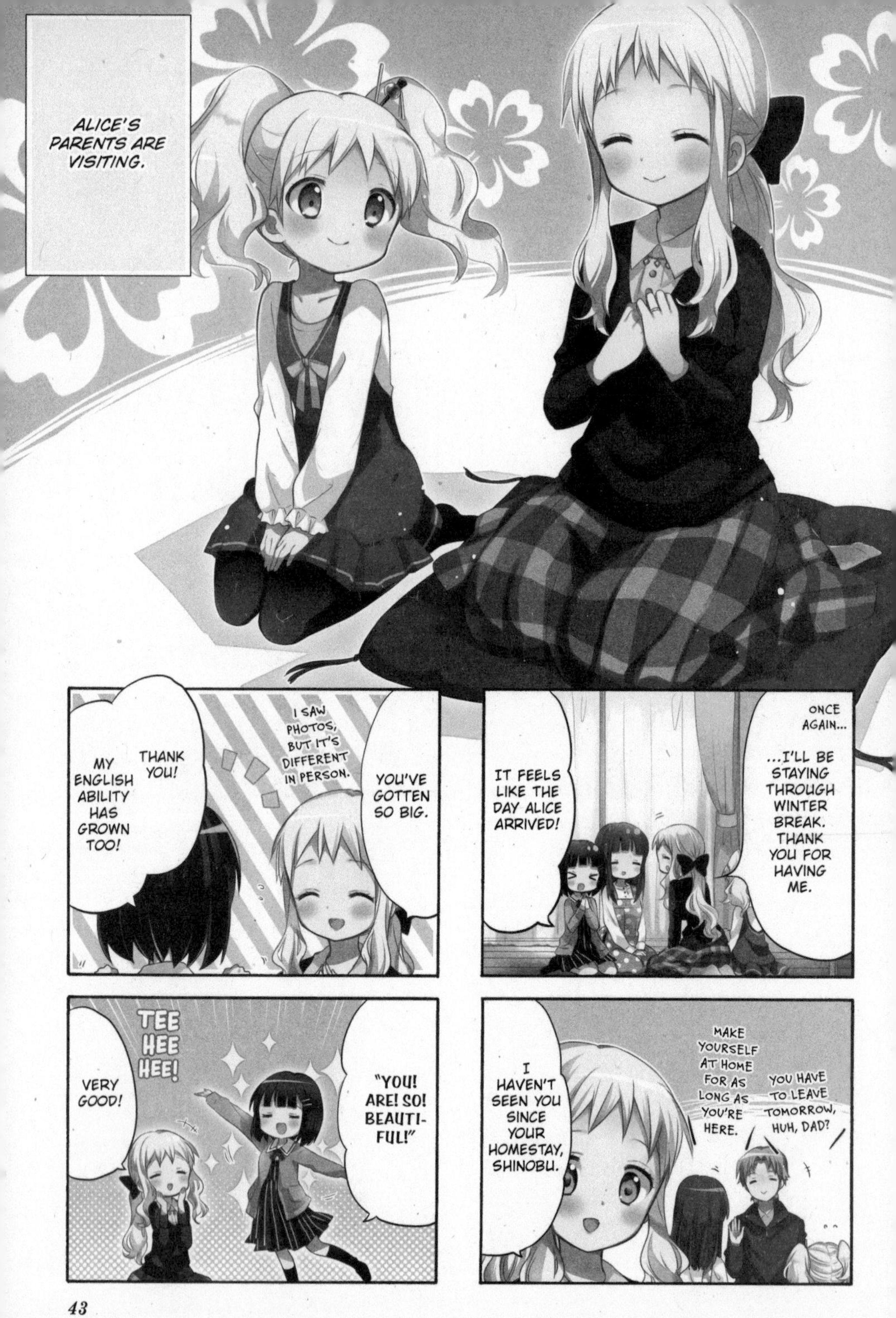
ALICE'S PARENTS ARE VISITING.
ONCE AGAIN...
...I'LL BE STAYING THROUGH WINTER BREAK. THANK YOU FOR HAVING ME.
IT FEELS LIKE THE DAY ALICE ARRIVED!
YOU'VE GOTTEN SO BIG.
I SAW PHOTOS, BUT IT'S DIFFERENT IN PERSON.
THANK YOU!
MY ENGLISH ABILITY HAS GROWN TOO!
MAKE YOURSELF AT HOME FOR AS LONG AS YOU'RE HERE.
YOU HAVE TO LEAVE TOMORROW, HUH, DAD?
I HAVEN'T SEEN YOU SINCE YOUR HOMESTAY, SHINOBU.
"YOU! ARE! SO! BEAUTI-FUL!"
TEE HEE HEE!
VERY GOOD!

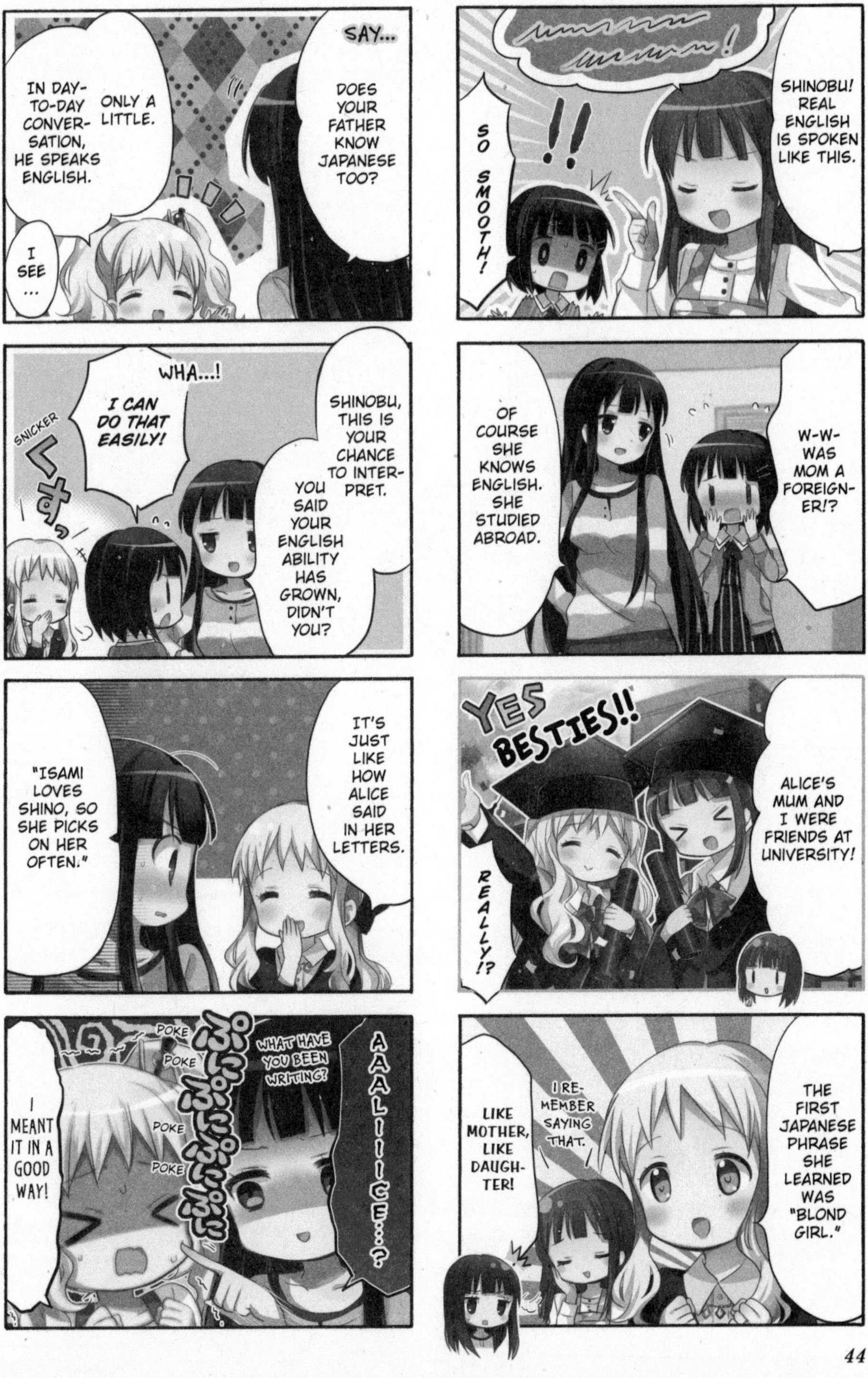
SHINOBU! REAL ENGLISH IS SPOKEN LIKE THIS.
!!
SO SMOOTH!
SAY...
DOES YOUR FATHER KNOW JAPANESE TOO?
ONLY A LITTLE.
IN DAY-TO-DAY CONVERSATION, HE SPEAKS ENGLISH.
I SEE...
W-W-WAS MOM A FOREIGNER!?
OF COURSE SHE KNOWS ENGLISH. SHE STUDIED ABROAD.
SHINOBU, THIS IS YOUR CHANCE TO INTERPRET.
YOU SAID YOUR ENGLISH ABILITY HAS GROWN, DIDN'T YOU?
WHA...!
I CAN DO THAT EASILY!
SNICKER
ALICE'S MUM AND I WERE FRIENDS AT UNIVERSITY!
YES BESTIES!!
REALLY!?
IT'S JUST LIKE HOW ALICE SAID IN HER LETTERS.
"ISAMI LOVES SHINO, SO SHE PICKS ON HER OFTEN."
THE FIRST JAPANESE PHRASE SHE LEARNED WAS "BLOND GIRL."
I REMEMBER SAYING THAT.
LIKE MOTHER, LIKE DAUGHTER!
AAALIIICE...?
WHAT HAVE YOU BEEN WRITING?
POKE
POKE
POKE
POKE
I MEANT IT IN A GOOD WAY!

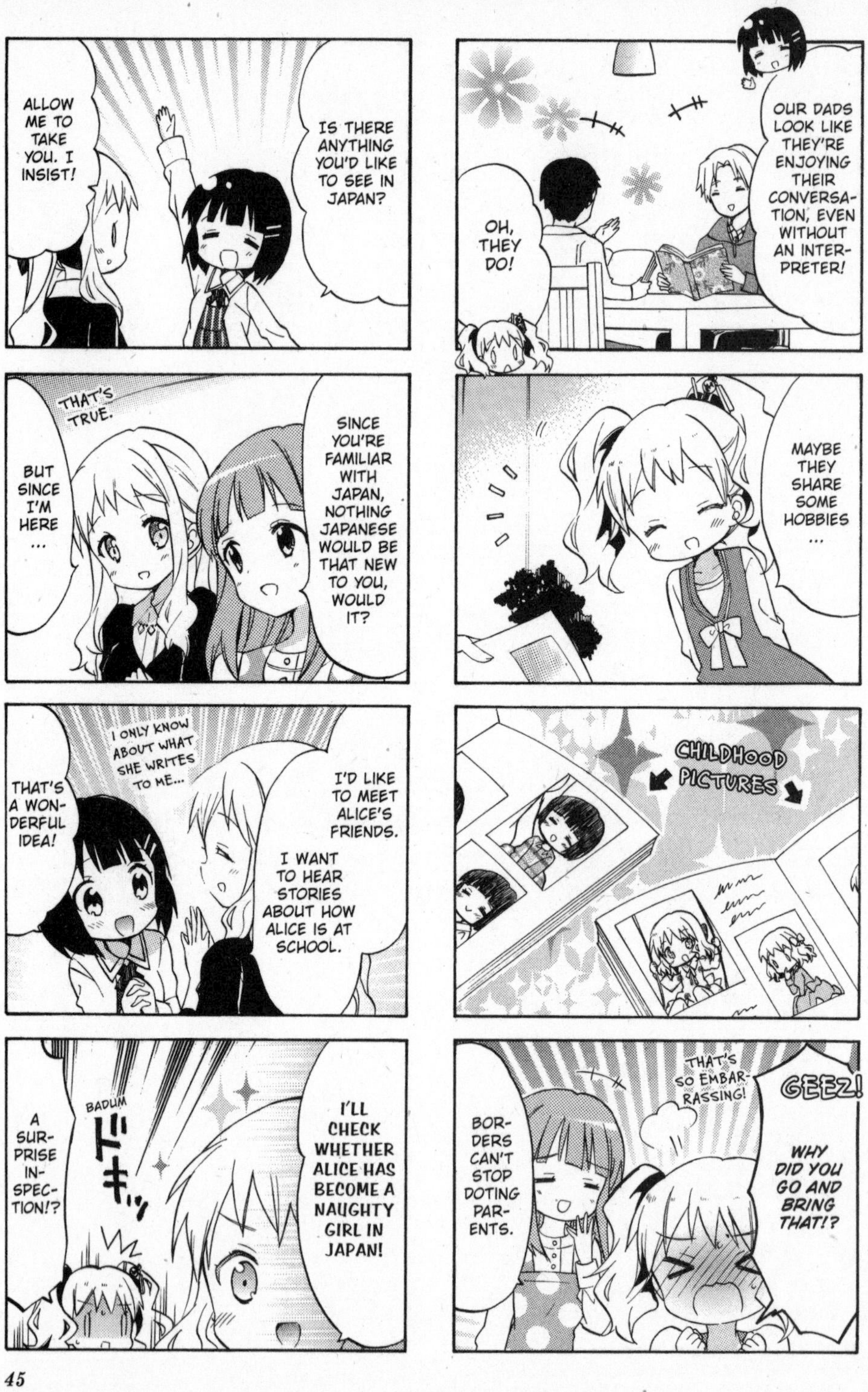
OUR DADS LOOK LIKE THEY'RE ENJOYING THEIR CONVERSATION, EVEN WITHOUT AN INTERPRETER!
OH, THEY DO!
MAYBE THEY SHARE SOME HOBBIES ...
CHILDHOOD PICTURES
GEEZ!
THAT'S SO EMBARRASSING!
WHY DID YOU GO AND BRING THAT!?
BORDERS CAN'T STOP DOTING PARENTS.
IS THERE ANYTHING YOU'D LIKE TO SEE IN JAPAN?
ALLOW ME TO TAKE YOU. I INSIST!
SINCE YOU'RE FAMILIAR WITH JAPAN, NOTHING JAPANESE WOULD BE THAT NEW TO YOU, WOULD IT?
THAT'S TRUE.
BUT SINCE I'M HERE ...
I'D LIKE TO MEET ALICE'S FRIENDS.
I WANT TO HEAR STORIES ABOUT HOW ALICE IS AT SCHOOL.
I ONLY KNOW ABOUT WHAT SHE WRITES TO ME...
THAT'S A WONDERFUL IDEA!
I'LL CHECK WHETHER ALICE HAS BECOME A NAUGHTY GIRL IN JAPAN!
BADUM
ドキッ
A SURPRISE INSPECTION!?

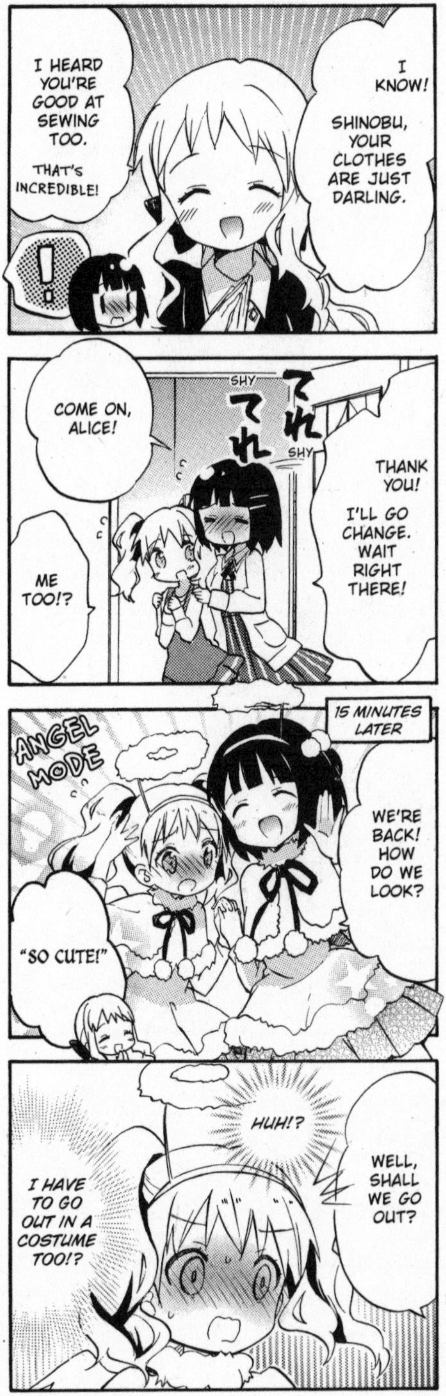
I KNOW!
SHINOBU, YOUR CLOTHES ARE JUST DARLING.
I HEARD YOU'RE GOOD AT SEWING TOO.
THAT'S INCREDIBLE!
!
てれ SHY
てれ SHY
THANK YOU!
I'LL GO CHANGE. WAIT RIGHT THERE!
COME ON, ALICE!
ME TOO!?
15 MINUTES LATER
WE'RE BACK! HOW DO WE LOOK?
ANGEL MODE
"SO CUTE!"
WELL, SHALL WE GO OUT?
HUH!?
I HAVE TO GO OUT IN A COSTUME TOO!?

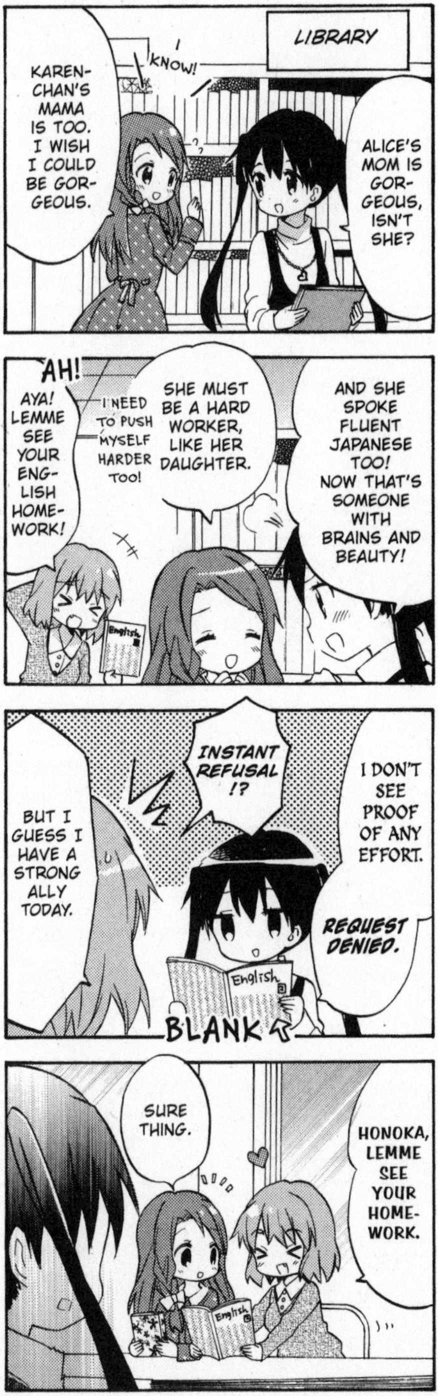
LIBRARY
ALICE'S MOM IS GORGEOUS, ISN'T SHE?
I KNOW!
KAREN-CHAN'S MAMA IS TOO. I WISH I COULD BE GORGEOUS.
AND SHE SPOKE FLUENT JAPANESE TOO! NOW THAT'S SOMEONE WITH BRAINS AND BEAUTY!
SHE MUST BE A HARD WORKER, LIKE HER DAUGHTER.
I NEED TO PUSH MYSELF HARDER TOO!
AH!
AYA! LEMME SEE YOUR ENGLISH HOMEWORK!
English
I DON'T SEE PROOF OF ANY EFFORT.
INSTANT REFUSAL!?
REQUEST DENIED.
BUT I GUESS I HAVE A STRONG ALLY TODAY.
English
BLANK
HONOKA, LEMME SEE YOUR HOMEWORK.
SURE THING.
English

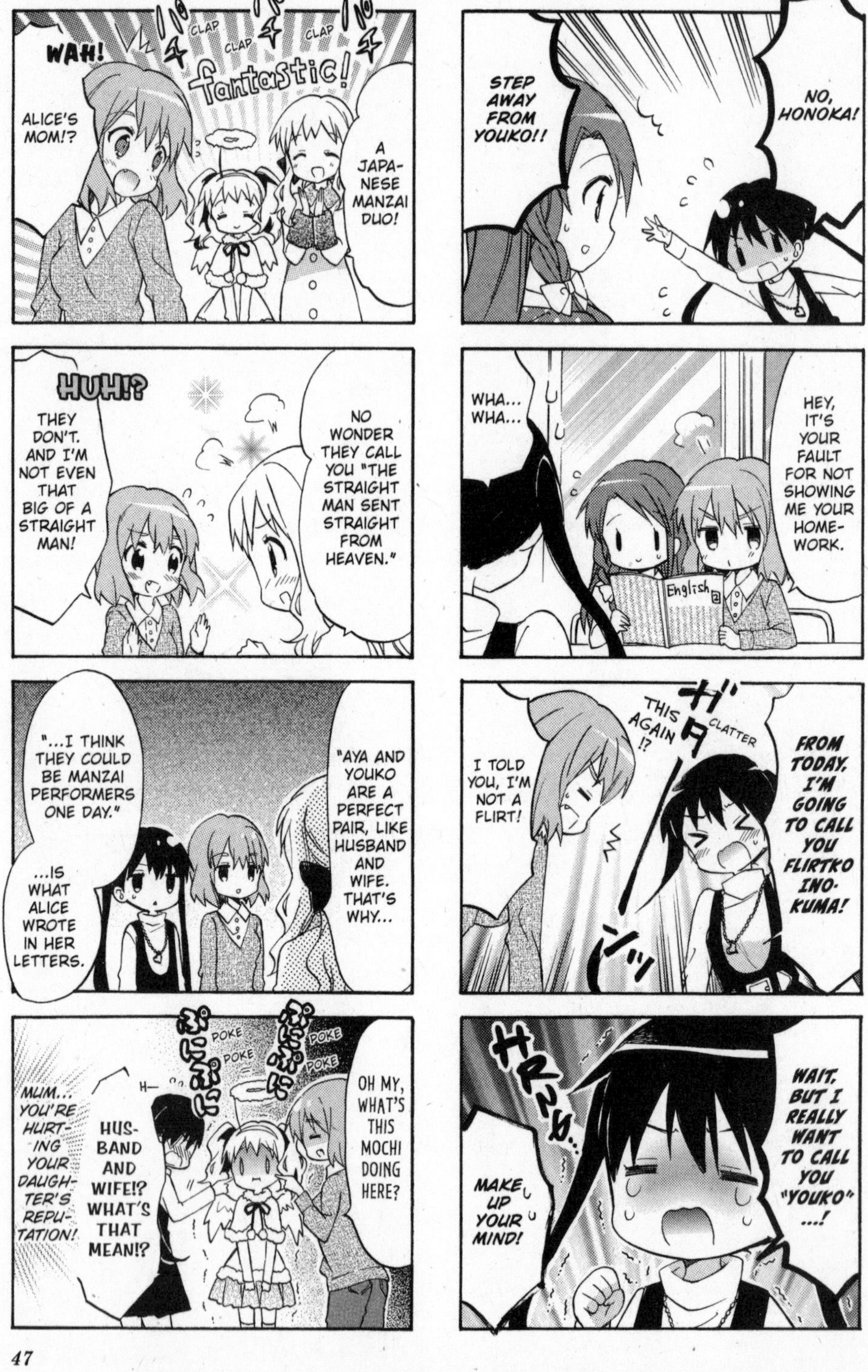
NO, HONOKA!
STEP AWAY FROM YOUKO!!
HEY, IT'S YOUR FAULT FOR NOT SHOWING ME YOUR HOMEWORK.
WHA... WHA...
English
FROM TODAY, I'M GOING TO CALL YOU FLIRTKO INOKUMA!
CLATTER
THIS AGAIN!?
I TOLD YOU, I'M NOT A FLIRT!
WAIT, BUT I REALLY WANT TO CALL YOU "YOUKO"...!
HRNN...
MAKE UP YOUR MIND!
CLAP CLAP CLAP
WAH!
fantastic!
A JAPANESE MANZAI DUO!
ALICE'S MOM!?
NO WONDER THEY CALL YOU "THE STRAIGHT MAN SENT STRAIGHT FROM HEAVEN."
HUH!?
THEY DON'T. AND I'M NOT EVEN THAT BIG OF A STRAIGHT MAN!
"AYA AND YOUKO ARE A PERFECT PAIR, LIKE HUSBAND AND WIFE. THAT'S WHY...
"...I THINK THEY COULD BE MANZAI PERFORMERS ONE DAY."
...IS WHAT ALICE WROTE IN HER LETTERS.
POKE POKE POKE POKE
OH MY, WHAT'S THIS MOCHI DOING HERE?
HUSBAND AND WIFE!? WHAT'S THAT MEAN!?
H—
MUM... YOU'RE HURTING YOUR DAUGHTER'S REPUTATION!

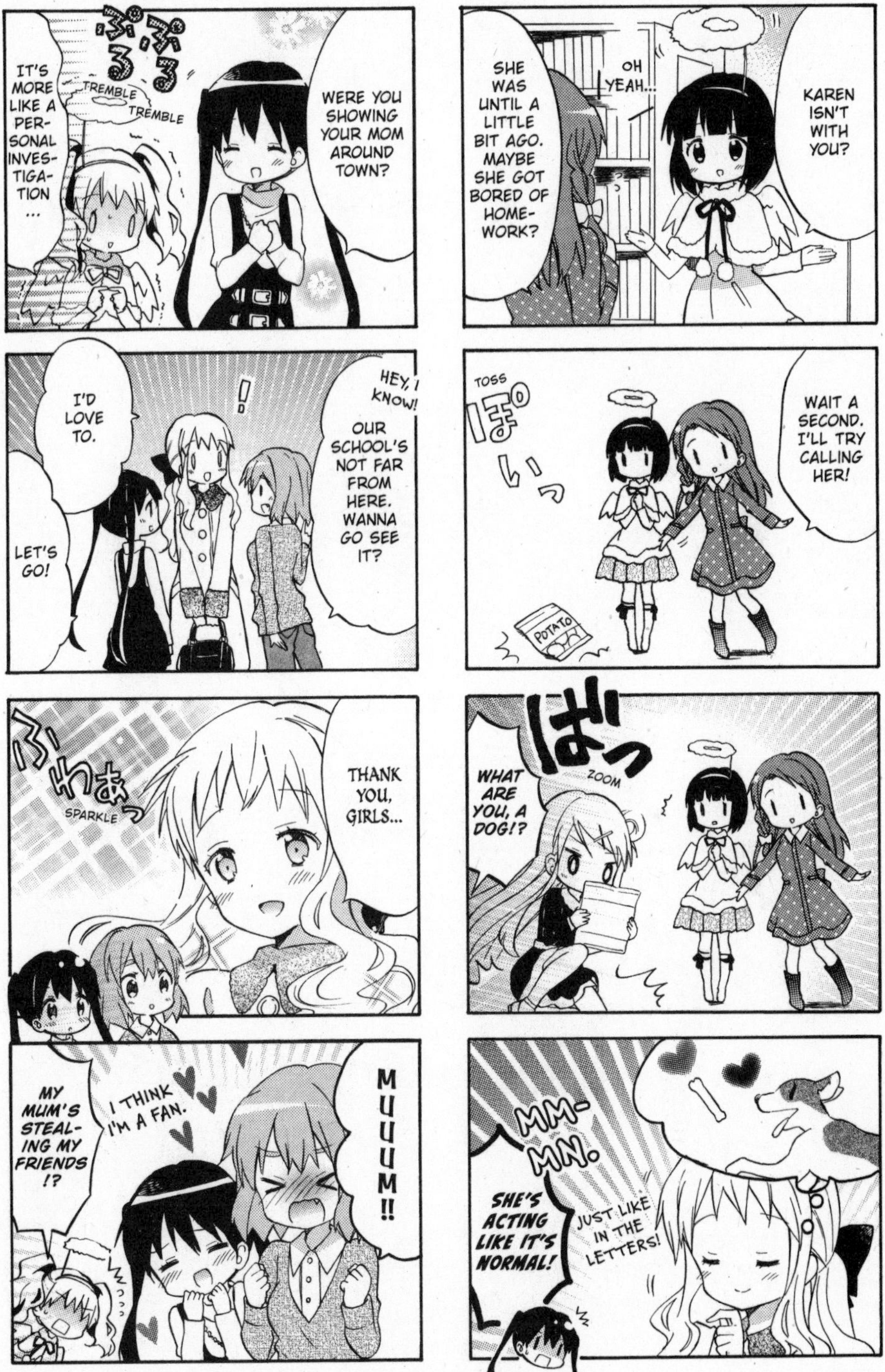
KAREN ISN'T WITH YOU?
OH YEAH...
SHE WAS UNTIL A LITTLE BIT AGO. MAYBE SHE GOT BORED OF HOMEWORK?
WAIT A SECOND. I'LL TRY CALLING HER!
ぽいっ
TOSS
POTATO
ばっ
ZOOM
WHAT ARE YOU, A DOG!?
MM-MN.
JUST LIKE IN THE LETTERS!
SHE'S ACTING LIKE IT'S NORMAL!
WERE YOU SHOWING YOUR MOM AROUND TOWN?
ぷるぷる
TREMBLE TREMBLE
IT'S MORE LIKE A PERSONAL INVESTIGATION...
HEY, I KNOW!
OUR SCHOOL'S NOT FAR FROM HERE. WANNA GO SEE IT?
!
I'D LOVE TO.
LET'S GO!
THANK YOU, GIRLS...
ふわあっ
SPARKLE
MUUUUM!!
I THINK I'M A FAN.
MY MUM'S STEALING MY FRIENDS!?

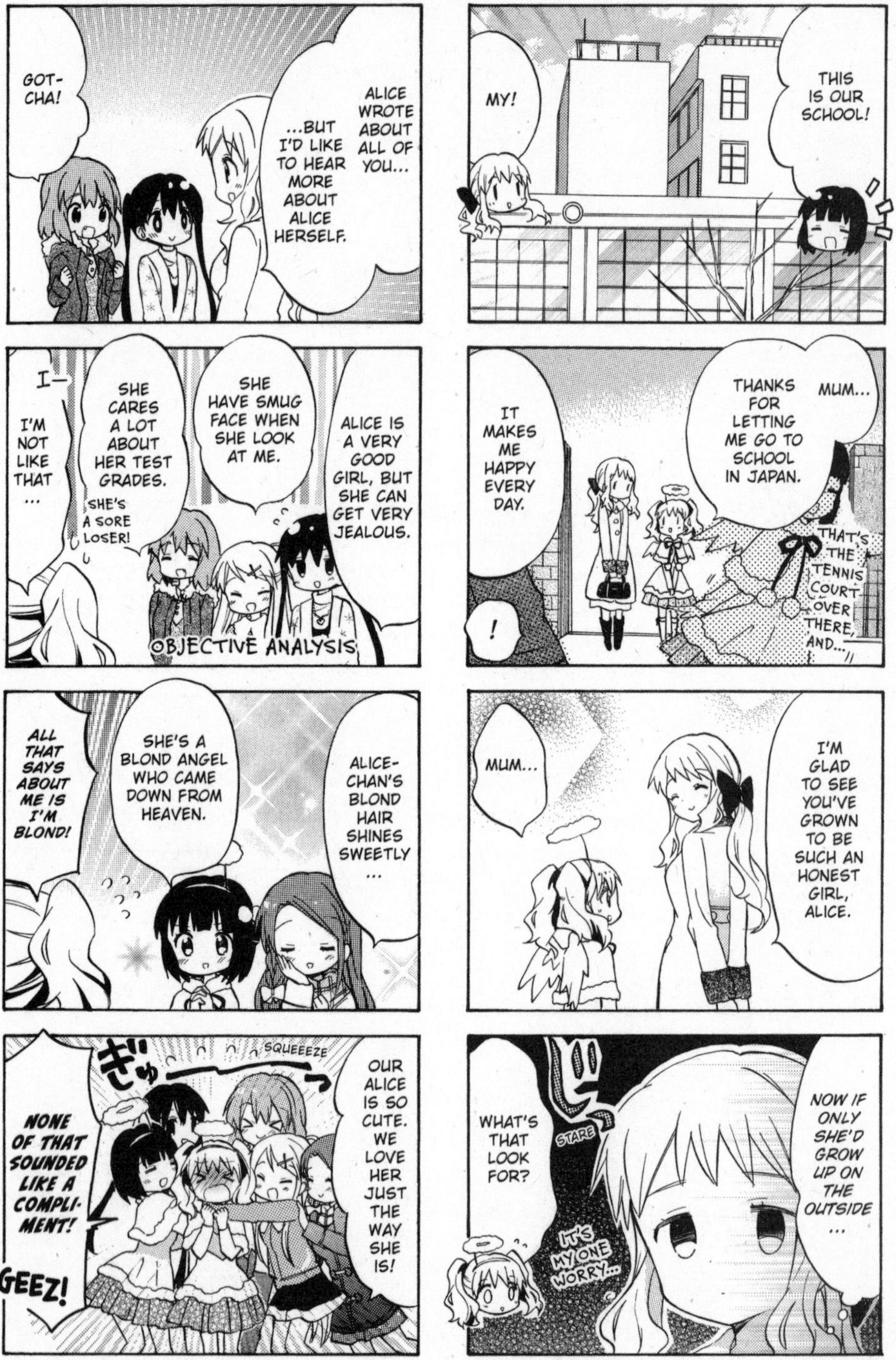
THIS IS OUR SCHOOL!
MY!
MUM...
THANKS FOR LETTING ME GO TO SCHOOL IN JAPAN.
THAT'S THE TENNIS COURT OVER THERE, AND...
IT MAKES ME HAPPY EVERY DAY.
!
I'M GLAD TO SEE YOU'VE GROWN TO BE SUCH AN HONEST GIRL, ALICE.
MUM...
NOW IF ONLY SHE'D GROW UP ON THE OUTSIDE...
じー
STARE
WHAT'S THAT LOOK FOR?
IT'S MY ONE WORRY...
ALICE WROTE ABOUT ALL OF YOU...
...BUT I'D LIKE TO HEAR MORE ABOUT ALICE HERSELF.
GOT-CHA!
ALICE IS A VERY GOOD GIRL, BUT SHE CAN GET VERY JEALOUS.
SHE HAVE SMUG FACE WHEN SHE LOOK AT ME.
SHE CARES A LOT ABOUT HER TEST GRADES.
SHE'S A SORE LOSER!
I—
I'M NOT LIKE THAT...
OBJECTIVE ANALYSIS
ALICE-CHAN'S BLOND HAIR SHINES SWEETLY...
SHE'S A BLOND ANGEL WHO CAME DOWN FROM HEAVEN.
ALL THAT SAYS ABOUT ME IS I'M BLOND!
OUR ALICE IS SO CUTE. WE LOVE HER JUST THE WAY SHE IS!
SQUEEEZE
ぎゅーっ
NONE OF THAT SOUNDED LIKE A COMPLIMENT!
GEEZ!

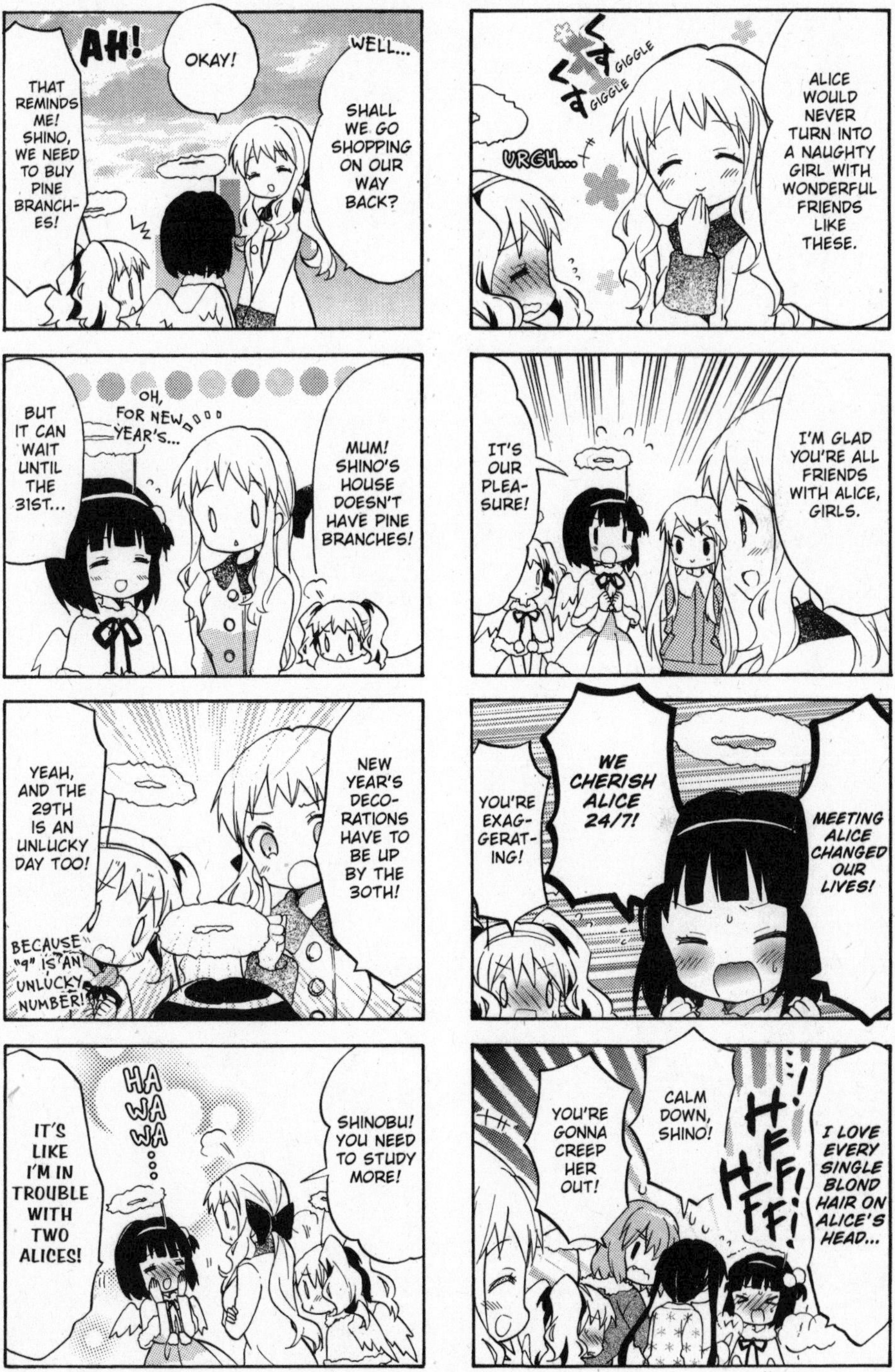

ALICE WOULD NEVER TURN INTO A NAUGHTY GIRL WITH WONDERFUL FRIENDS LIKE THESE.
くすくす GIGGLE GIGGLE
URGH...
I'M GLAD YOU'RE ALL FRIENDS WITH ALICE, GIRLS.
IT'S OUR PLEASURE!
MEETING ALICE CHANGED OUR LIVES!
WE CHERISH ALICE 24/7!
YOU'RE EXAGGERATING!
I LOVE EVERY SINGLE BLOND HAIR ON ALICE'S HEAD...
HFF! HFF! HFF!
CALM DOWN, SHINO!
YOU'RE GONNA CREEP HER OUT!
WELL... SHALL WE GO SHOPPING ON OUR WAY BACK?
OKAY!
AH! THAT REMINDS ME! SHINO, WE NEED TO BUY PINE BRANCHES!
MUM! SHINO'S HOUSE DOESN'T HAVE PINE BRANCHES!
OH, FOR NEW YEAR'S...
BUT IT CAN WAIT UNTIL THE 31ST...
NEW YEAR'S DECORATIONS HAVE TO BE UP BY THE 30TH!
YEAH, AND THE 29TH IS AN UNLUCKY DAY TOO!
BECAUSE "9" IS AN UNLUCKY NUMBER!
SHINOBU! YOU NEED TO STUDY MORE!
HAWAWA...
IT'S LIKE I'M IN TROUBLE WITH TWO ALICES!

SHINOBU GETS DEEP

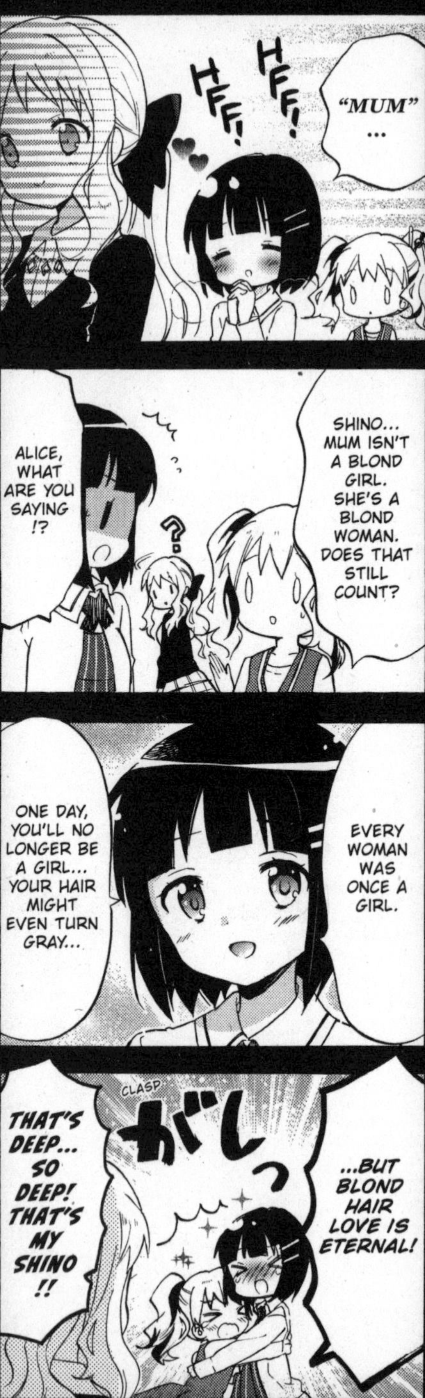
"MUM" ...
HFF! HFF!
SHINO... MUM ISN'T A BLOND GIRL. SHE'S A BLOND WOMAN. DOES THAT STILL COUNT?
ALICE, WHAT ARE YOU SAYING !?
EVERY WOMAN WAS ONCE A GIRL.
ONE DAY, YOU'LL NO LONGER BE A GIRL... YOUR HAIR MIGHT EVEN TURN GRAY...
...BUT BLOND HAIR LOVE IS ETERNAL!
がしっ
CLASP
THAT'S DEEP... SO DEEP! THAT'S MY SHINO !!

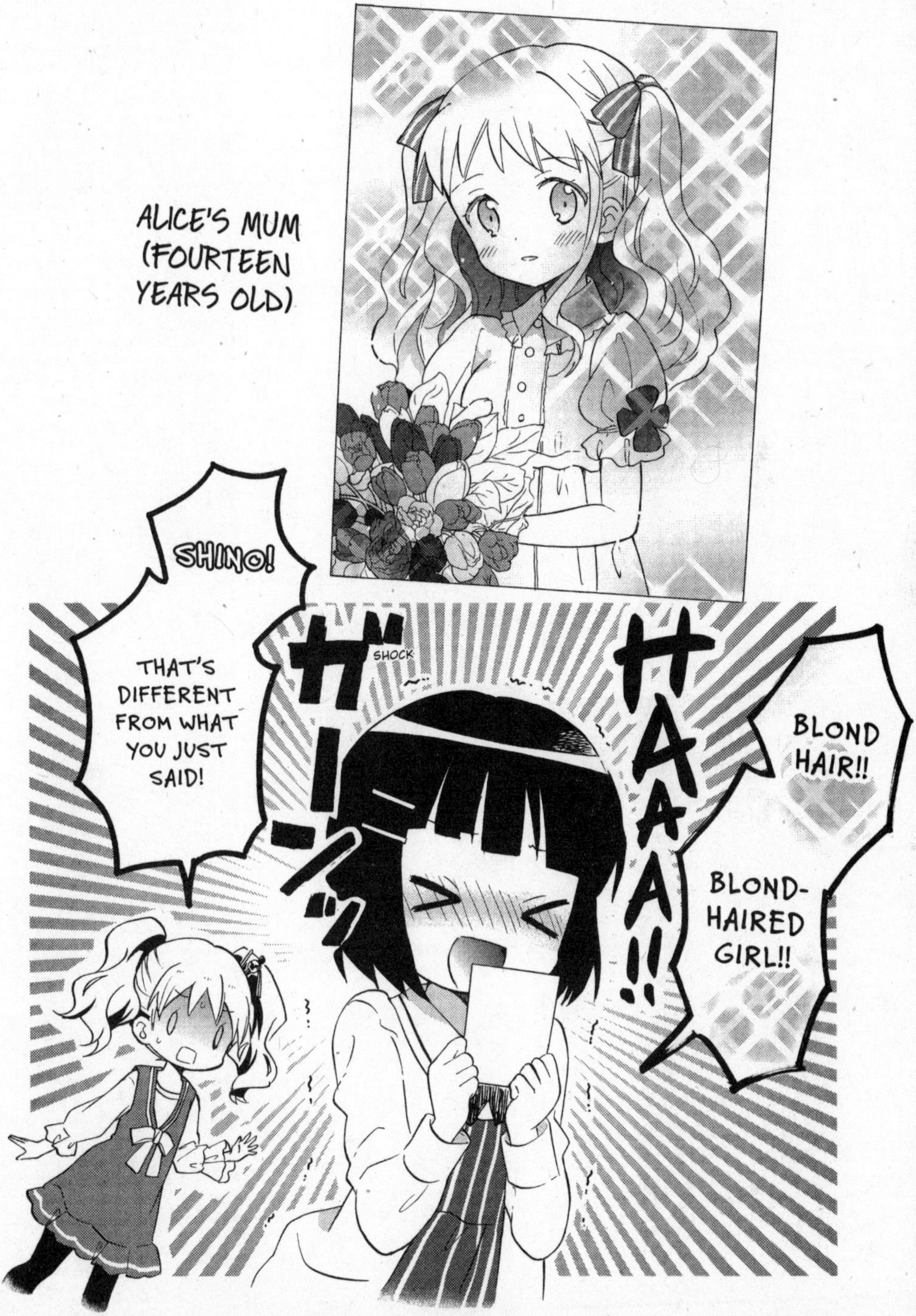
ALICE'S MUM (FOURTEEN YEARS OLD)
BLOND HAIR!!
BLOND-HAIRED GIRL!!
HAAAA!!
ザー
SHOCK
SHINO!
THAT'S DIFFERENT FROM WHAT YOU JUST SAID!

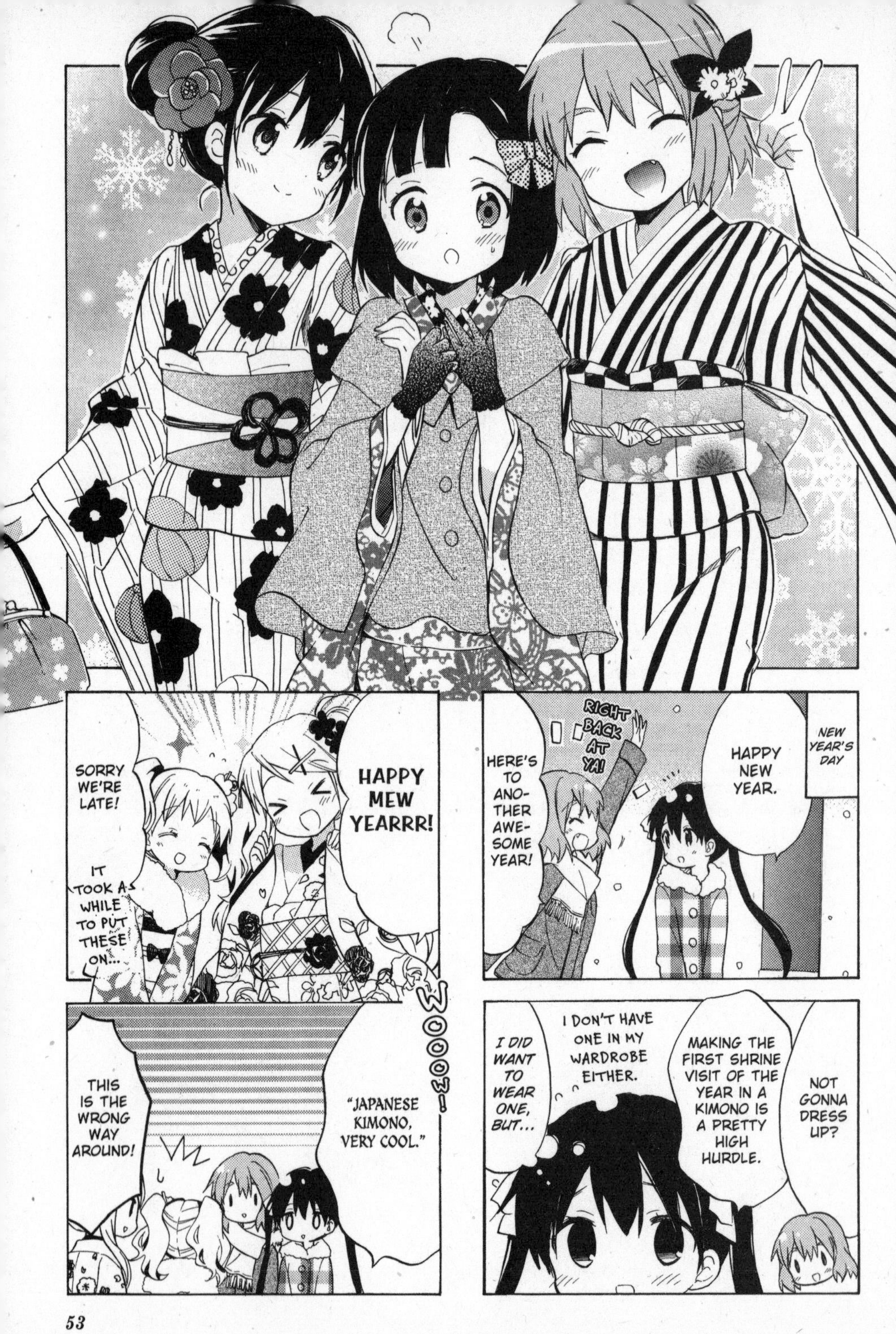
NEW YEAR'S DAY
HAPPY NEW YEAR.
RIGHT BACK AT YA!
HERE'S TO ANOTHER AWESOME YEAR!
HAPPY MEW YEARRR!
SORRY WE'RE LATE!
IT TOOK A WHILE TO PUT THESE ON...
NOT GONNA DRESS UP?
MAKING THE FIRST SHRINE VISIT OF THE YEAR IN A KIMONO IS A PRETTY HIGH HURDLE.
I DON'T HAVE ONE IN MY WARDROBE EITHER.
I DID WANT TO WEAR ONE, BUT...
WOOOOW!
"JAPANESE KIMONO, VERY COOL."
THIS IS THE WRONG WAY AROUND!

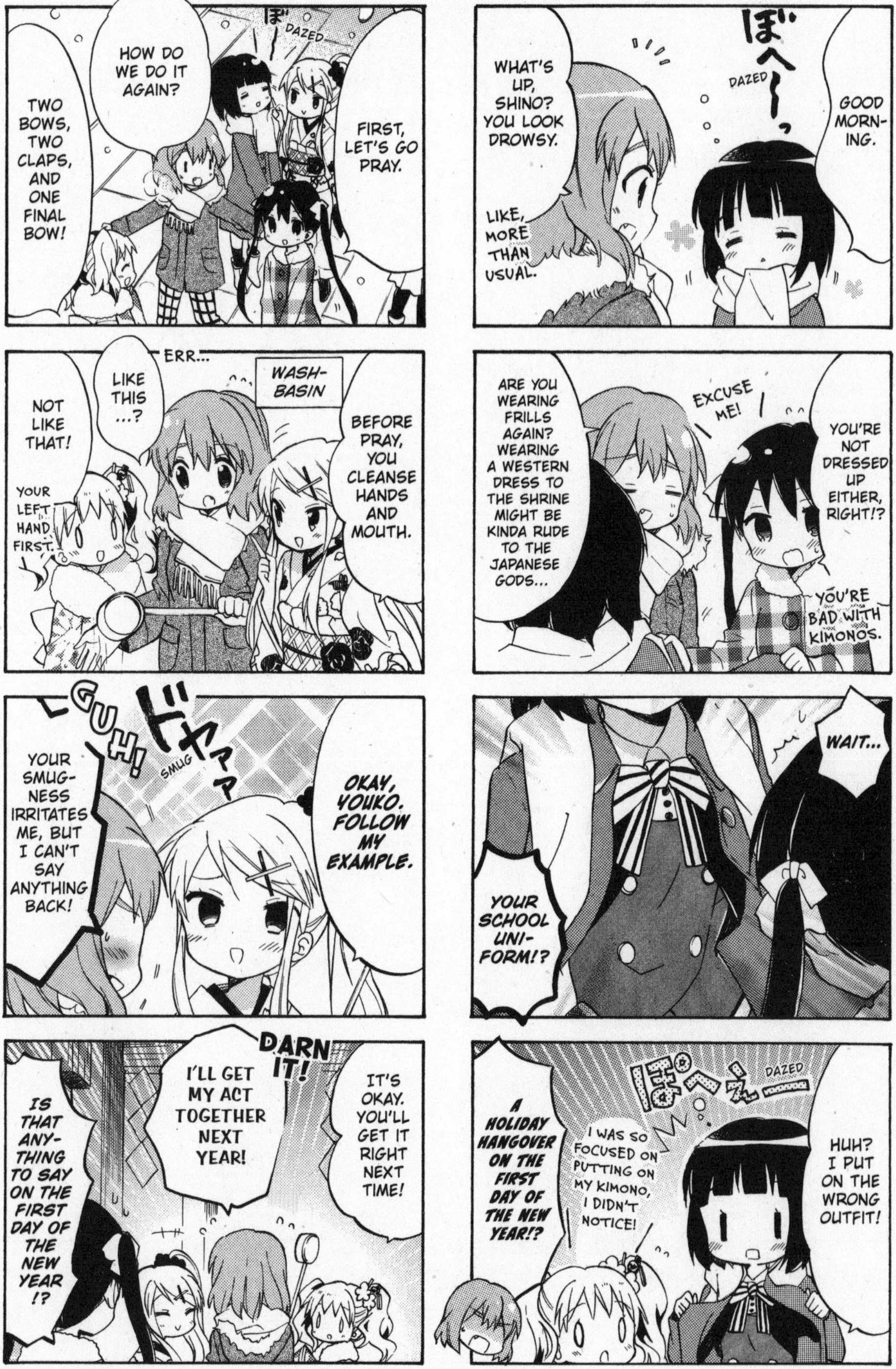
GOOD MORNING.
ぼへ～っ
DAZED
WHAT'S UP, SHINO? YOU LOOK DROWSY.
LIKE, MORE THAN USUAL.
YOU'RE NOT DRESSED UP EITHER, RIGHT!?
EXCUSE ME!
ARE YOU WEARING FRILLS AGAIN? WEARING A WESTERN DRESS TO THE SHRINE MIGHT BE KINDA RUDE TO THE JAPANESE GODS...
YOU'RE BAD WITH KIMONOS.
WAIT...
YOUR SCHOOL UNIFORM!?
HUH? I PUT ON THE WRONG OUTFIT!
ぽへえ～
DAZED
I WAS SO FOCUSED ON PUTTING ON MY KIMONO, I DIDN'T NOTICE!
A HOLIDAY HANGOVER ON THE FIRST DAY OF THE NEW YEAR!?
FIRST, LET'S GO PRAY.
ぼ
DAZED
HOW DO WE DO IT AGAIN?
TWO BOWS, TWO CLAPS, AND ONE FINAL BOW!
BEFORE PRAY, YOU CLEANSE HANDS AND MOUTH.
WASH-BASIN
ERR...
LIKE THIS ...?
NOT LIKE THAT!
YOUR LEFT HAND FIRST.
OKAY, YOUKO. FOLLOW MY EXAMPLE.
ドヤァァ
SMUG
GUH!
YOUR SMUGNESS IRRITATES ME, BUT I CAN'T SAY ANYTHING BACK!
IT'S OKAY. YOU'LL GET IT RIGHT NEXT TIME!
DARN IT!
I'LL GET MY ACT TOGETHER NEXT YEAR!
IS THAT ANYTHING TO SAY ON THE FIRST DAY OF THE NEW YEAR!?

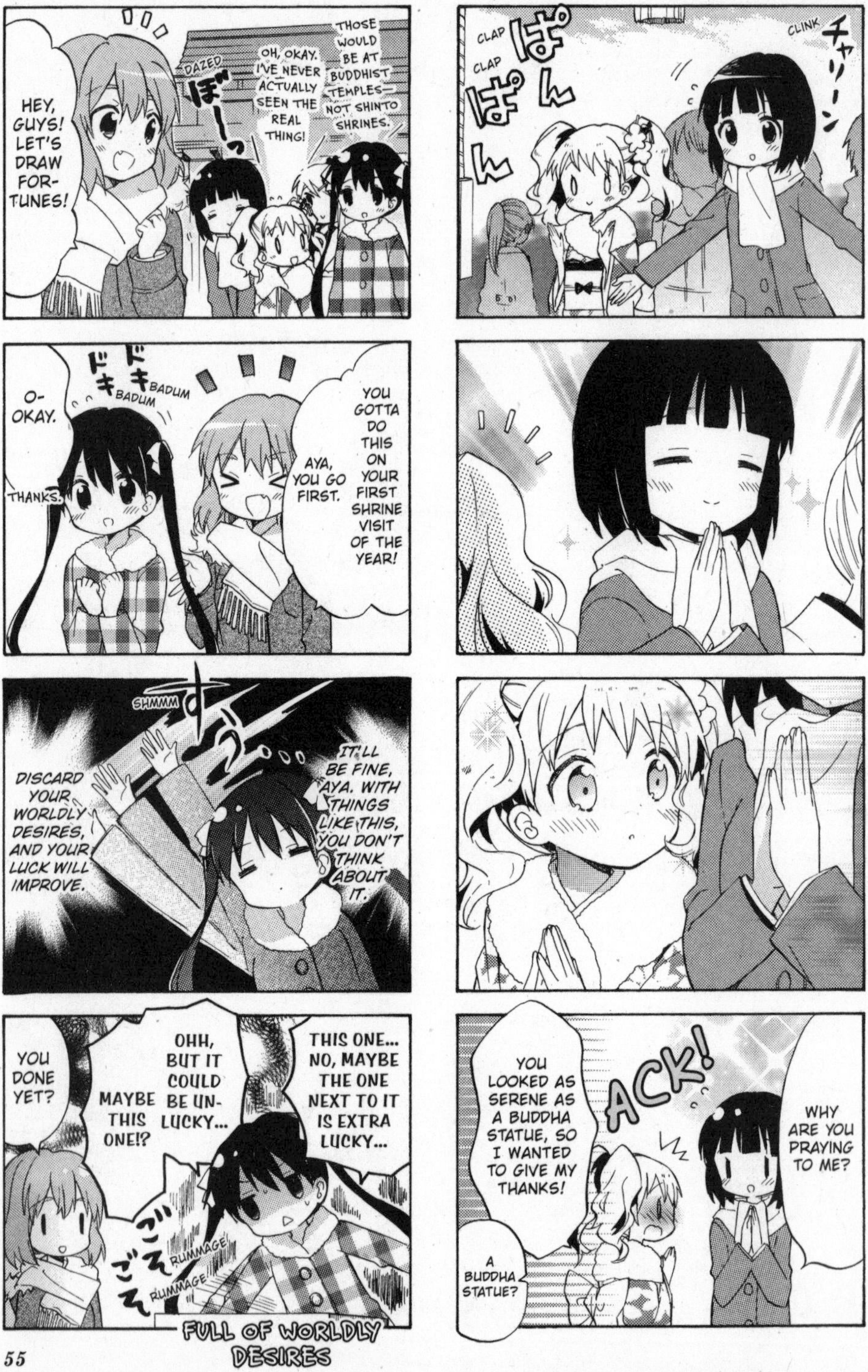
CLAP
ぱん
CLAP
ぱん
CLINK
チャリーン
WHY ARE YOU PRAYING TO ME?
ACK!
YOU LOOKED AS SERENE AS A BUDDHA STATUE, SO I WANTED TO GIVE MY THANKS!
A BUDDHA STATUE?
THOSE WOULD BE AT BUDDHIST TEMPLES— NOT SHINTO SHRINES.
OH, OKAY. I'VE NEVER ACTUALLY SEEN THE REAL THING!
DAZED
ぼーっ
HEY, GUYS! LET'S DRAW FOR-TUNES!
YOU GOTTA DO THIS ON YOUR FIRST SHRINE VISIT OF THE YEAR!
AYA, YOU GO FIRST.
ドキドキ
BADUM BADUM
O-OKAY.
THANKS.
IT'LL BE FINE, AYA. WITH THINGS LIKE THIS, YOU DON'T THINK ABOUT IT.
SHMMM
DISCARD YOUR WORLDLY DESIRES, AND YOUR LUCK WILL IMPROVE.
THIS ONE... NO, MAYBE THE ONE NEXT TO IT IS EXTRA LUCKY...
OHH, BUT IT COULD BE UN-LUCKY...
MAYBE THIS ONE!?
YOU DONE YET?
ごそごそ
RUMMAGE RUMMAGE
FULL OF WORLDLY DESIRES

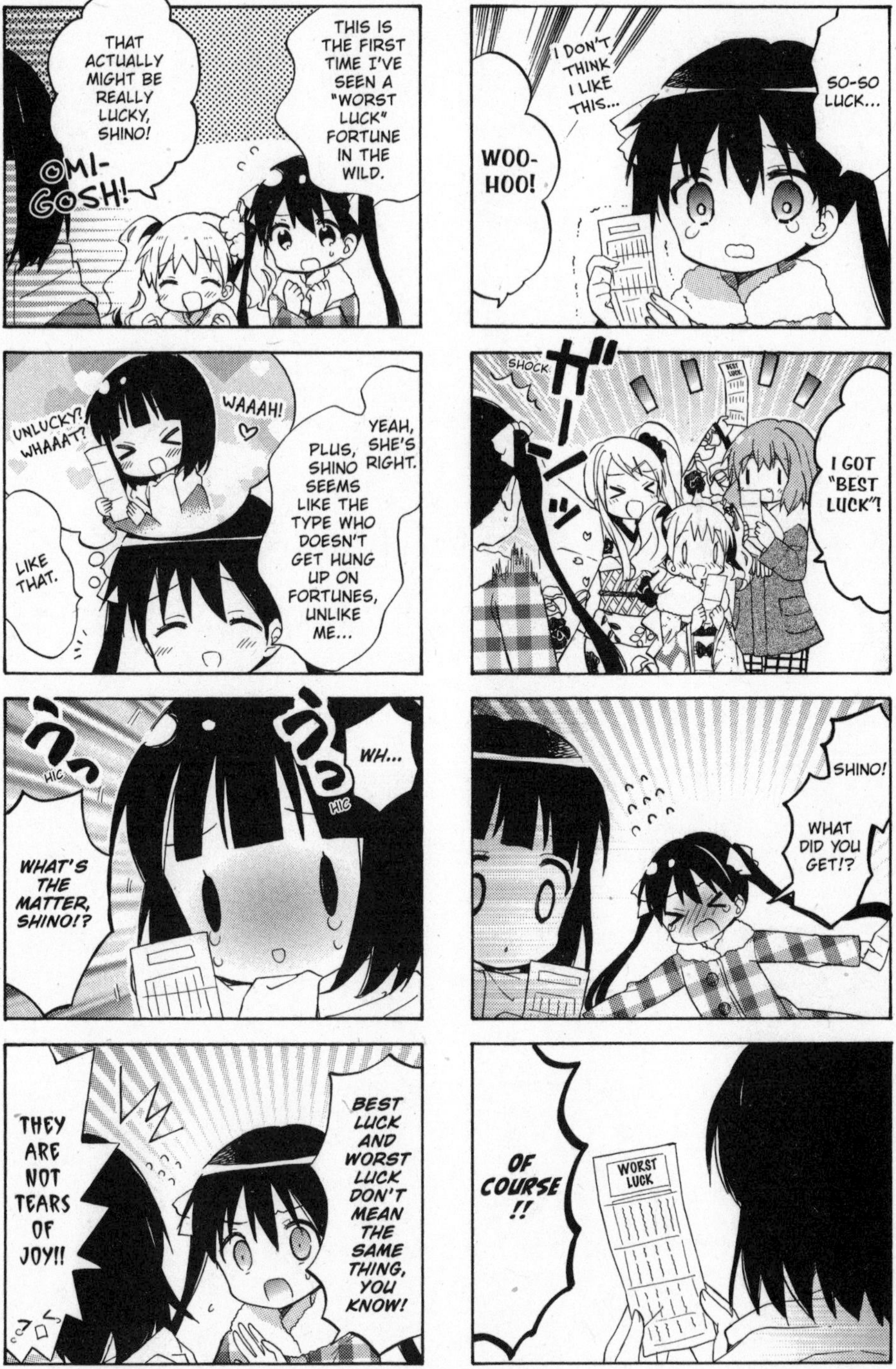
SO-SO LUCK...
I DON'T THINK I LIKE THIS...
WOO-HOO!
THIS IS THE FIRST TIME I'VE SEEN A "WORST LUCK" FORTUNE IN THE WILD.
THAT ACTUALLY MIGHT BE REALLY LUCKY, SHINO!
OMI-GOSH!
SHOCK
BEST LUCK
I GOT "BEST LUCK"!
YEAH, SHE'S RIGHT.
PLUS, SHINO SEEMS LIKE THE TYPE WHO DOESN'T GET HUNG UP ON FORTUNES, UNLIKE ME...
WAAAH!
UNLUCKY? WHAAAT?
LIKE THAT.
SHINO!
WHAT DID YOU GET!?
WH...
HIC
HIC
WHAT'S THE MATTER, SHINO!?
WORST LUCK
OF COURSE!!
BEST LUCK AND WORST LUCK DON'T MEAN THE SAME THING, YOU KNOW!
THEY ARE NOT TEARS OF JOY!!

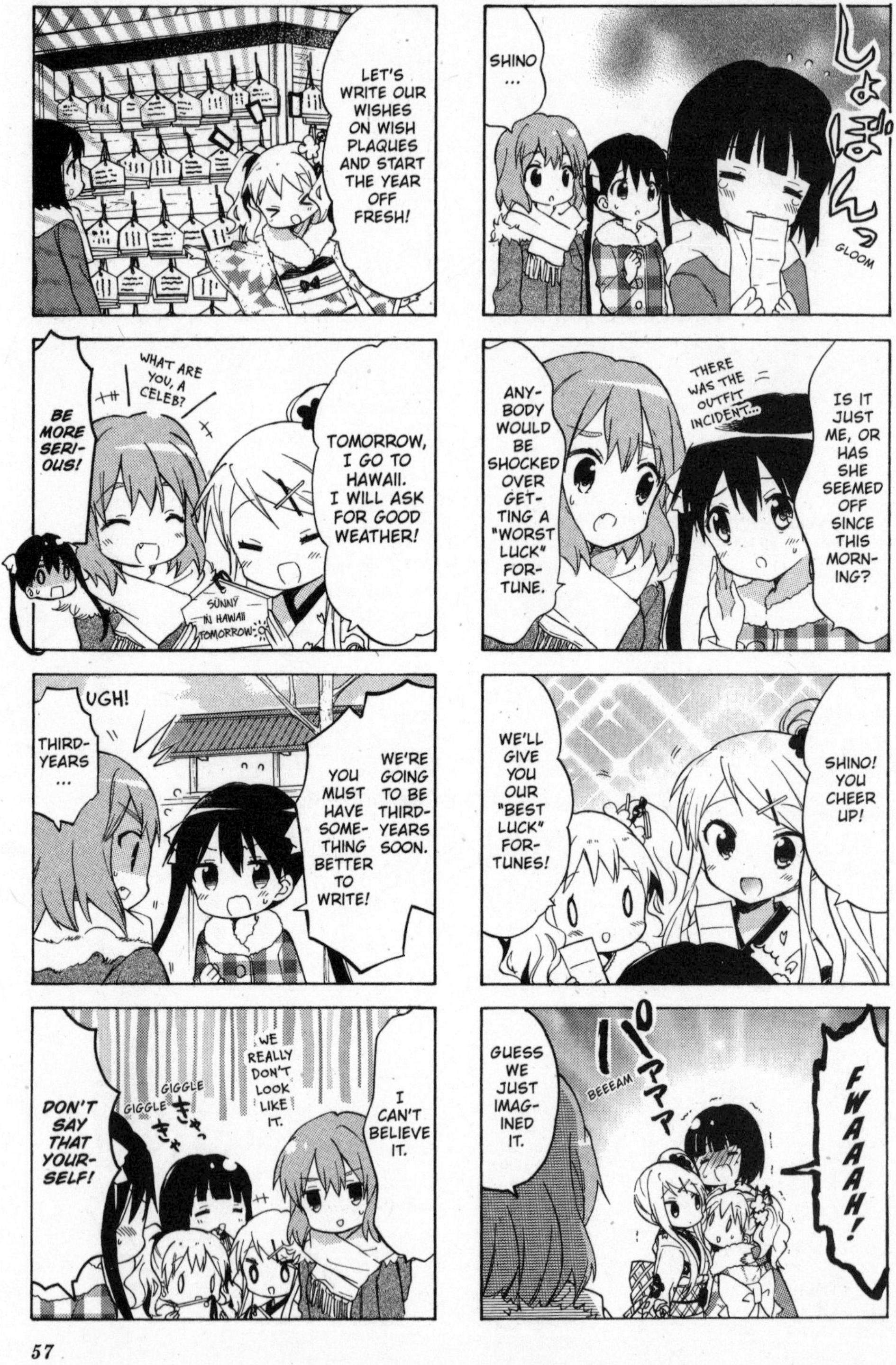
しょぼんっ
GLOOM
SHINO ...
IS IT JUST ME, OR HAS SHE SEEMED OFF SINCE THIS MORNING?
THERE WAS THE OUTFIT INCIDENT...
ANYBODY WOULD BE SHOCKED OVER GETTING A "WORST LUCK" FORTUNE.
SHINO! YOU CHEER UP!
WE'LL GIVE YOU OUR "BEST LUCK" FORTUNES!
FWAAAH!
パアアア
BEEEEAM
GUESS WE JUST IMAGINED IT.
LET'S WRITE OUR WISHES ON WISH PLAQUES AND START THE YEAR OFF FRESH!
TOMORROW, I GO TO HAWAII. I WILL ASK FOR GOOD WEATHER!
SUNNY IN HAWAII TOMORROW
WHAT ARE YOU, A CELEB?
BE MORE SERIOUS!
WE'RE GOING TO BE THIRD-YEARS SOON.
YOU MUST HAVE SOMETHING BETTER TO WRITE!
UGH!
THIRD-YEARS ...
I CAN'T BELIEVE IT.
WE REALLY DON'T LOOK LIKE IT.
きゃっきゃ
GIGGLE GIGGLE
DON'T SAY THAT YOURSELF!

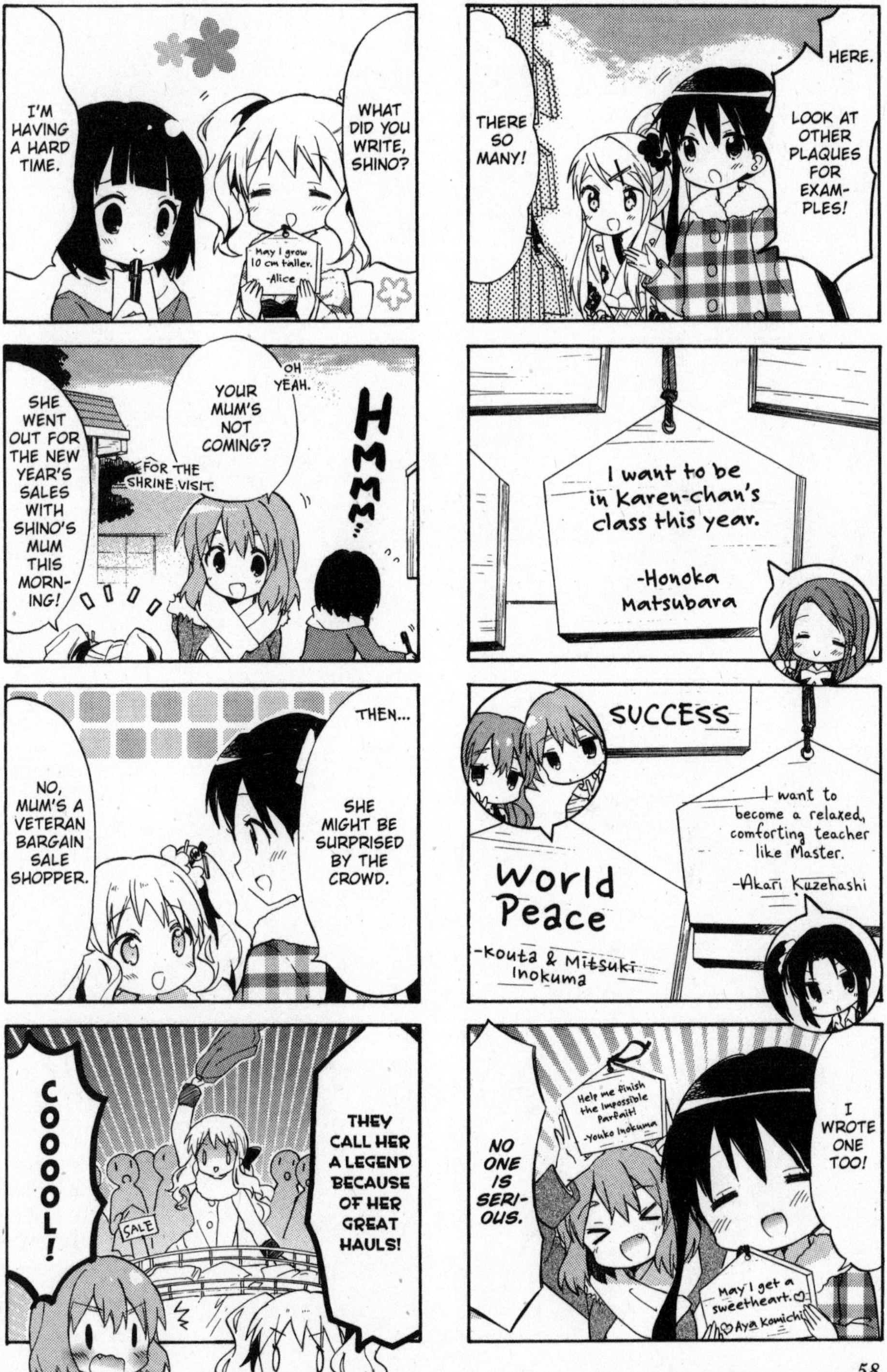
HERE.
LOOK AT OTHER PLAQUES FOR EXAMPLES!
THERE SO MANY!
I want to be in Karen-chan's class this year.
-Honoka Matsubara
SUCCESS
I want to become a relaxed, comforting teacher like Master.
-Akari Kuzehashi
World Peace
-Kouta & Mitsuki Inokuma
I WROTE ONE TOO!
May I get a sweetheart. ♡Aya Komichi
Help me finish the Impossible Parfait! -Youko Inokuma
NO ONE IS SERIOUS.
WHAT DID YOU WRITE, SHINO?
May I grow 10 cm taller. -Alice
I'M HAVING A HARD TIME.
HMMM...
OH YEAH.
YOUR MUM'S NOT COMING?
FOR THE SHRINE VISIT.
SHE WENT OUT FOR THE NEW YEAR'S SALES WITH SHINO'S MUM THIS MORNING!
THEN...
SHE MIGHT BE SURPRISED BY THE CROWD.
NO, MUM'S A VETERAN BARGAIN SALE SHOPPER.
THEY CALL HER A LEGEND BECAUSE OF HER GREAT HAULS!
SALE
COOOOOL!

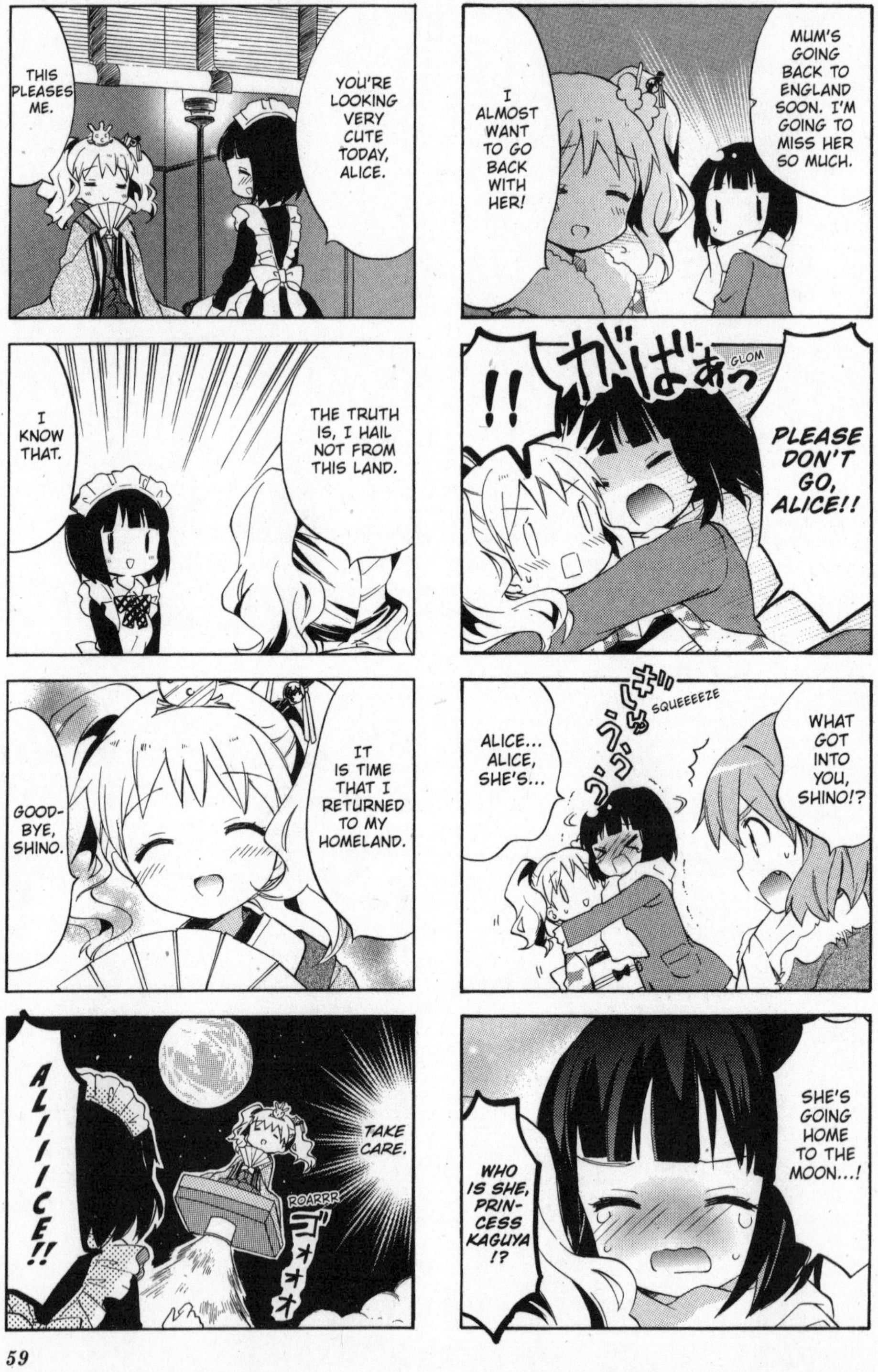

MUM'S GOING BACK TO ENGLAND SOON. I'M GOING TO MISS HER SO MUCH.
I ALMOST WANT TO GO BACK WITH HER!
がばあっ
GLOM
PLEASE DON'T GO, ALICE!!
!!
WHAT GOT INTO YOU, SHINO!?
ぎゅううう
SQUEEEEZE
ALICE... ALICE, SHE'S...
SHE'S GOING HOME TO THE MOON...!
WHO IS SHE, PRINCESS KAGUYA!?
YOU'RE LOOKING VERY CUTE TODAY, ALICE.
THIS PLEASES ME.
THE TRUTH IS, I HAIL NOT FROM THIS LAND.
I KNOW THAT.
IT IS TIME THAT I RETURNED TO MY HOMELAND.
GOOD-BYE, SHINO.
TAKE CARE.
ROARRR
ゴオオオ
ALIIIICE!!

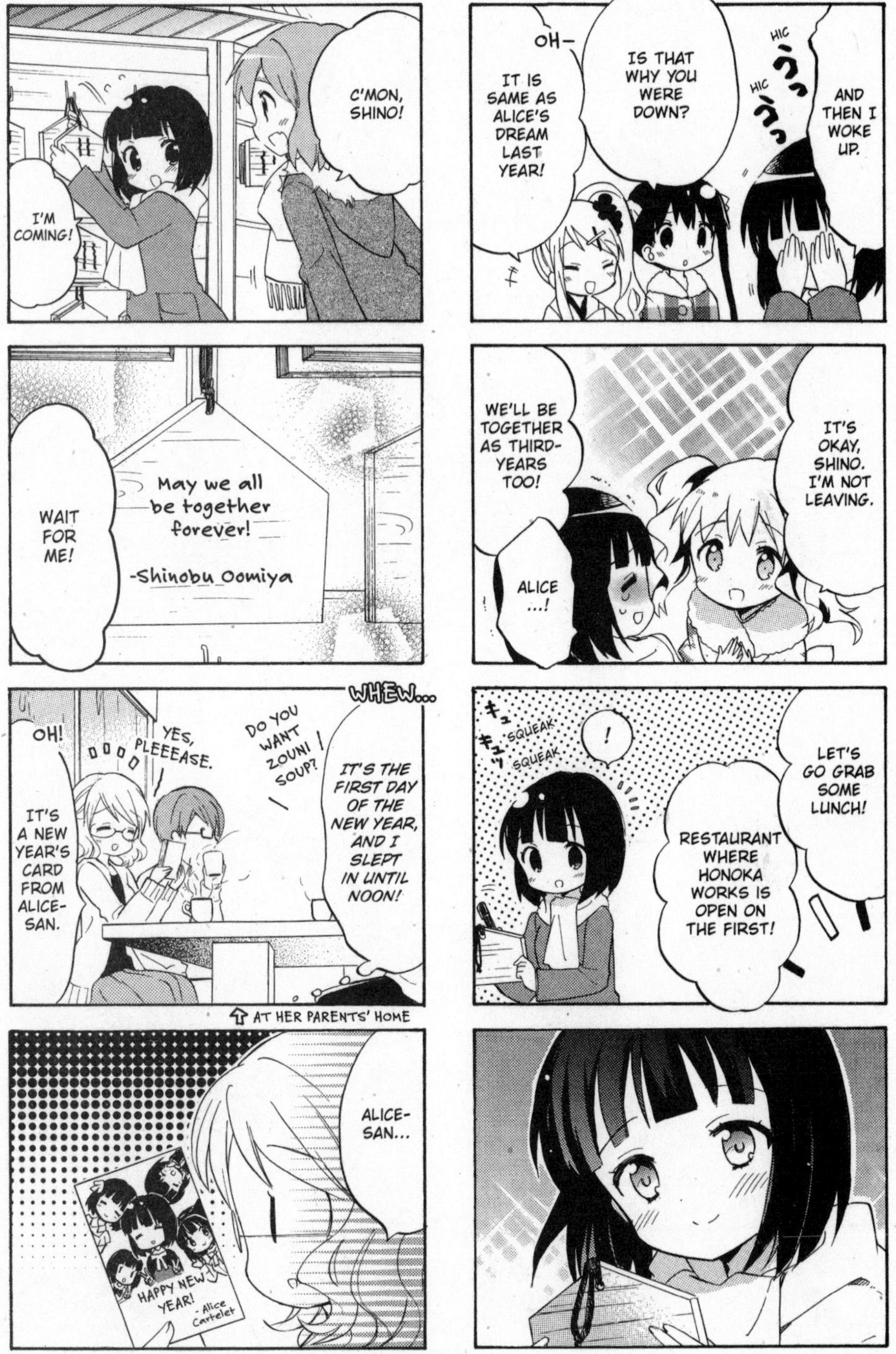
HIC
HIC
AND THEN I WOKE UP.
IS THAT WHY YOU WERE DOWN?
OH—
IT IS SAME AS ALICE'S DREAM LAST YEAR!
IT'S OKAY, SHINO. I'M NOT LEAVING.
WE'LL BE TOGETHER AS THIRD-YEARS TOO!
ALICE ...!
LET'S GO GRAB SOME LUNCH!
RESTAURANT WHERE HONOKA WORKS IS OPEN ON THE FIRST!
!
SQUEAK
SQUEAK
C'MON, SHINO!
I'M COMING!
WAIT FOR ME!
May we all be together forever!
-Shinobu Oomiya
WHEW...
IT'S THE FIRST DAY OF THE NEW YEAR, AND I SLEPT IN UNTIL NOON!
DO YOU WANT ZOUNI SOUP?
YES, PLEEEASE.
OH!
IT'S A NEW YEAR'S CARD FROM ALICE-SAN.
AT HER PARENTS' HOME
ALICE-SAN...
HAPPY NEW YEAR!
- Alice Cartelet

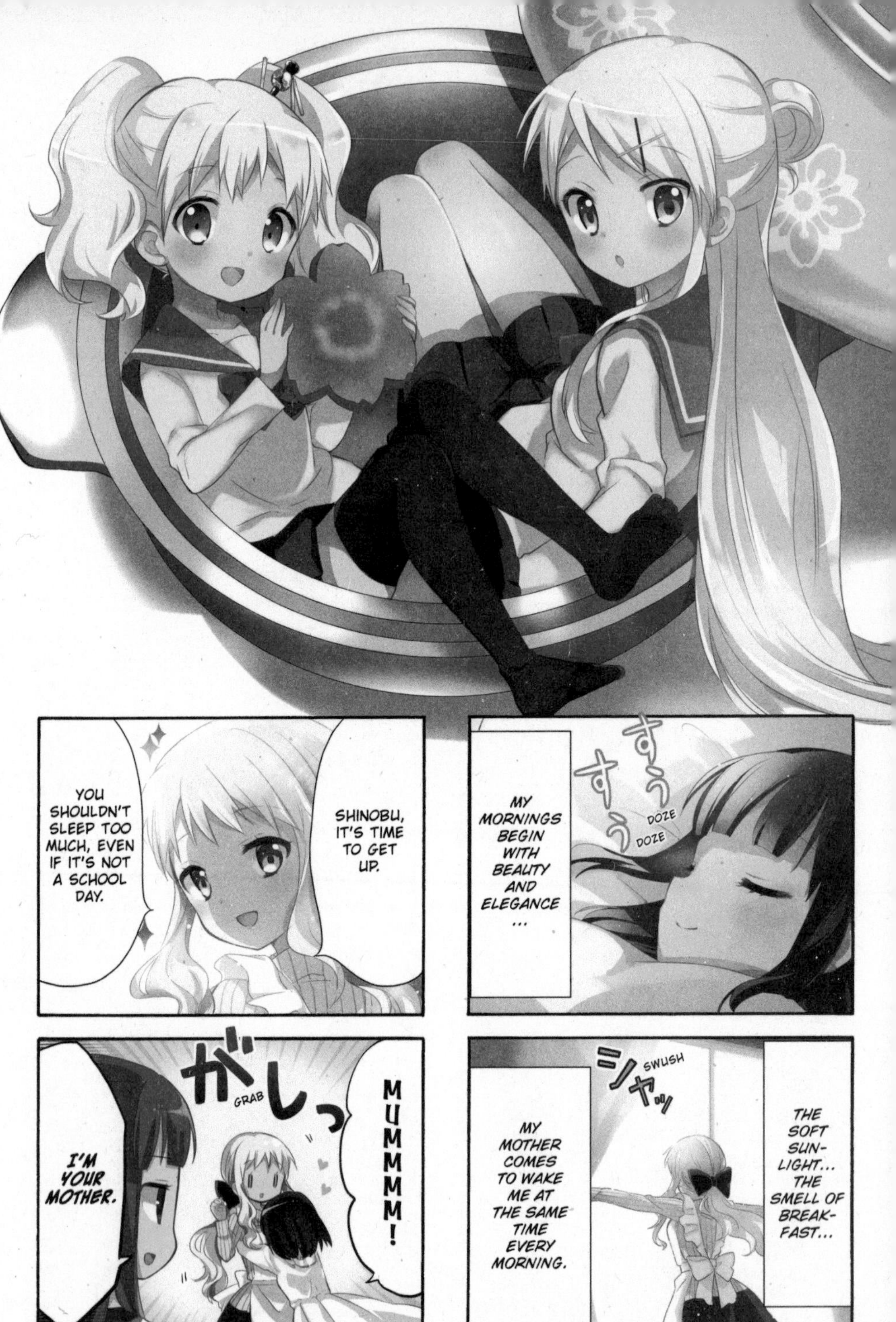
MY MORNINGS BEGIN WITH BEAUTY AND ELEGANCE...
すう すう
DOZE DOZE
THE SOFT SUN-LIGHT... THE SMELL OF BREAK-FAST...
シャッ
SWUSH
MY MOTHER COMES TO WAKE ME AT THE SAME TIME EVERY MORNING.
SHINOBU, IT'S TIME TO GET UP.
YOU SHOULDN'T SLEEP TOO MUCH, EVEN IF IT'S NOT A SCHOOL DAY.
MUMMMM!
がしっ
GRAB
I'M YOUR MOTHER.

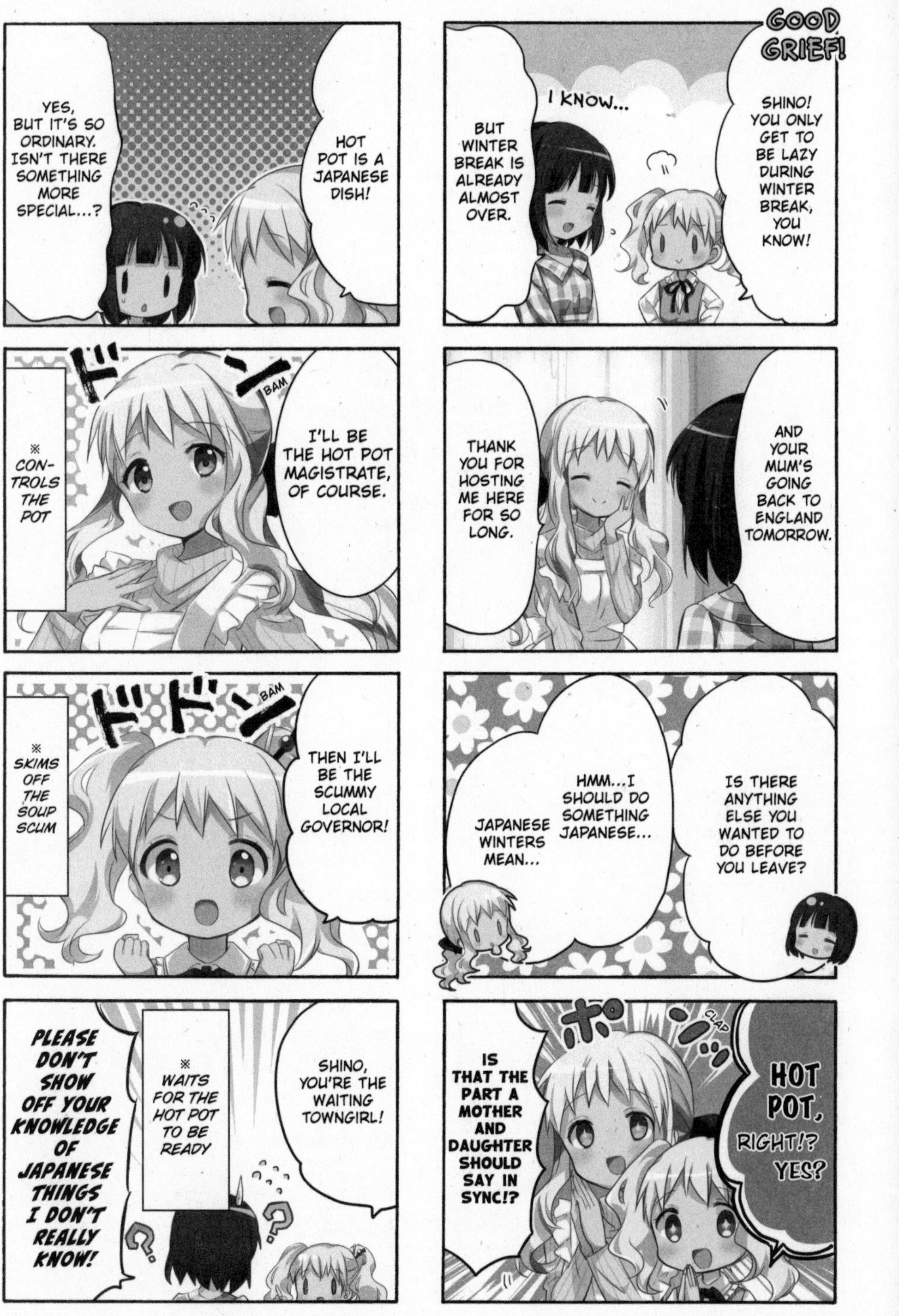
SHINO! YOU ONLY GET TO BE LAZY DURING WINTER BREAK, YOU KNOW!
BUT WINTER BREAK IS ALREADY ALMOST OVER.
I KNOW...
GOOD GRIEF!
AND YOUR MUM'S GOING BACK TO ENGLAND TOMORROW.
THANK YOU FOR HOSTING ME HERE FOR SO LONG.
IS THERE ANYTHING ELSE YOU WANTED TO DO BEFORE YOU LEAVE?
HMM...I SHOULD DO SOMETHING JAPANESE...
JAPANESE WINTERS MEAN...
CLAP
HOT POT, RIGHT!? YES?
IS THAT THE PART A MOTHER AND DAUGHTER SHOULD SAY IN SYNC!?
HOT POT IS A JAPANESE DISH!
YES, BUT IT'S SO ORDINARY. ISN'T THERE SOMETHING MORE SPECIAL...?
BAM
I'LL BE THE HOT POT MAGISTRATE, OF COURSE.
※ CONTROLS THE POT
BAM
THEN I'LL BE THE SCUMMY LOCAL GOVERNOR!
※ SKIMS OFF THE SOUP SCUM
SHINO, YOU'RE THE WAITING TOWNGIRL!
※ WAITS FOR THE HOT POT TO BE READY
PLEASE DON'T SHOW OFF YOUR KNOWLEDGE OF JAPANESE THINGS I DON'T REALLY KNOW!

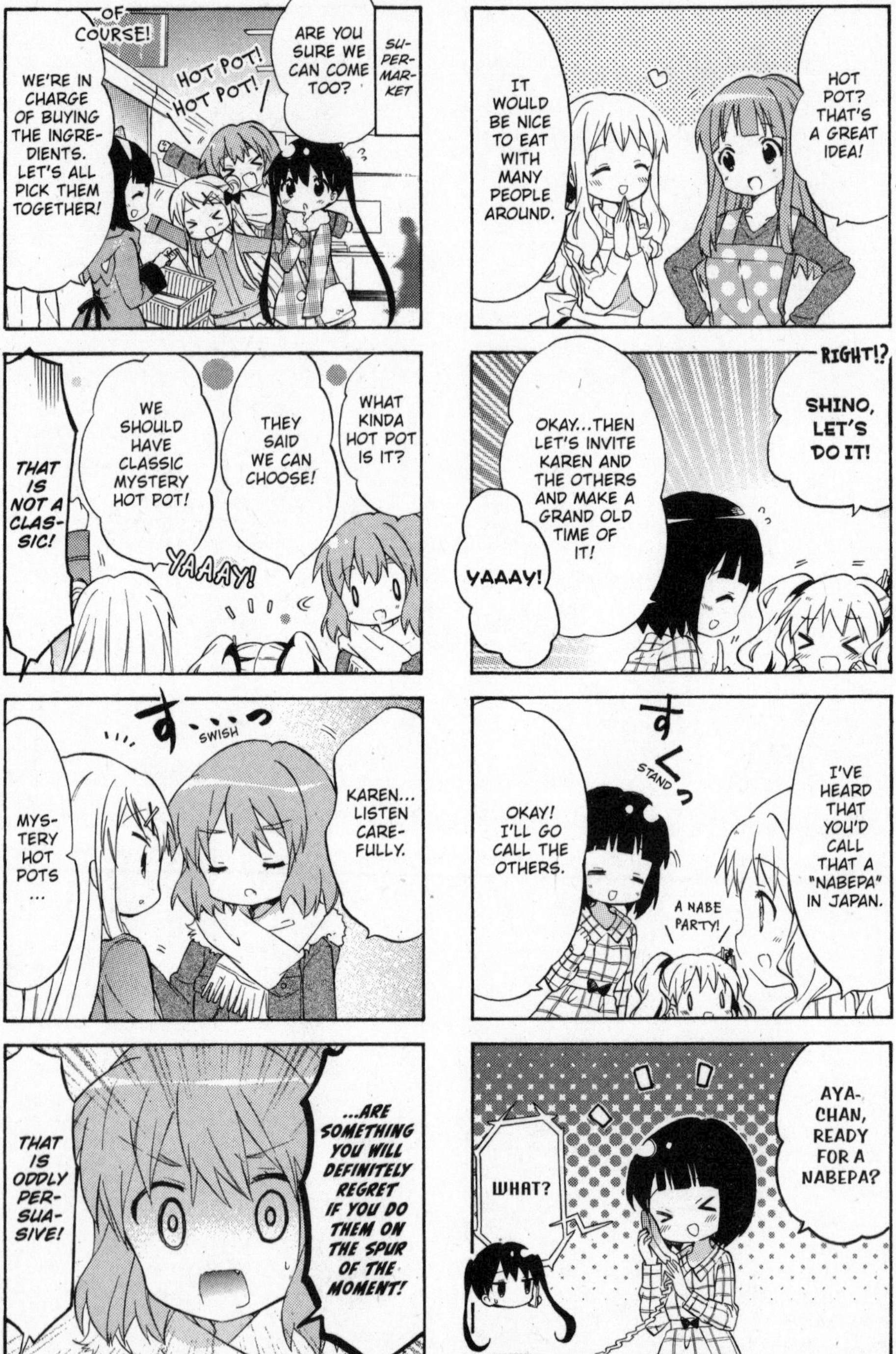

HOT POT? THAT'S A GREAT IDEA!
IT WOULD BE NICE TO EAT WITH MANY PEOPLE AROUND.
RIGHT!? SHINO, LET'S DO IT!
OKAY...THEN LET'S INVITE KAREN AND THE OTHERS AND MAKE A GRAND OLD TIME OF IT!
YAAAY!
I'VE HEARD THAT YOU'D CALL THAT A "NABEPA" IN JAPAN.
A NABE PARTY!
すくっ
STAND
OKAY! I'LL GO CALL THE OTHERS.
AYA-CHAN, READY FOR A NABEPA?
WHAT?
SUPER-MARKET
ARE YOU SURE WE CAN COME TOO?
HOT POT! HOT POT!
OF COURSE!
WE'RE IN CHARGE OF BUYING THE INGREDIENTS. LET'S ALL PICK THEM TOGETHER!
WHAT KINDA HOT POT IS IT?
THEY SAID WE CAN CHOOSE!
WE SHOULD HAVE CLASSIC MYSTERY HOT POT!
YAAAAY!
THAT IS NOT A CLASSIC!
KAREN... LISTEN CAREFULLY.
すーっ
SWISH
MYSTERY HOT POTS ...
...ARE SOMETHING YOU WILL DEFINITELY REGRET IF YOU DO THEM ON THE SPUR OF THE MOMENT!
THAT IS ODDLY PERSUASIVE!

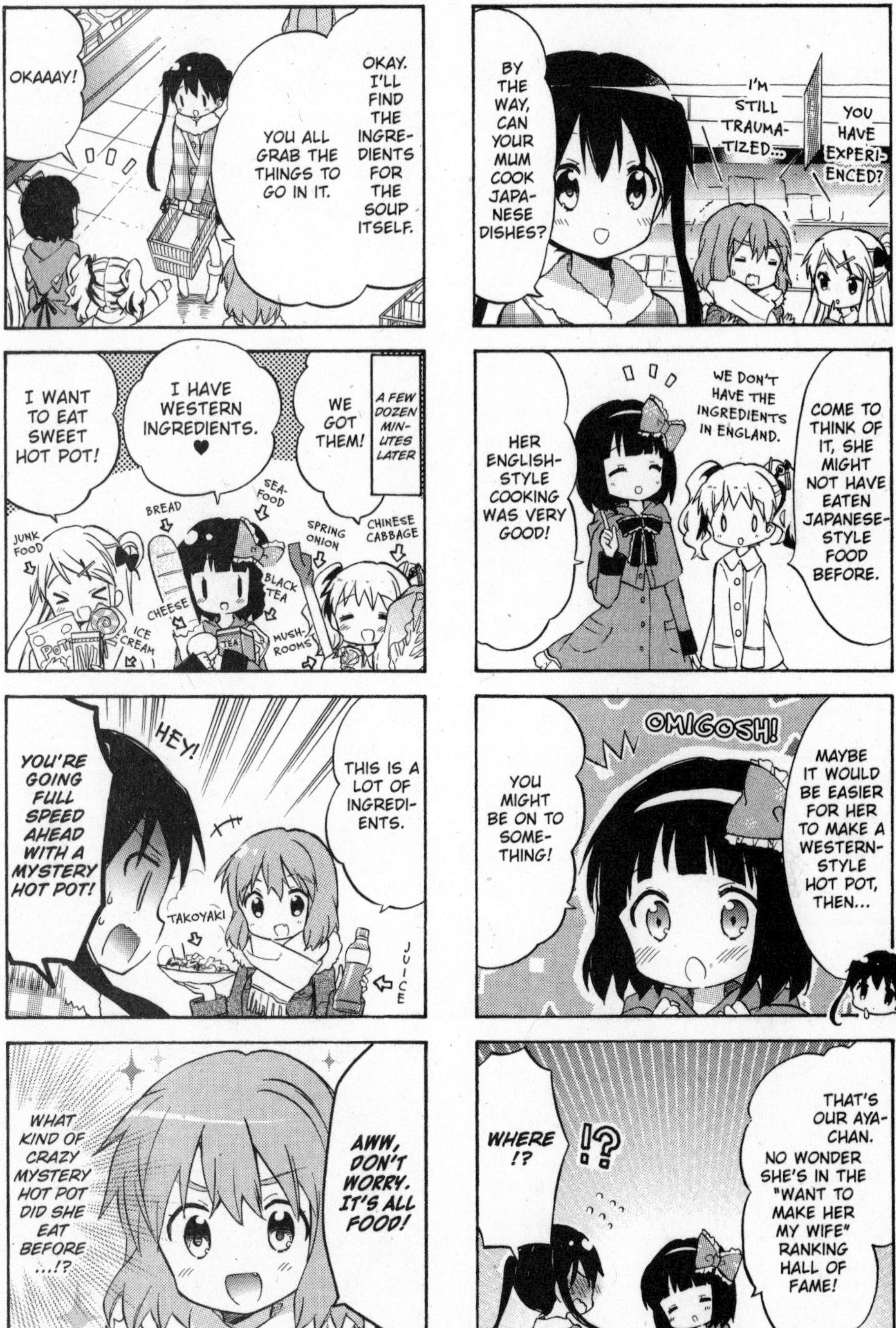
YOU HAVE EXPERIENCED?
I'M STILL TRAUMATIZED...
BY THE WAY, CAN YOUR MUM COOK JAPANESE DISHES?
COME TO THINK OF IT, SHE MIGHT NOT HAVE EATEN JAPANESE-STYLE FOOD BEFORE.
WE DON'T HAVE THE INGREDIENTS IN ENGLAND.
HER ENGLISH-STYLE COOKING WAS VERY GOOD!
MAYBE IT WOULD BE EASIER FOR HER TO MAKE A WESTERN-STYLE HOT POT, THEN...
OMIGOSH!
YOU MIGHT BE ON TO SOMETHING!
THAT'S OUR AYA-CHAN. NO WONDER SHE'S IN THE "WANT TO MAKE HER MY WIFE" RANKING HALL OF FAME!
!?
WHERE !?
OKAY. I'LL FIND THE INGREDIENTS FOR THE SOUP ITSELF.
YOU ALL GRAB THE THINGS TO GO IN IT.
OKAAAY!
A FEW DOZEN MINUTES LATER
WE GOT THEM!
I HAVE WESTERN INGREDIENTS. ♥
I WANT TO EAT SWEET HOT POT!
CHINESE CABBAGE
SPRING ONION
MUSHROOMS
SEAFOOD
BLACK TEA
BREAD
CHEESE
ICE CREAM
JUNK FOOD
THIS IS A LOT OF INGREDIENTS.
HEY!
YOU'RE GOING FULL SPEED AHEAD WITH A MYSTERY HOT POT!
JUICE
TAKOYAKI
AWW, DON'T WORRY. IT'S ALL FOOD!
WHAT KIND OF CRAZY MYSTERY HOT POT DID SHE EAT BEFORE ...!?

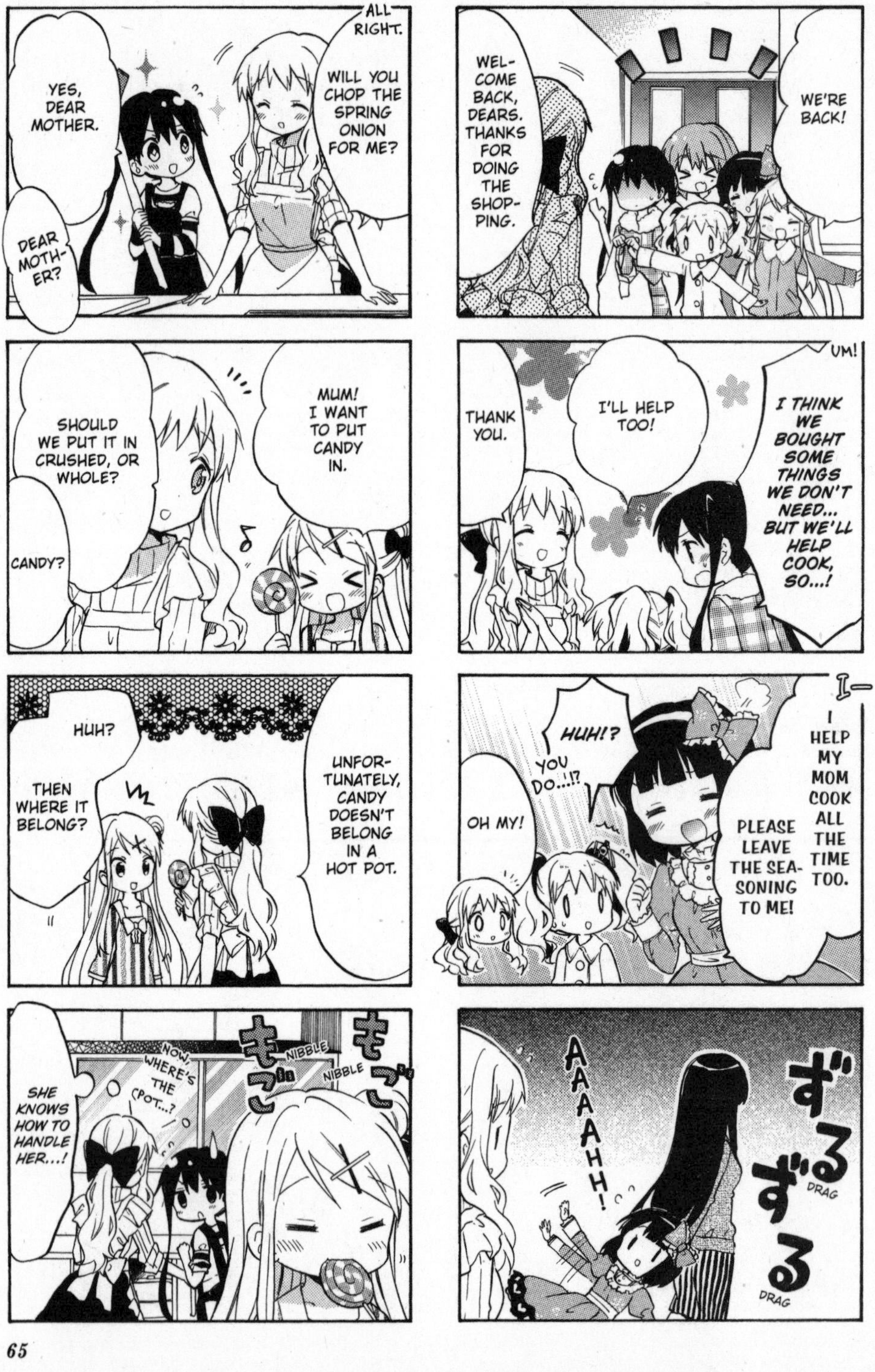
WE'RE BACK!
WEL-COME BACK, DEARS. THANKS FOR DOING THE SHOP-PING.
UM!
I THINK WE BOUGHT SOME THINGS WE DON'T NEED... BUT WE'LL HELP COOK, SO...!
I'LL HELP TOO!
THANK YOU.
I—
I HELP MY MOM COOK ALL THE TIME TOO.
PLEASE LEAVE THE SEA-SONING TO ME!
HUH!?
YOU DO...!?
OH MY!
ずるずる
DRAG
DRAG
AAAAHH!
ALL RIGHT.
WILL YOU CHOP THE SPRING ONION FOR ME?
YES, DEAR MOTHER.
DEAR MOTH-ER?
MUM! I WANT TO PUT CANDY IN.
SHOULD WE PUT IT IN CRUSHED, OR WHOLE?
CANDY?
UNFOR-TUNATELY, CANDY DOESN'T BELONG IN A HOT POT.
HUH?
THEN WHERE IT BELONG?
もご もご
NIBBLE
NIBBLE
NOW, WHERE'S THE POT...?
SHE KNOWS HOW TO HANDLE HER...!

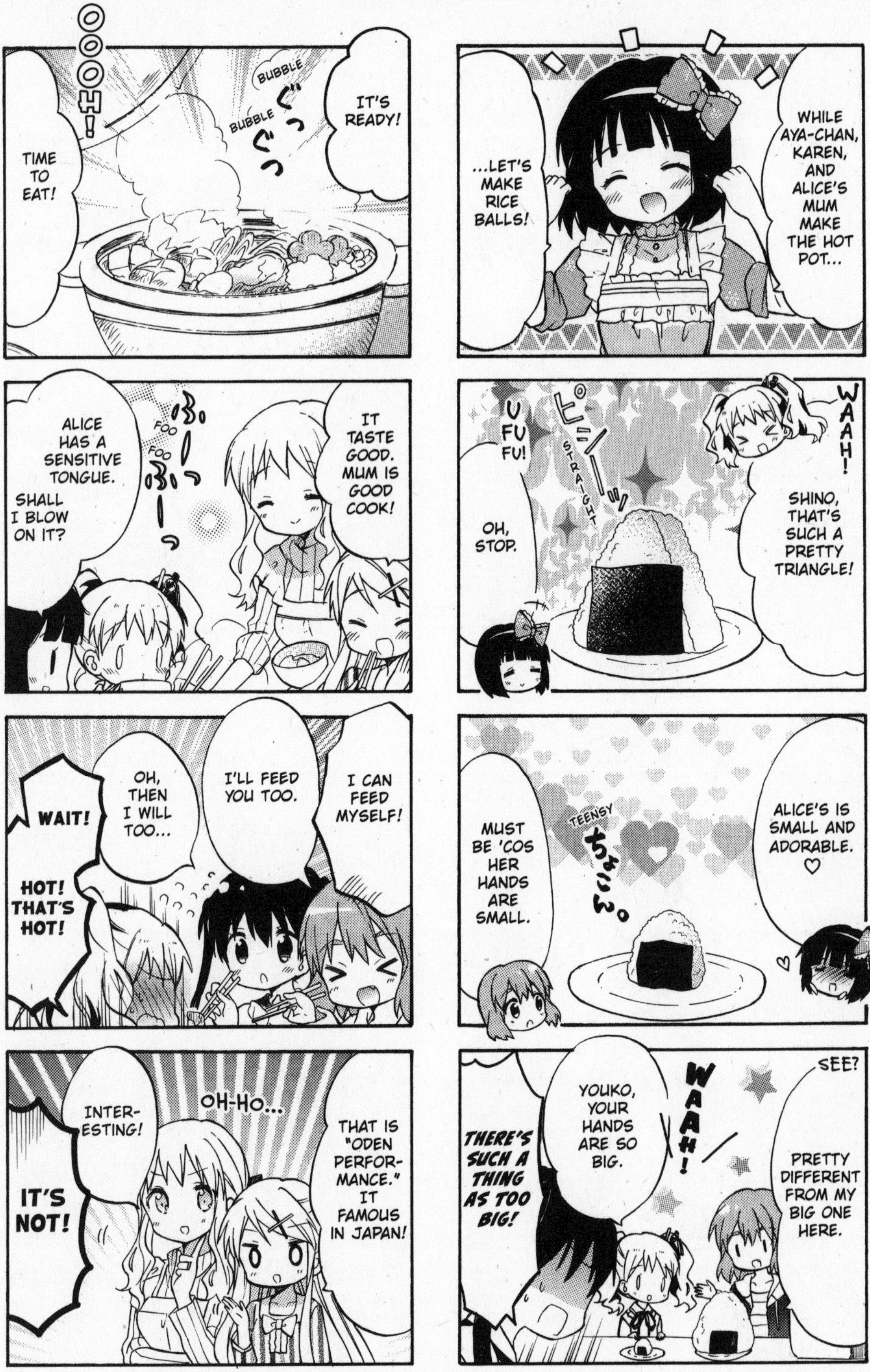

WHILE AYA-CHAN, KAREN, AND ALICE'S MUM MAKE THE HOT POT...
...LET'S MAKE RICE BALLS!
WAAAH!
SHINO, THAT'S SUCH A PRETTY TRIANGLE!
STRAIGHT
UFUFU!
OH, STOP.
ALICE'S IS SMALL AND ADORABLE. ♡
TEENSY
ちょこん。
MUST BE 'COS HER HANDS ARE SMALL.
SEE?
PRETTY DIFFERENT FROM MY BIG ONE HERE.
WAAAH!
YOUKO, YOUR HANDS ARE SO BIG.
THERE'S SUCH A THING AS TOO BIG!
IT'S READY!
BUBBLE
BUBBLE
OOOOH!
TIME TO EAT!
IT TASTE GOOD. MUM IS GOOD COOK!
FOO
FOO
ALICE HAS A SENSITIVE TONGUE.
SHALL I BLOW ON IT?
I CAN FEED MYSELF!
I'LL FEED YOU TOO.
OH, THEN I WILL TOO...
WAIT!
HOT! THAT'S HOT!
THAT IS "ODEN PERFORMANCE." IT FAMOUS IN JAPAN!
OH-HO...
INTER-ESTING!
IT'S NOT!

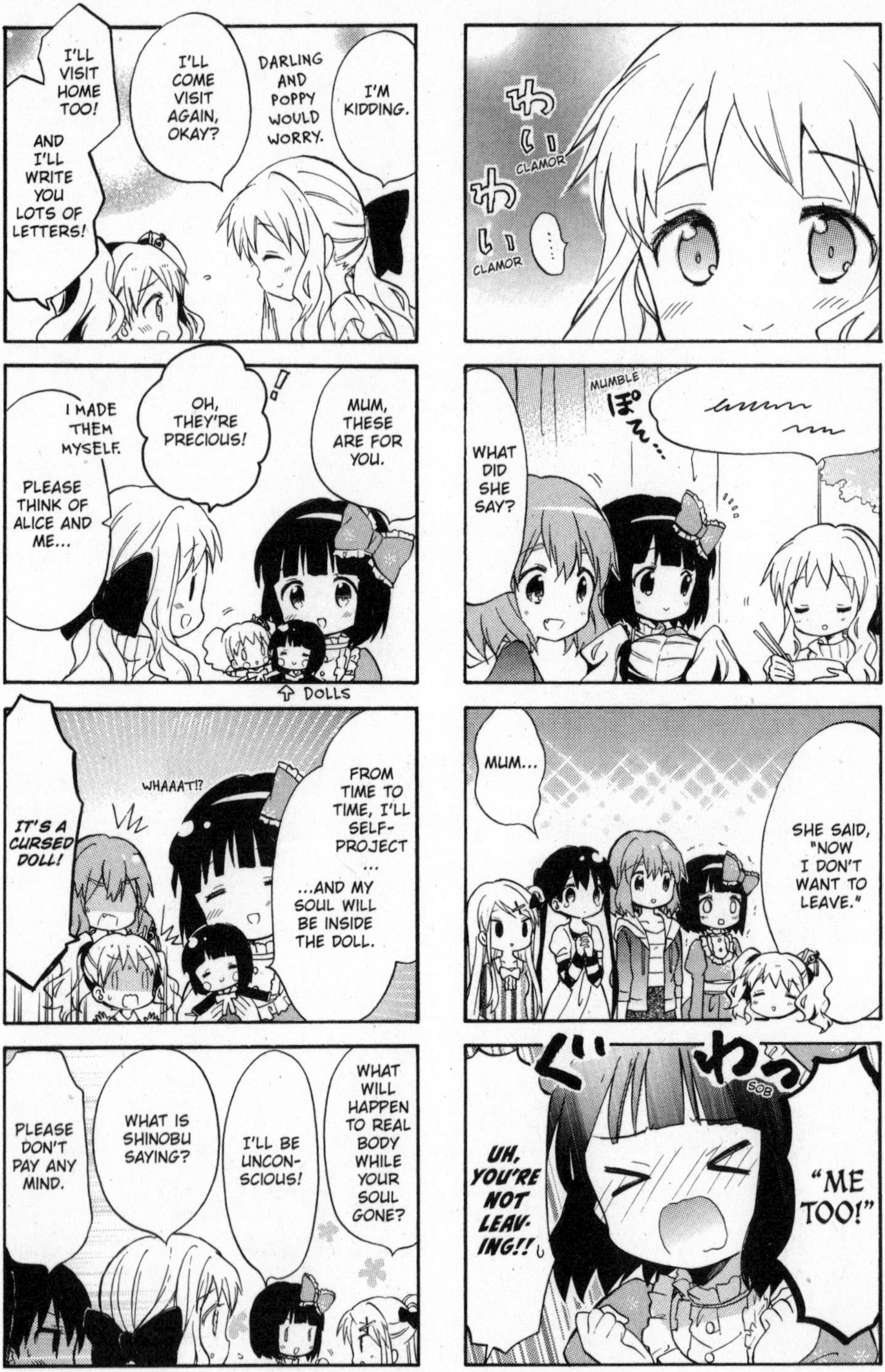

わい
CLAMOR
わい
CLAMOR
...
I'M KIDDING.
DARLING AND POPPY WOULD WORRY.
I'LL COME VISIT AGAIN, OKAY?
I'LL VISIT HOME TOO!
AND I'LL WRITE YOU LOTS OF LETTERS!
MUMBLE
ぽそ...
WHAT DID SHE SAY?
MUM, THESE ARE FOR YOU.
!
OH, THEY'RE PRECIOUS!
I MADE THEM MYSELF.
PLEASE THINK OF ALICE AND ME...
⇧ DOLLS
SHE SAID, "NOW I DON'T WANT TO LEAVE."
MUM...
FROM TIME TO TIME, I'LL SELF-PROJECT ...
...AND MY SOUL WILL BE INSIDE THE DOLL.
WHAAAT!?
IT'S A CURSED DOLL!
ぐわっ
SOB
"ME TOO!"
UH, YOU'RE NOT LEAVING!!
WHAT WILL HAPPEN TO REAL BODY WHILE YOUR SOUL GONE?
I'LL BE UNCONSCIOUS!
WHAT IS SHINOBU SAYING?
PLEASE DON'T PAY ANY MIND.

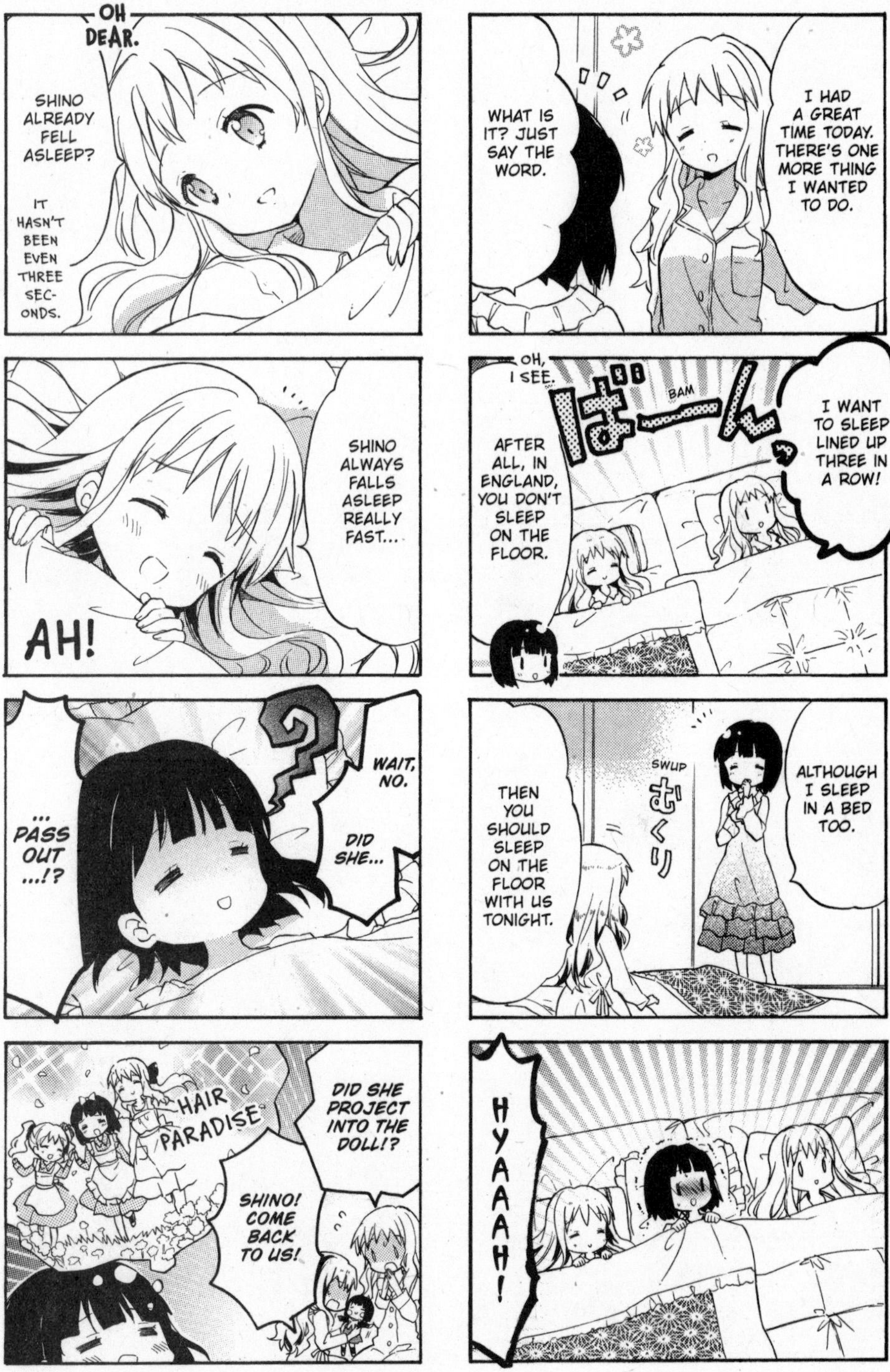
I HAD A GREAT TIME TODAY. THERE'S ONE MORE THING I WANTED TO DO.
WHAT IS IT? JUST SAY THE WORD.
I WANT TO SLEEP LINED UP THREE IN A ROW!
ばーーん
BAM
OH, I SEE.
AFTER ALL, IN ENGLAND, YOU DON'T SLEEP ON THE FLOOR.
ALTHOUGH I SLEEP IN A BED TOO.
SWUP
むくり
THEN YOU SHOULD SLEEP ON THE FLOOR WITH US TONIGHT.
HYAAAAH!
OH DEAR.
SHINO ALREADY FELL ASLEEP?
IT HASN'T BEEN EVEN THREE SEC-ONDS.
SHINO ALWAYS FALLS ASLEEP REALLY FAST...
AH!
WAIT, NO.
DID SHE...
...PASS OUT ...!?
DID SHE PROJECT INTO THE DOLL!?
HAIR PARADISE
SHINO! COME BACK TO US!

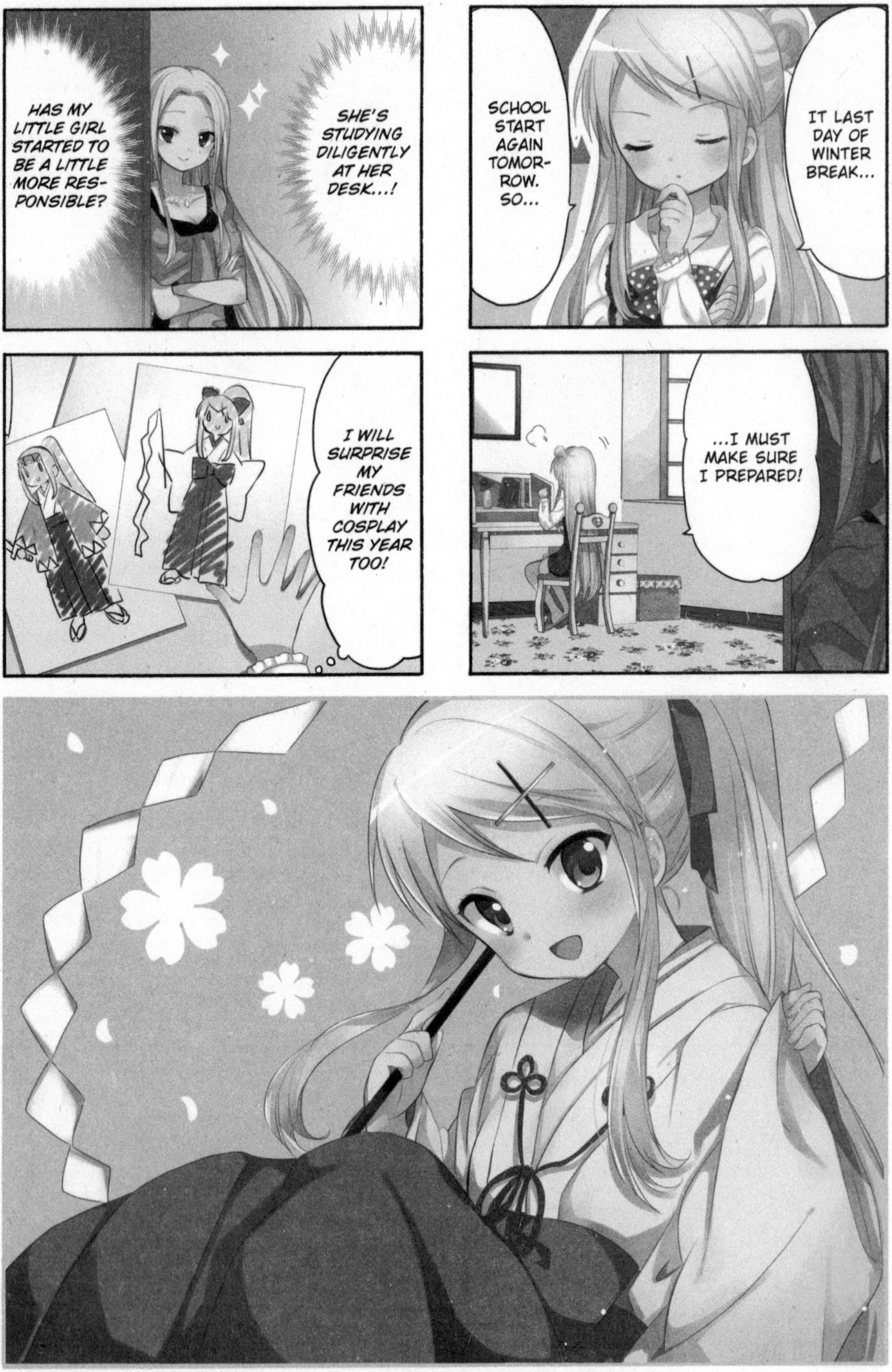
IT LAST DAY OF WINTER BREAK...
SCHOOL START AGAIN TOMORROW. SO...
SHE'S STUDYING DILIGENTLY AT HER DESK...!
HAS MY LITTLE GIRL STARTED TO BE A LITTLE MORE RESPONSIBLE?
...I MUST MAKE SURE I PREPARED!
I WILL SURPRISE MY FRIENDS WITH COSPLAY THIS YEAR TOO!

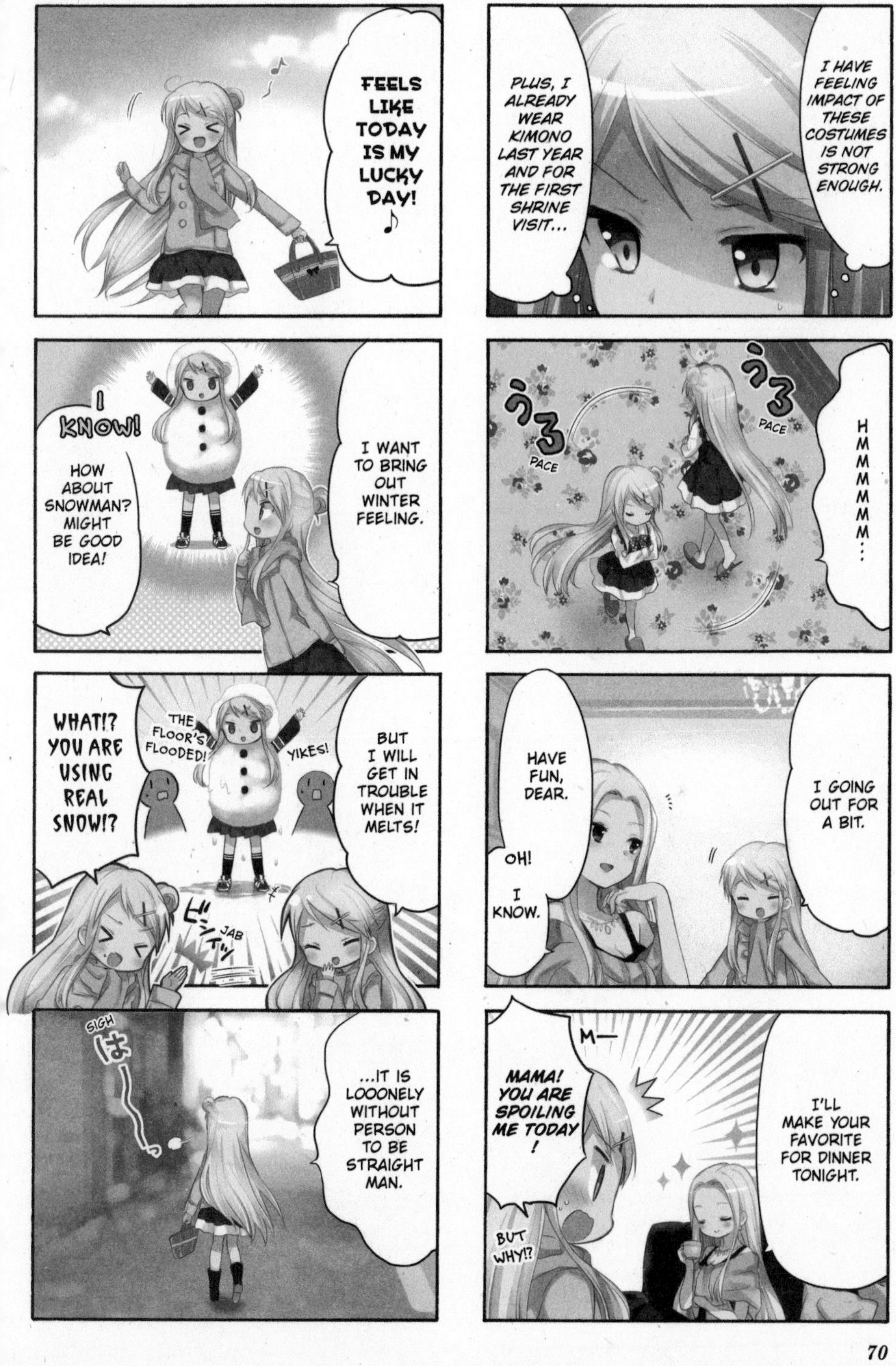
I HAVE FEELING IMPACT OF THESE COSTUMES IS NOT STRONG ENOUGH.
PLUS, I ALREADY WEAR KIMONO LAST YEAR AND FOR THE FIRST SHRINE VISIT...
HMMMMMM...
うろ
PACE
うろ
PACE
I GOING OUT FOR A BIT.
HAVE FUN, DEAR.
OH!
I KNOW.
I'LL MAKE YOUR FAVORITE FOR DINNER TONIGHT.
M—
MAMA! YOU ARE SPOILING ME TODAY!
BUT WHY!?
FEELS LIKE TODAY IS MY LUCKY DAY! ♪
I WANT TO BRING OUT WINTER FEELING.
I KNOW!
HOW ABOUT SNOWMAN? MIGHT BE GOOD IDEA!
BUT I WILL GET IN TROUBLE WHEN IT MELTS!
YIKES!
THE FLOOR'S FLOODED!
WHAT!? YOU ARE USING REAL SNOW!?
JAB
...IT IS LOOONELY WITHOUT PERSON TO BE STRAIGHT MAN.
SIGH
はー

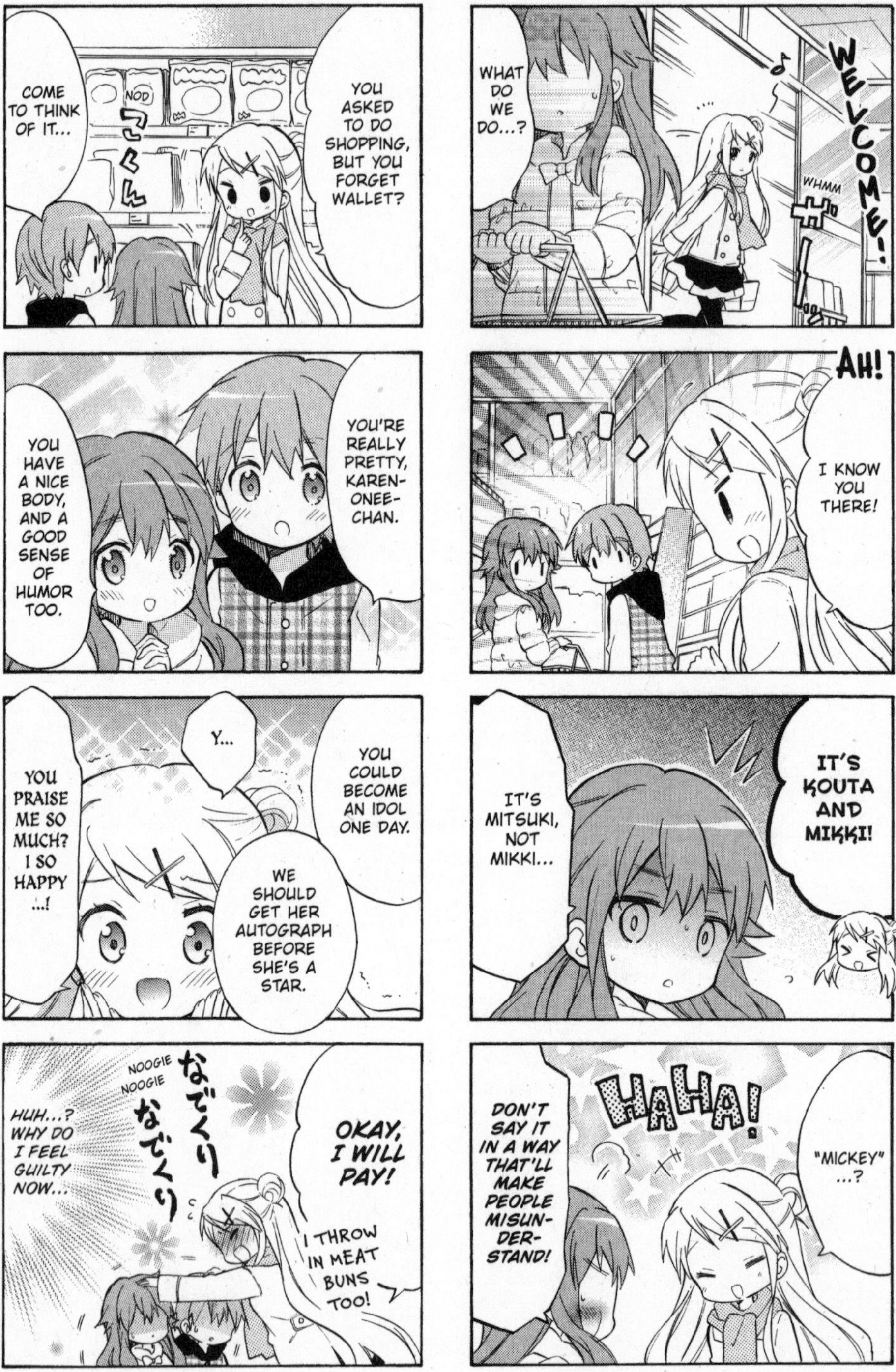
WELCOME!
WHMM
...
WHAT DO WE DO...?
YOU ASKED TO DO SHOPPING, BUT YOU FORGET WALLET?
NOD
こくん
COME TO THINK OF IT...
AH!
I KNOW YOU THERE!
YOU'RE REALLY PRETTY, KAREN-ONEE-CHAN.
YOU HAVE A NICE BODY, AND A GOOD SENSE OF HUMOR TOO.
IT'S KOUTA AND MIKKI!
IT'S MITSUKI, NOT MIKKI...
YOU COULD BECOME AN IDOL ONE DAY.
WE SHOULD GET HER AUTOGRAPH BEFORE SHE'S A STAR.
Y...
YOU PRAISE ME SO MUCH? I SO HAPPY ...!
"MICKEY" ...?
HAHA!
DON'T SAY IT IN A WAY THAT'LL MAKE PEOPLE MISUNDERSTAND!
OKAY, I WILL PAY!
I THROW IN MEAT BUNS TOO!
なでくり なでくり
NOOGIE NOOGIE
HUH...? WHY DO I FEEL GUILTY NOW...

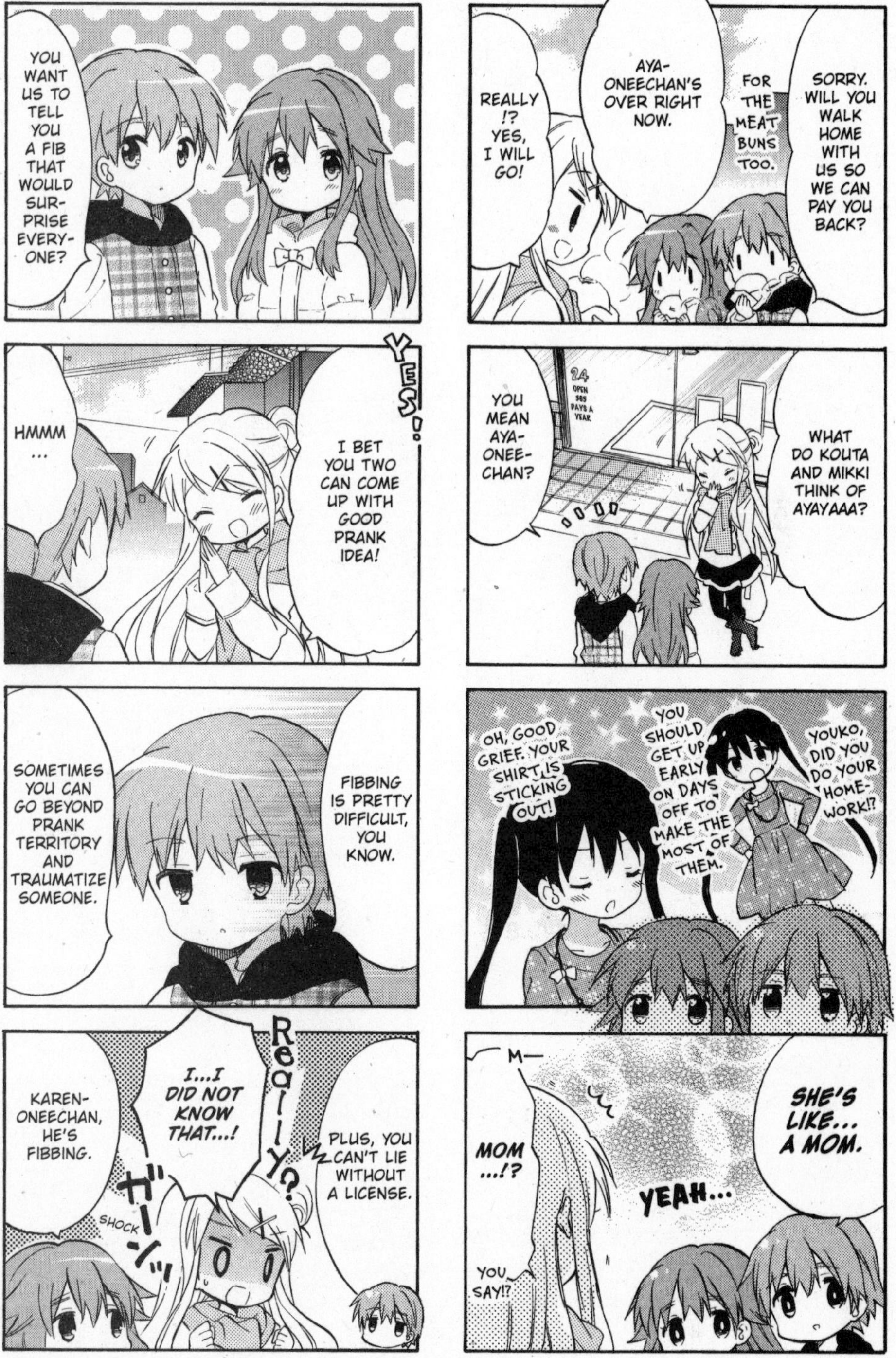
SORRY. WILL YOU WALK HOME WITH US SO WE CAN PAY YOU BACK?
FOR THE MEAT BUNS TOO.
AYA-ONEECHAN'S OVER RIGHT NOW.
REALLY!? YES, I WILL GO!
WHAT DO KOUTA AND MIKKI THINK OF AYAYAAA?
YOU MEAN AYA-ONEE-CHAN?
YOUKO, DID YOU DO YOUR HOME-WORK!?
YOU SHOULD GET UP EARLY ON DAYS OFF TO MAKE THE MOST OF THEM.
OH, GOOD GRIEF. YOUR SHIRT IS STICKING OUT!
SHE'S LIKE... A MOM.
YEAH...
M—
MOM...!?
YOU SAY!?
YOU WANT US TO TELL YOU A FIB THAT WOULD SURPRISE EVERY-ONE?
YES!
I BET YOU TWO CAN COME UP WITH GOOD PRANK IDEA!
HMMM...
FIBBING IS PRETTY DIFFICULT, YOU KNOW.
SOMETIMES YOU CAN GO BEYOND PRANK TERRITORY AND TRAUMATIZE SOMEONE.
Really?
PLUS, YOU CAN'T LIE WITHOUT A LICENSE.
I...I DID NOT KNOW THAT...!
KAREN-ONEECHAN, HE'S FIBBING.
SHOCK

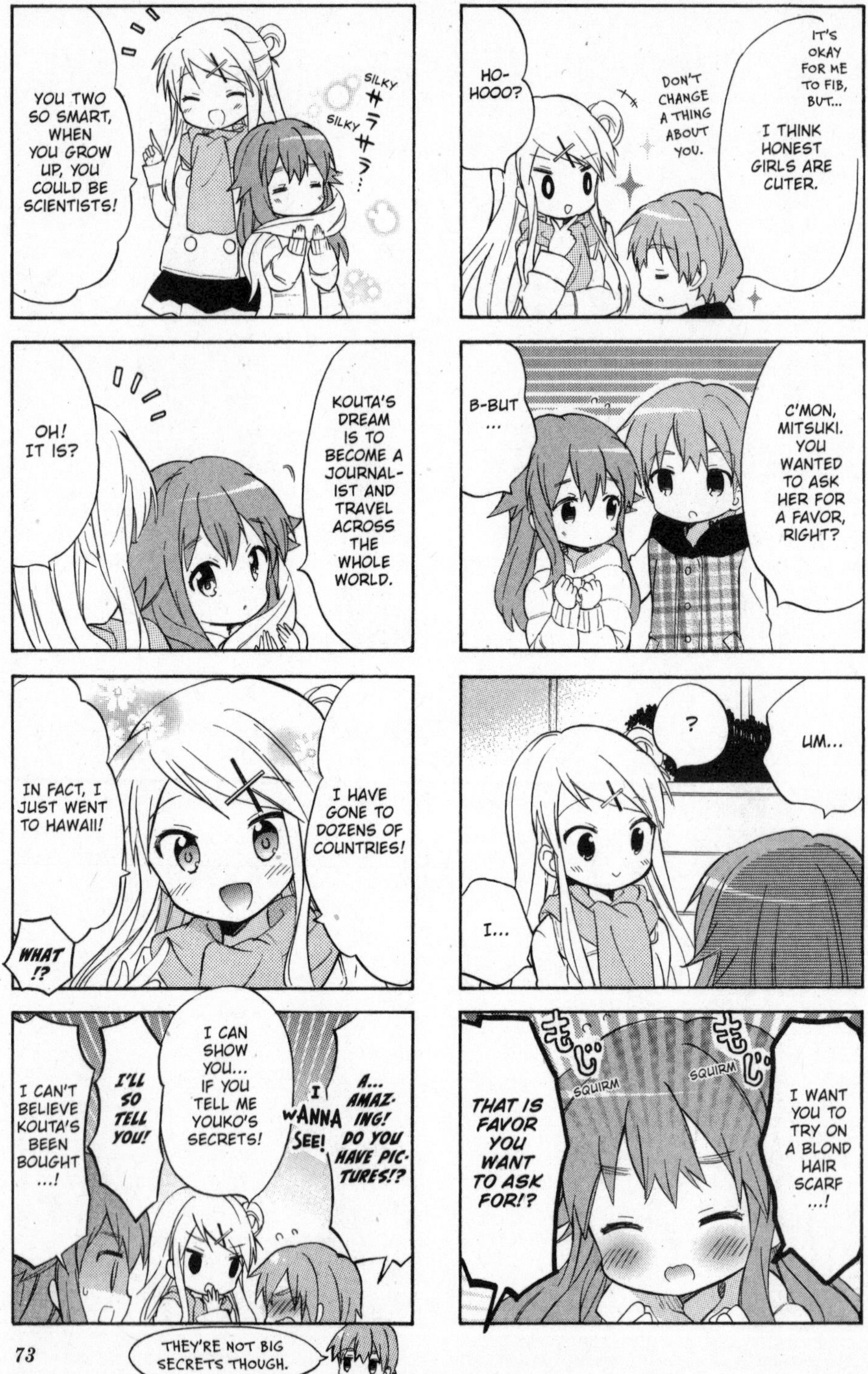
IT'S OKAY FOR ME TO FIB, BUT...
I THINK HONEST GIRLS ARE CUTER.
DON'T CHANGE A THING ABOUT YOU.
HO-HOOO?
C'MON, MITSUKI. YOU WANTED TO ASK HER FOR A FAVOR, RIGHT?
B-BUT ...
UM...
?
I...
SQUIRM
SQUIRM
I WANT YOU TO TRY ON A BLOND HAIR SCARF ...!
THAT IS FAVOR YOU WANT TO ASK FOR!?
SILKY
SILKY
YOU TWO SO SMART, WHEN YOU GROW UP, YOU COULD BE SCIENTISTS!
KOUTA'S DREAM IS TO BECOME A JOURNAL-IST AND TRAVEL ACROSS THE WHOLE WORLD.
OH! IT IS?
I HAVE GONE TO DOZENS OF COUNTRIES!
IN FACT, I JUST WENT TO HAWAII!
WHAT !?
A... AMAZ-ING! DO YOU HAVE PIC-TURES!?
I WANNA SEE!
I CAN SHOW YOU... IF YOU TELL ME YOUKO'S SECRETS!
I'LL SO TELL YOU!
I CAN'T BELIEVE KOUTA'S BEEN BOUGHT ...!
THEY'RE NOT BIG SECRETS THOUGH.

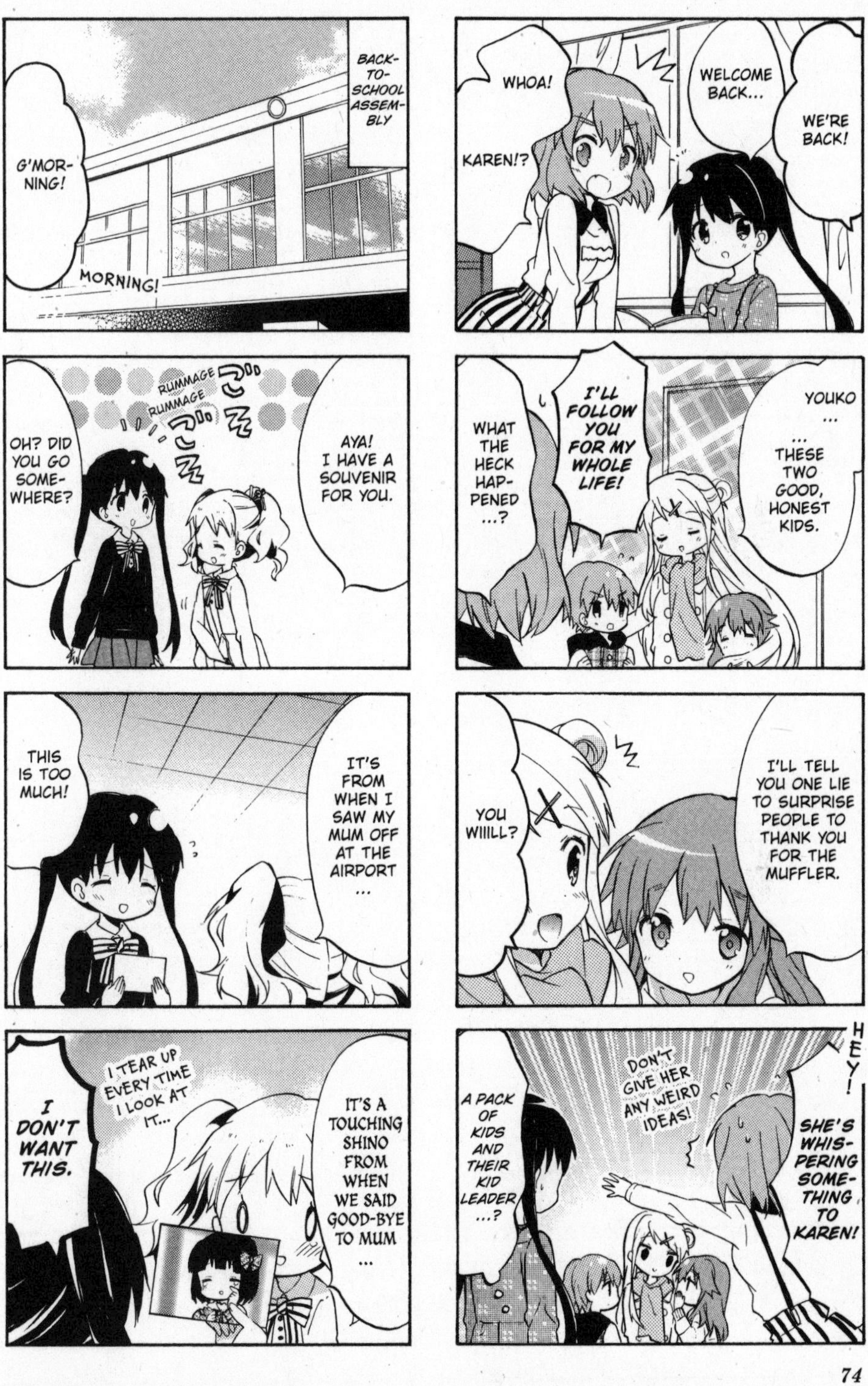
WELCOME BACK...
WE'RE BACK!
WHOA!
KAREN!?
YOUKO ... ... THESE TWO GOOD, HONEST KIDS.
I'LL FOLLOW YOU FOR MY WHOLE LIFE!
WHAT THE HECK HAPPENED ...?
I'LL TELL YOU ONE LIE TO SURPRISE PEOPLE TO THANK YOU FOR THE MUFFLER.
YOU WIIILL?
HEY!
SHE'S WHISPERING SOMETHING TO KAREN!
DON'T GIVE HER ANY WEIRD IDEAS!
A PACK OF KIDS AND THEIR KID LEADER ...?
BACK-TO-SCHOOL ASSEMBLY
G'MORNING!
MORNING!
AYA! I HAVE A SOUVENIR FOR YOU.
RUMMAGE
RUMMAGE
OH? DID YOU GO SOMEWHERE?
IT'S FROM WHEN I SAW MY MUM OFF AT THE AIRPORT ...
THIS IS TOO MUCH!
IT'S A TOUCHING SHINO FROM WHEN WE SAID GOOD-BYE TO MUM ...
I TEAR UP EVERY TIME I LOOK AT IT...
I DON'T WANT THIS.

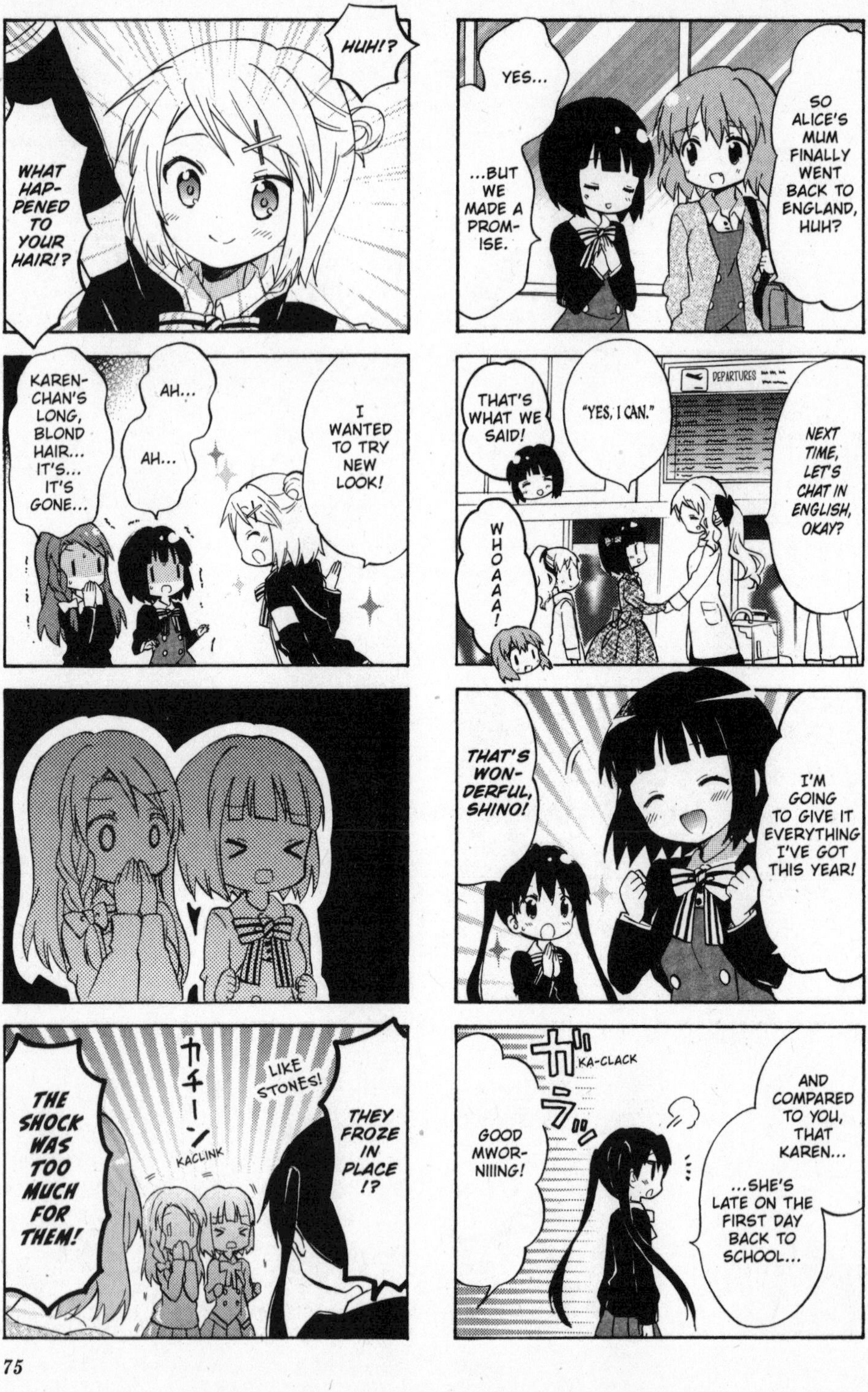
SO ALICE'S MUM FINALLY WENT BACK TO ENGLAND, HUH?
YES...
...BUT WE MADE A PROMISE.
NEXT TIME, LET'S CHAT IN ENGLISH, OKAY?
DEPARTURES
"YES, I CAN."
THAT'S WHAT WE SAID!
WHOAAAA!
I'M GOING TO GIVE IT EVERYTHING I'VE GOT THIS YEAR!
THAT'S WONDERFUL, SHINO!
AND COMPARED TO YOU, THAT KAREN...
...SHE'S LATE ON THE FIRST DAY BACK TO SCHOOL...
ガラッ
KA-CLACK
GOOD MWORNIIING!
HUH!?
WHAT HAPPENED TO YOUR HAIR!?
I WANTED TO TRY NEW LOOK!
AH...
AH...
KAREN-CHAN'S LONG, BLOND HAIR... IT'S... IT'S GONE...
THEY FROZE IN PLACE!?
LIKE STONES!
カチーン
KACLINK
THE SHOCK WAS TOO MUCH FOR THEM!

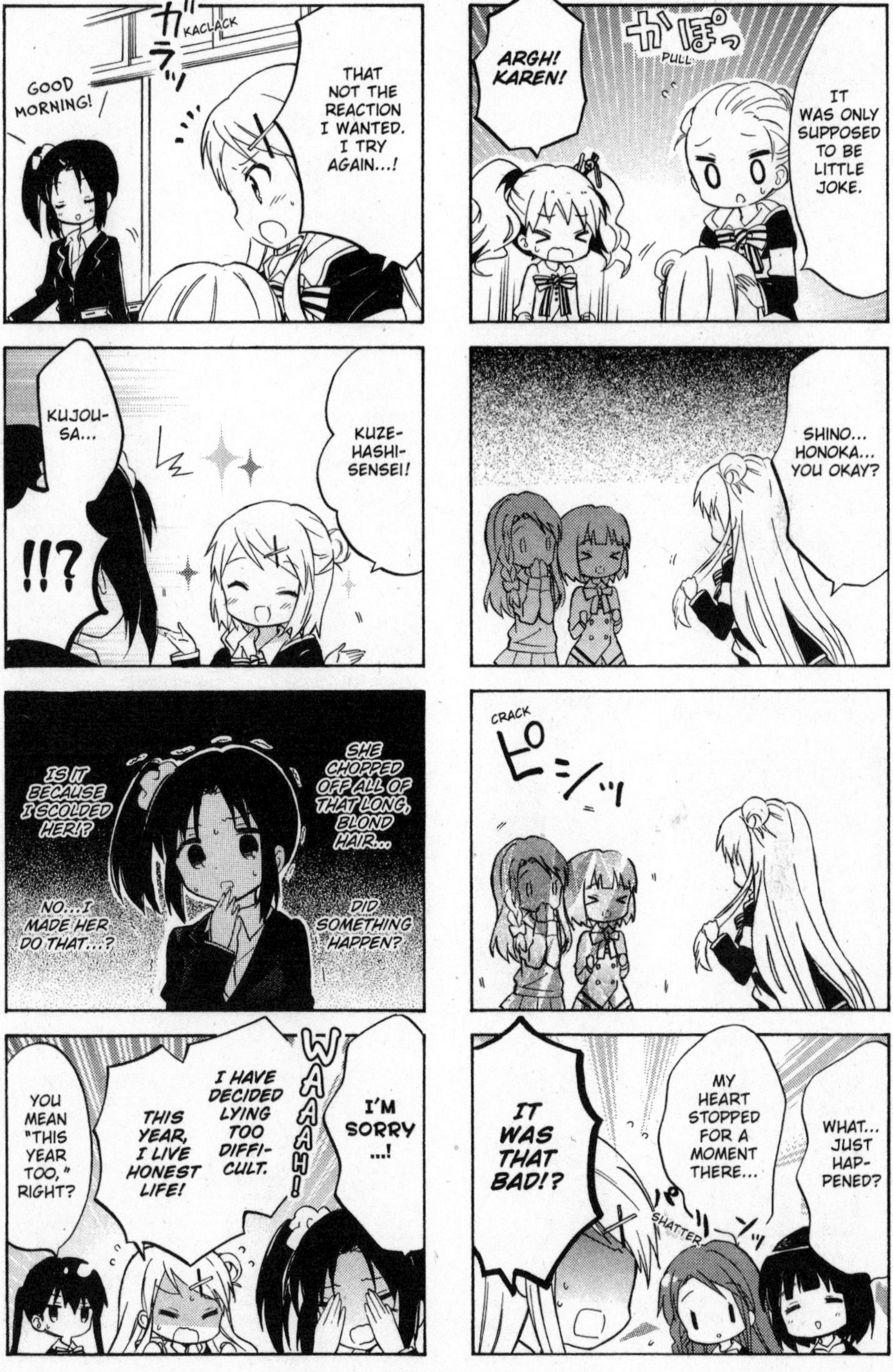
PULL
ARGH! KAREN!
IT WAS ONLY SUPPOSED TO BE LITTLE JOKE.
SHINO... HONOKA... YOU OKAY?
CRACK
WHAT... JUST HAP-PENED?
MY HEART STOPPED FOR A MOMENT THERE...
IT WAS THAT BAD!?
SHATTER
KACLACK
GOOD MORNING!
THAT NOT THE REACTION I WANTED. I TRY AGAIN...!
KUZE-HASHI-SENSEI!
KUJOU-SA...
!!?
SHE CHOPPED OFF ALL OF THAT LONG, BLOND HAIR...
DID SOMETHING HAPPEN?
IS IT BECAUSE I SCOLDED HER!?
NO... I MADE HER DO THAT...?
I'M SORRY...!
WAAAAH!
I HAVE DECIDED LYING TOO DIFFI-CULT.
THIS YEAR, I LIVE HONEST LIFE!
YOU MEAN "THIS YEAR TOO," RIGHT?

LEVEL OF SURPRISE

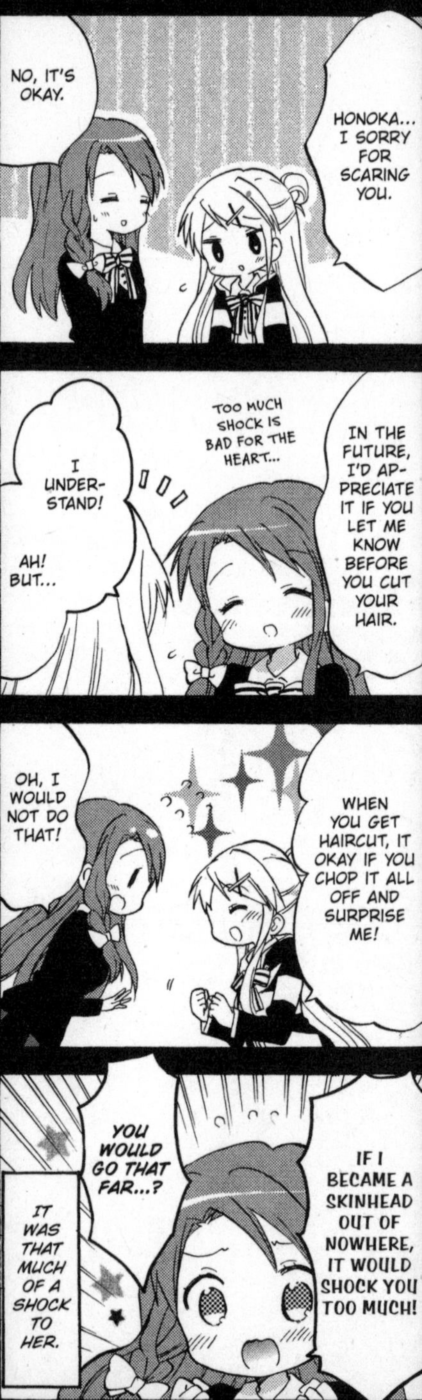
HONOKA... I SORRY FOR SCARING YOU.
NO, IT'S OKAY.
IN THE FUTURE, I'D AP-PRECIATE IT IF YOU LET ME KNOW BEFORE YOU CUT YOUR HAIR.
TOO MUCH SHOCK IS BAD FOR THE HEART...
I UNDER-STAND!
AH! BUT...
WHEN YOU GET HAIRCUT, IT OKAY IF YOU CHOP IT ALL OFF AND SURPRISE ME!
OH, I WOULD NOT DO THAT!
IF I BECAME A SKINHEAD OUT OF NOWHERE, IT WOULD SHOCK YOU TOO MUCH!
YOU WOULD GO THAT FAR...?
IT WAS THAT MUCH OF A SHOCK TO HER.

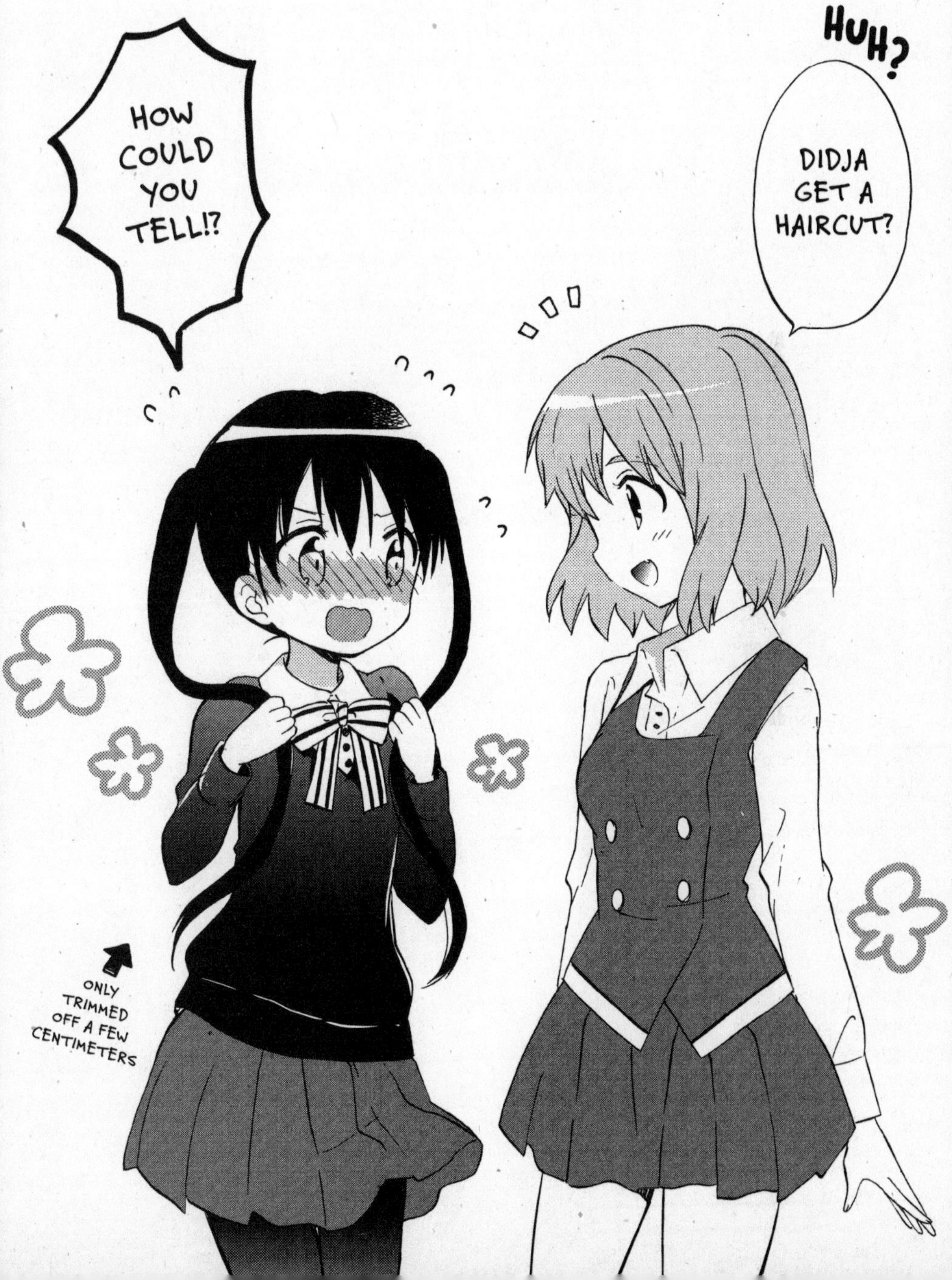
HUH?
DIDJA GET A HAIRCUT?
HOW COULD YOU TELL!?
ONLY TRIMMED OFF A FEW CENTIMETERS

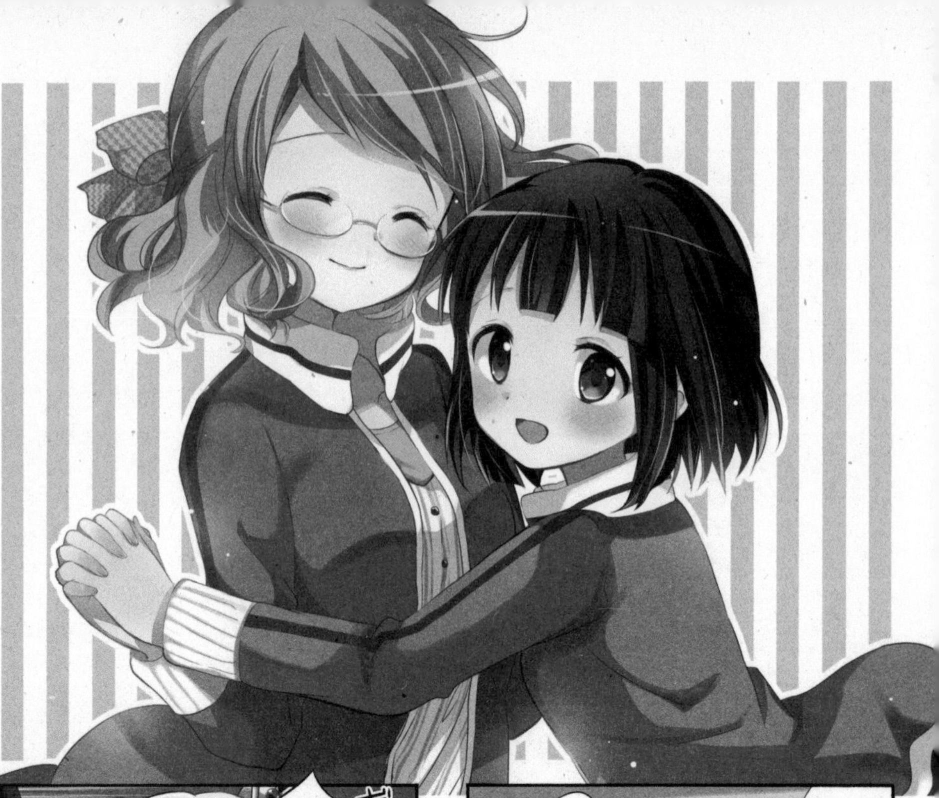

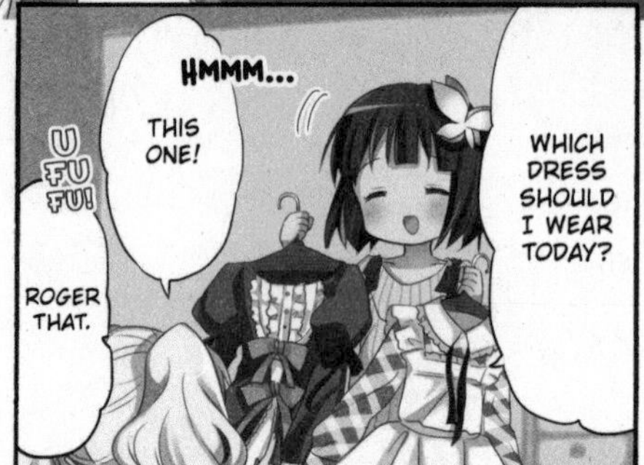
WHICH DRESS SHOULD I WEAR TODAY?
HMMM...
THIS ONE!
U FU FU!
ROGER THAT.

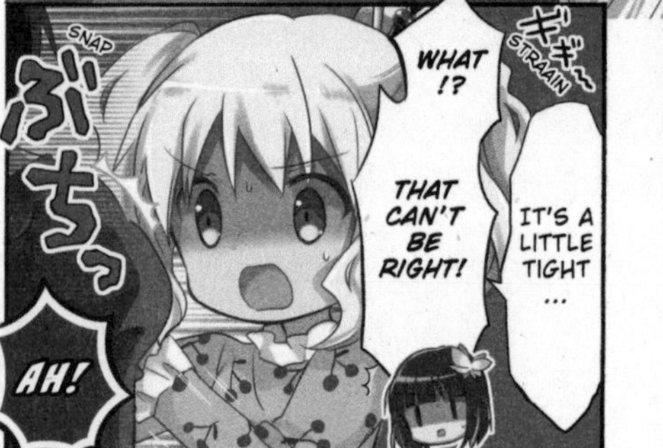
ギギ~
STRAAIN
WHAT !?
IT'S A LITTLE TIGHT ...
THAT CAN'T BE RIGHT!
SNAP
ぶちっ
AH!

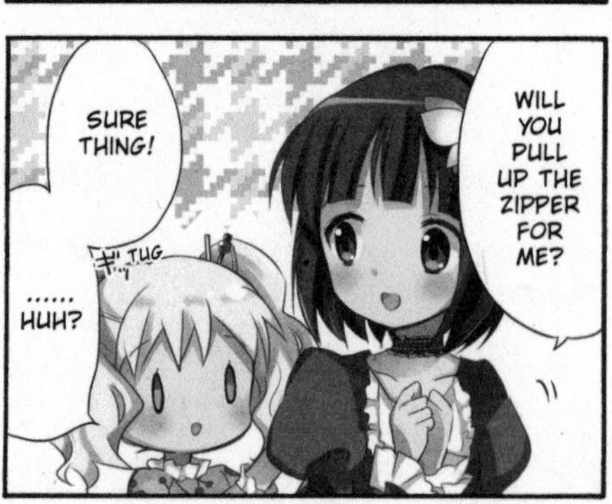
WILL YOU PULL UP THE ZIPPER FOR ME?
SURE THING!
TUG
...... HUH?

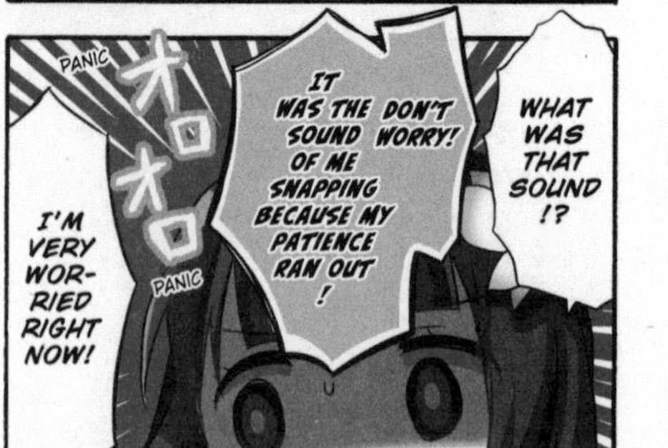
WHAT WAS THAT SOUND !?
DON'T WORRY!
IT WAS THE SOUND OF ME SNAPPING BECAUSE MY PATIENCE RAN OUT !
PANIC
オロオロ
PANIC
I'M VERY WOR-RIED RIGHT NOW!

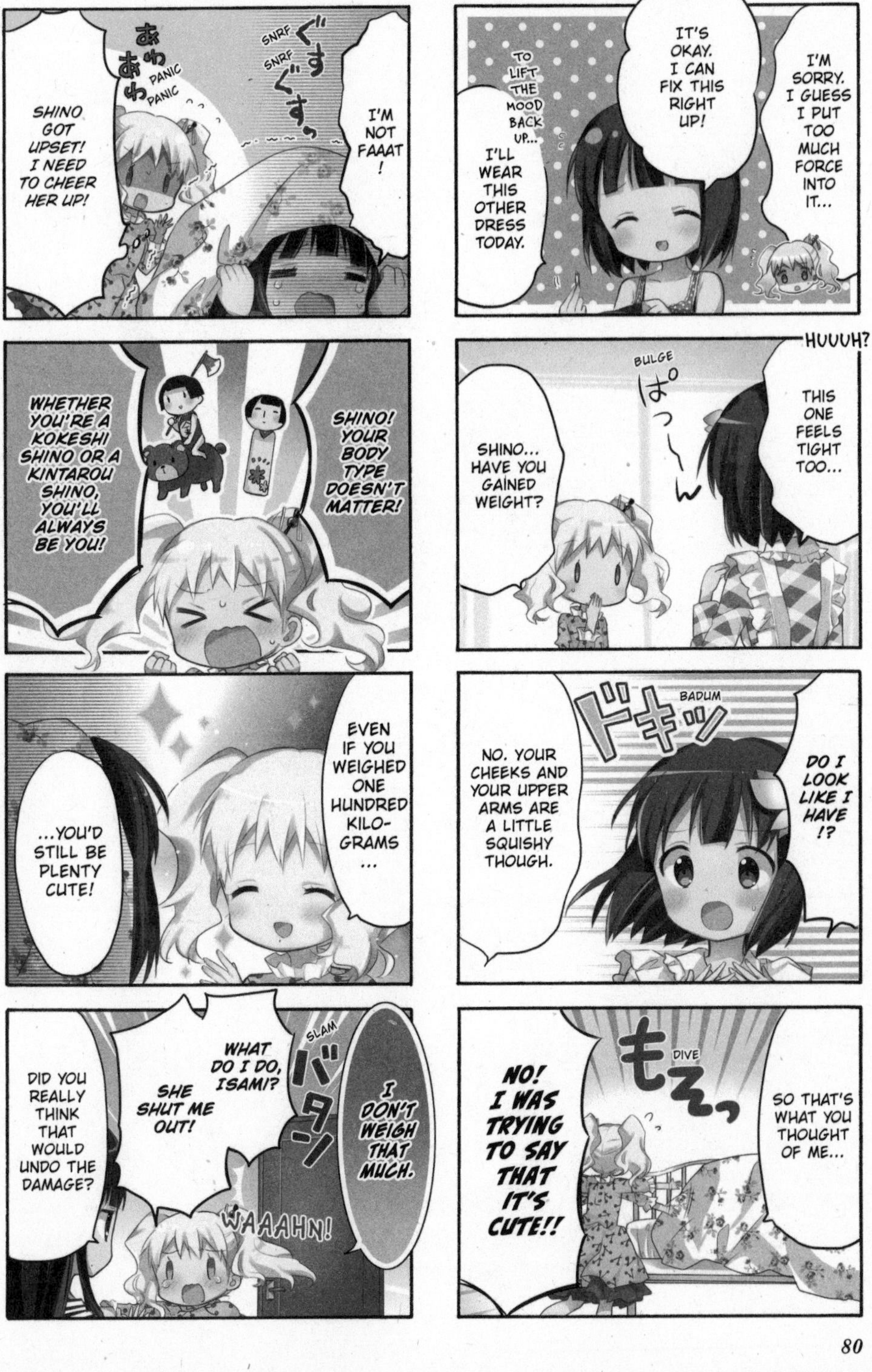
I'M SORRY. I GUESS I PUT TOO MUCH FORCE INTO IT...
IT'S OKAY. I CAN FIX THIS RIGHT UP!
TO LIFT THE MOOD BACK UP...
I'LL WEAR THIS OTHER DRESS TODAY.
HUUUH?
THIS ONE FEELS TIGHT TOO...
ぱっつ～ん
BULGE
SHINO... HAVE YOU GAINED WEIGHT?
DO I LOOK LIKE I HAVE!?
ドキッ
BADUM
NO. YOUR CHEEKS AND YOUR UPPER ARMS ARE A LITTLE SQUISHY THOUGH.
SO THAT'S WHAT YOU THOUGHT OF ME...
もぞっ
DIVE
NO! I WAS TRYING TO SAY THAT IT'S CUTE!!
I'M NOT FAAAT!
ぐすぐすっ
SNRF SNRF
あわあわ
PANIC PANIC
SHINO GOT UPSET! I NEED TO CHEER HER UP!
SHINO! YOUR BODY TYPE DOESN'T MATTER!
WHETHER YOU'RE A KOKESHI SHINO OR A KINTAROU SHINO, YOU'LL ALWAYS BE YOU!
EVEN IF YOU WEIGHED ONE HUNDRED KILO-GRAMS...
...YOU'D STILL BE PLENTY CUTE!
I DON'T WEIGH THAT MUCH.
バタン
SLAM
WHAT DO I DO, ISAMI?
SHE SHUT ME OUT!
WAAAHN!
DID YOU REALLY THINK THAT WOULD UNDO THE DAMAGE?

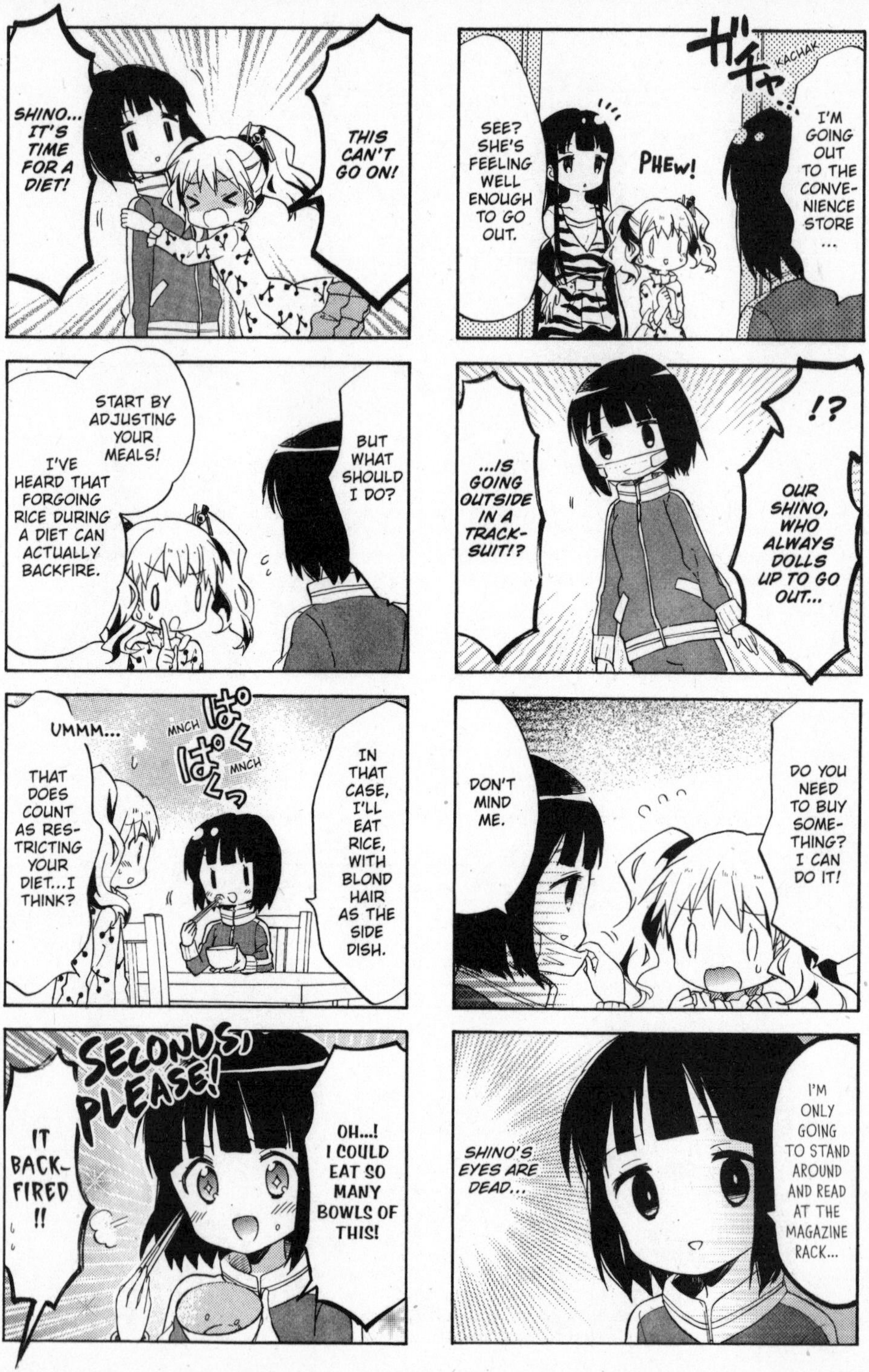
ガチャ
KACHAK
I'M GOING OUT TO THE CONVENIENCE STORE...
PHEW!
SEE? SHE'S FEELING WELL ENOUGH TO GO OUT.
!?
OUR SHINO, WHO ALWAYS DOLLS UP TO GO OUT...
...IS GOING OUTSIDE IN A TRACKSUIT!?
DO YOU NEED TO BUY SOMETHING? I CAN DO IT!
DON'T MIND ME.
I'M ONLY GOING TO STAND AROUND AND READ AT THE MAGAZINE RACK...
SHINO'S EYES ARE DEAD...
THIS CAN'T GO ON!
SHINO... IT'S TIME FOR A DIET!
BUT WHAT SHOULD I DO?
START BY ADJUSTING YOUR MEALS!
I'VE HEARD THAT FORGOING RICE DURING A DIET CAN ACTUALLY BACKFIRE.
IN THAT CASE, I'LL EAT RICE, WITH BLOND HAIR AS THE SIDE DISH.
ぱくぱくっ
MNCH MNCH
UMMM...
THAT DOES COUNT AS RESTRICTING YOUR DIET...I THINK?
OH...! I COULD EAT SO MANY BOWLS OF THIS!
SECONDS, PLEASE!
IT BACKFIRED!!

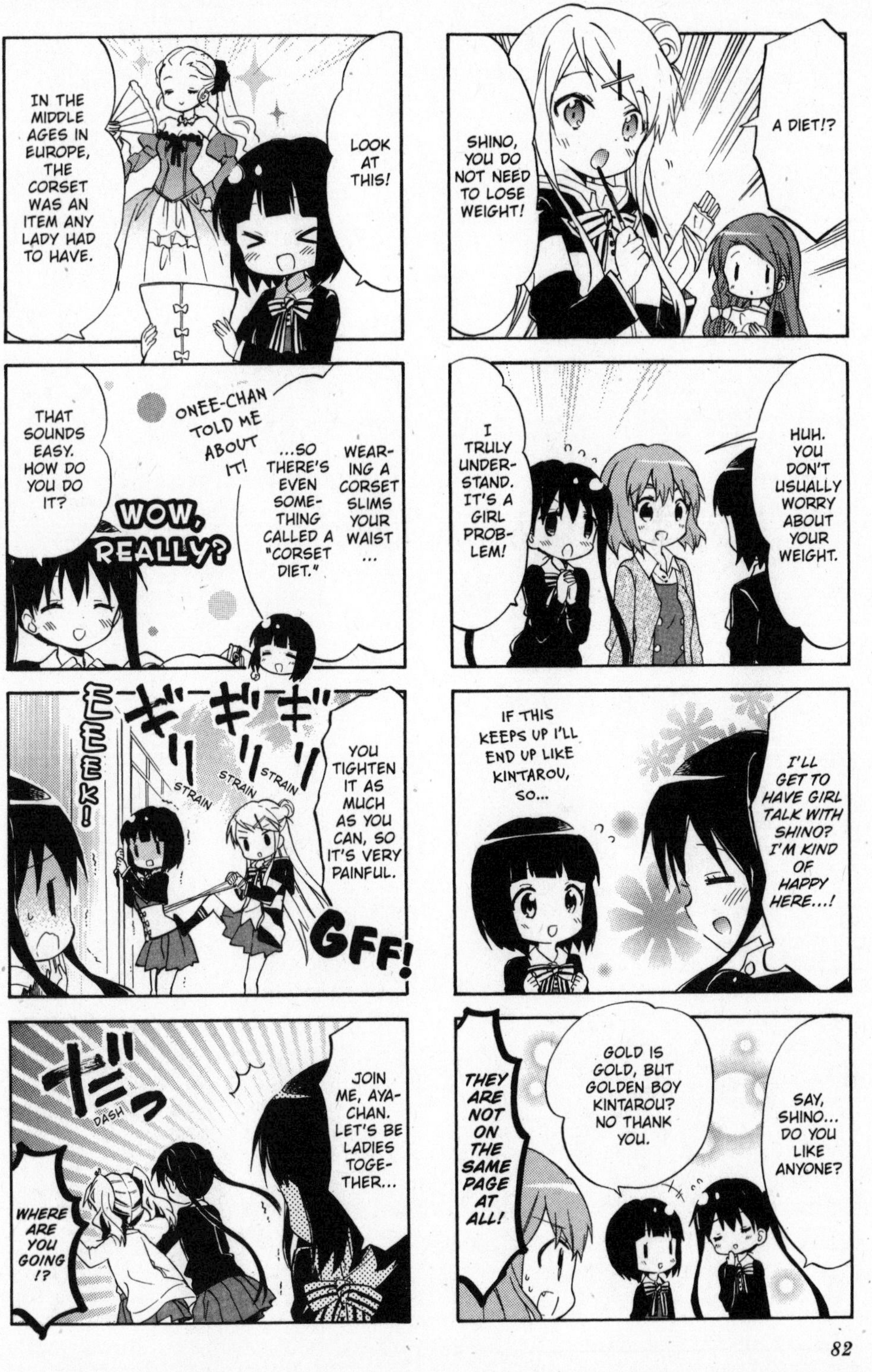
A DIET!?
SHINO, YOU DO NOT NEED TO LOSE WEIGHT!
HUH. YOU DON'T USUALLY WORRY ABOUT YOUR WEIGHT.
I TRULY UNDER-STAND. IT'S A GIRL PROB-LEM!
I'LL GET TO HAVE GIRL TALK WITH SHINO? I'M KIND OF HAPPY HERE...!
IF THIS KEEPS UP I'LL END UP LIKE KINTAROU, SO...
SAY, SHINO... DO YOU LIKE ANYONE?
GOLD IS GOLD, BUT GOLDEN BOY KINTAROU? NO THANK YOU.
THEY ARE NOT ON THE SAME PAGE AT ALL!
LOOK AT THIS!
IN THE MIDDLE AGES IN EUROPE, THE CORSET WAS AN ITEM ANY LADY HAD TO HAVE.
WEAR-ING A CORSET SLIMS YOUR WAIST...
...SO THERE'S EVEN SOME-THING CALLED A "CORSET DIET."
ONEE-CHAN TOLD ME ABOUT IT!
WOW, REALLY?
THAT SOUNDS EASY. HOW DO YOU DO IT?
YOU TIGHTEN IT AS MUCH AS YOU CAN, SO IT'S VERY PAINFUL.
STRAIN
STRAIN
STRAIN
GFF!
EEEEK!
JOIN ME, AYA-CHAN. LET'S BE LADIES TOGE-THER...
DASH
WHERE ARE YOU GOING!?

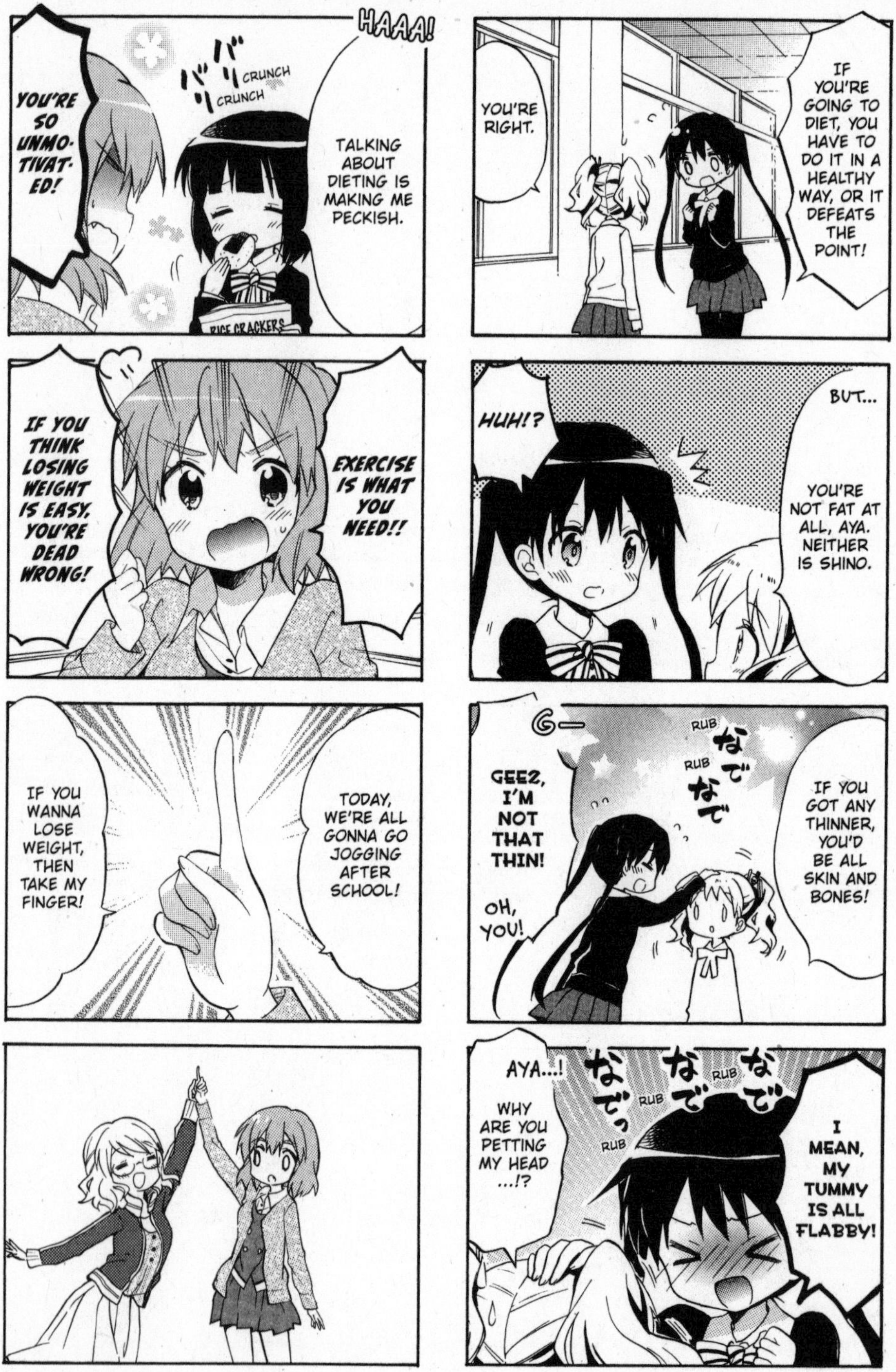
IF YOU'RE GOING TO DIET, YOU HAVE TO DO IT IN A HEALTHY WAY, OR IT DEFEATS THE POINT!
YOU'RE RIGHT.
BUT...
YOU'RE NOT FAT AT ALL, AYA. NEITHER IS SHINO.
HUH!?
IF YOU GOT ANY THINNER, YOU'D BE ALL SKIN AND BONES!
なで RUB
なで RUB
GEEZ, I'M NOT THAT THIN!
OH, YOU!
G—
I MEAN, MY TUMMY IS ALL FLABBY!
なで RUB
なで RUB
なでっ RUB
AYA...!
WHY ARE YOU PETTING MY HEAD ...!?
HAAA!
TALKING ABOUT DIETING IS MAKING ME PECKISH.
バリ CRUNCH
バリ CRUNCH
RICE CRACKERS
YOU'RE SO UNMOTIVATED!
EXERCISE IS WHAT YOU NEED!!
IF YOU THINK LOSING WEIGHT IS EASY, YOU'RE DEAD WRONG!
TODAY, WE'RE ALL GONNA GO JOGGING AFTER SCHOOL!
IF YOU WANNA LOSE WEIGHT, THEN TAKE MY FINGER!

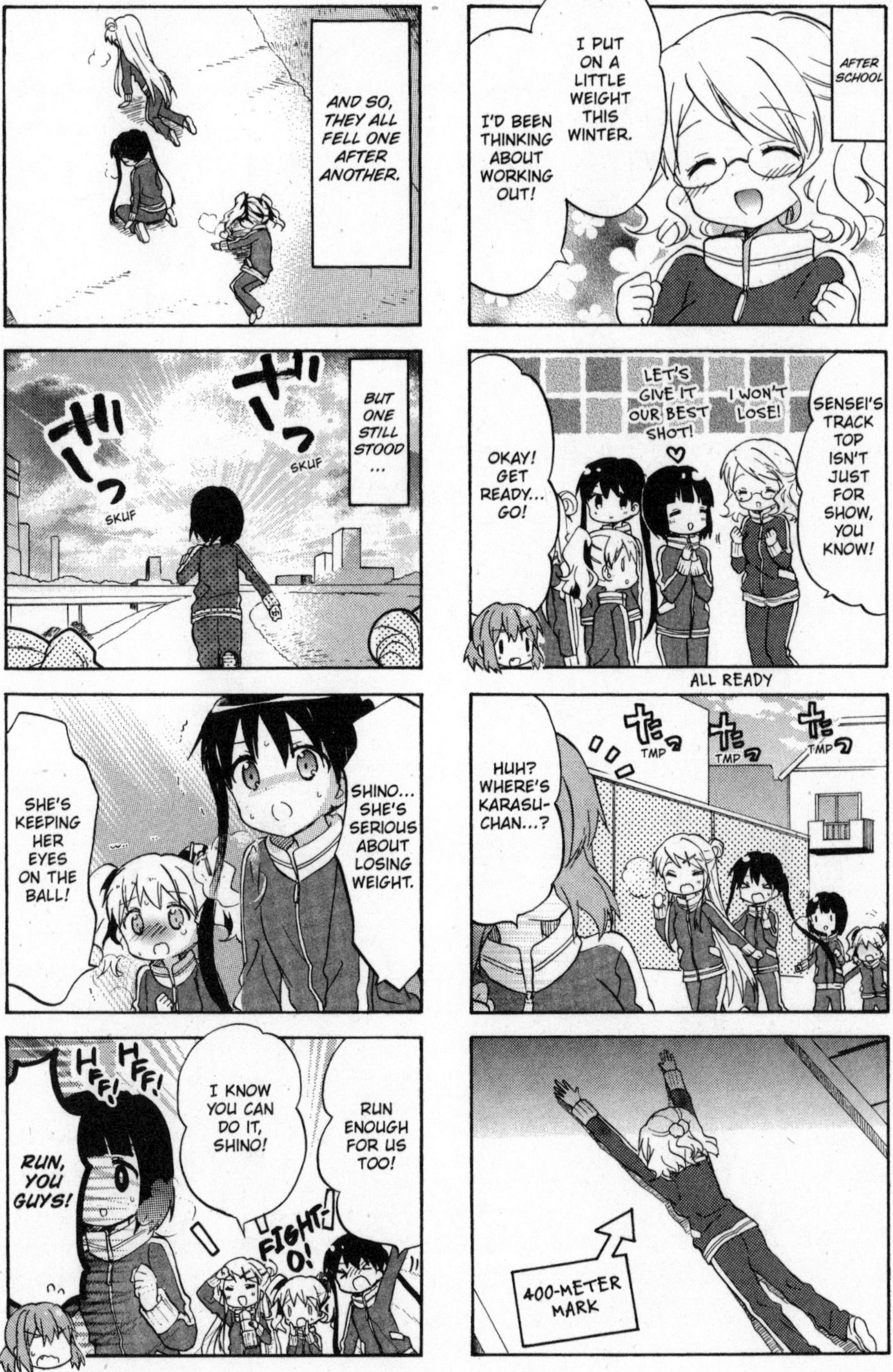
AFTER SCHOOL
I PUT ON A LITTLE WEIGHT THIS WINTER.
I'D BEEN THINKING ABOUT WORKING OUT!
AND SO, THEY ALL FELL ONE AFTER ANOTHER.
SENSEI'S TRACK TOP ISN'T JUST FOR SHOW, YOU KNOW!
I WON'T LOSE!
LET'S GIVE IT OUR BEST SHOT! ♥
OKAY! GET READY... GO!
ALL READY
BUT ONE STILL STOOD ...
SKUF
SKUF
TMP
TMP
TMP
HUH? WHERE'S KARASU-CHAN...?
SHINO... SHE'S SERIOUS ABOUT LOSING WEIGHT.
SHE'S KEEPING HER EYES ON THE BALL!
400-METER MARK
RUN ENOUGH FOR US TOO!
I KNOW YOU CAN DO IT, SHINO!
HFF! HFF!
FIGHT-O!
RUN, YOU GUYS!

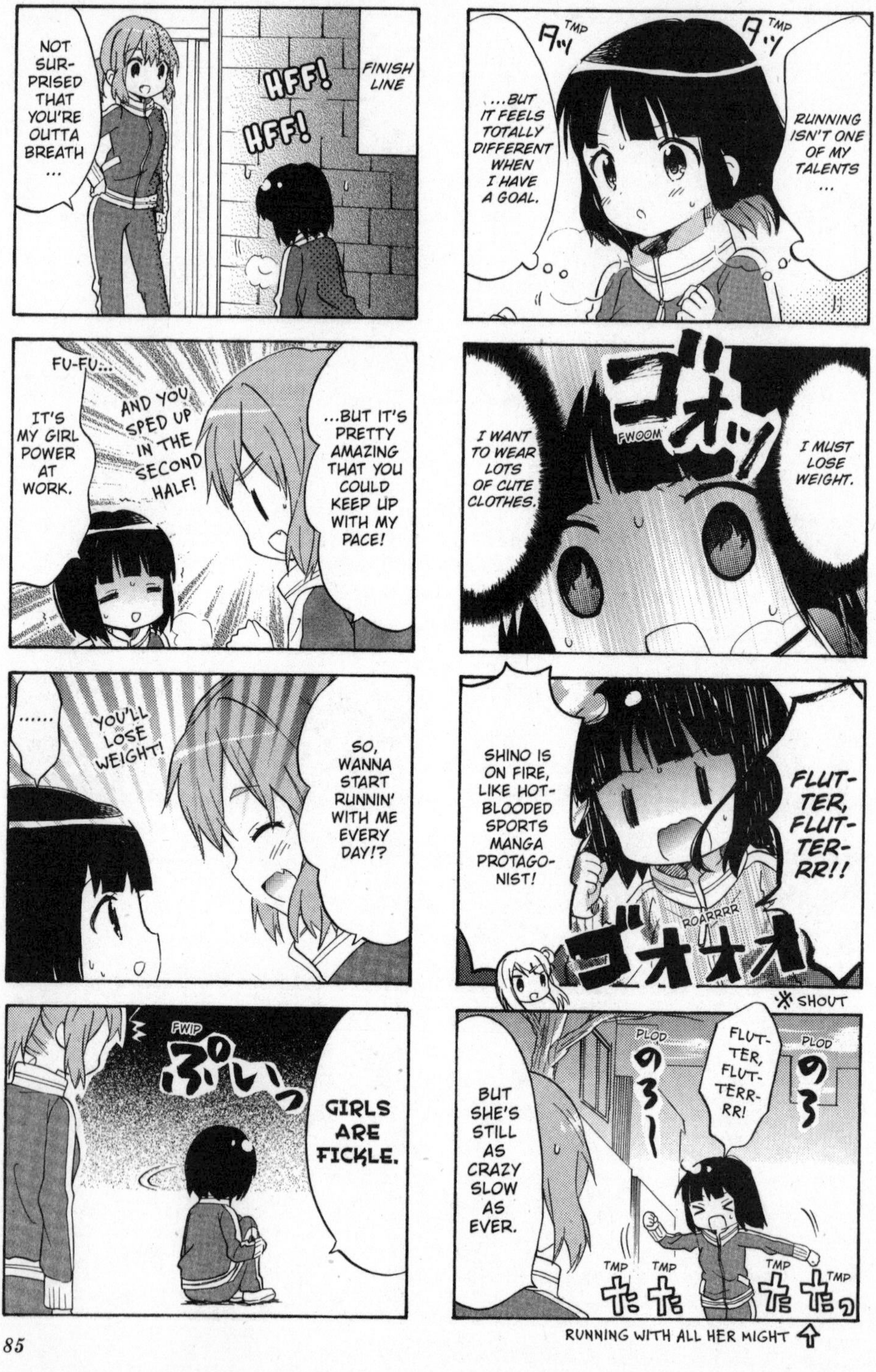
TMP
TMP
RUNNING ISN'T ONE OF MY TALENTS ...
...BUT IT FEELS TOTALLY DIFFERENT WHEN I HAVE A GOAL.
I MUST LOSE WEIGHT.
FWOOM
I WANT TO WEAR LOTS OF CUTE CLOTHES.
FLUTTER, FLUTTERRR!!
SHINO IS ON FIRE, LIKE HOT-BLOODED SPORTS MANGA PROTAGONIST!
ROARRRR
※SHOUT
PLOD
FLUTTER, FLUTTERRR!
PLOD
BUT SHE'S STILL AS CRAZY SLOW AS EVER.
TMP TMP TMP TMP
FINISH LINE
HFF!
HFF!
NOT SURPRISED THAT YOU'RE OUTTA BREATH ...
...BUT IT'S PRETTY AMAZING THAT YOU COULD KEEP UP WITH MY PACE!
AND YOU SPED UP IN THE SECOND HALF!
FU-FU...
IT'S MY GIRL POWER AT WORK.
SO, WANNA START RUNNIN' WITH ME EVERY DAY!?
YOU'LL LOSE WEIGHT!
......
GIRLS ARE FICKLE.
FWIP

RUNNING WITH ALL HER MIGHT ⇧

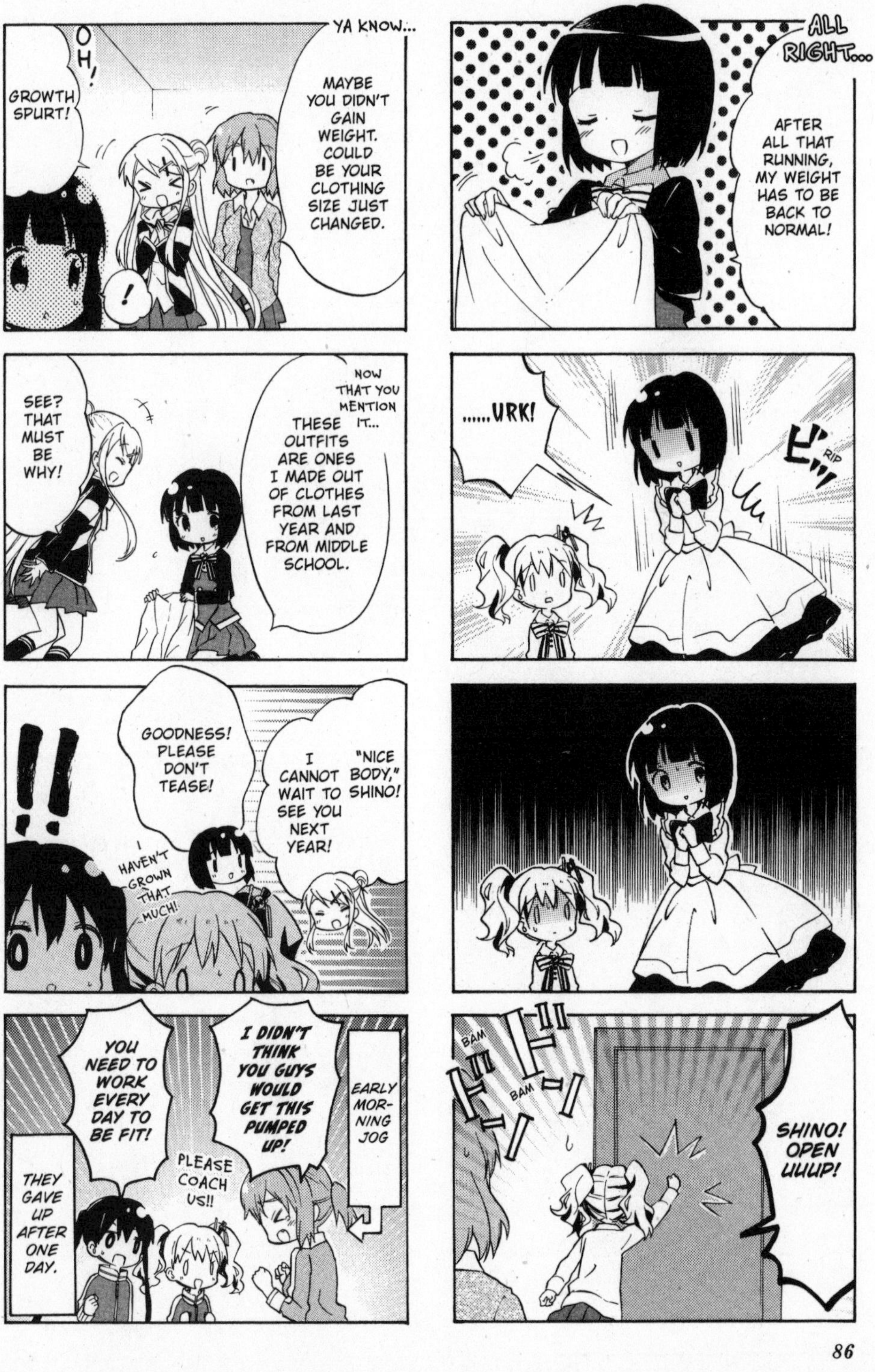

ALL RIGHT...
AFTER ALL THAT RUNNING, MY WEIGHT HAS TO BE BACK TO NORMAL!
......URK!
RIP
BAM
BAM
SHINO! OPEN UUUP!
YA KNOW...
MAYBE YOU DIDN'T GAIN WEIGHT. COULD BE YOUR CLOTHING SIZE JUST CHANGED.
OH!
GROWTH SPURT!
!
NOW THAT YOU MENTION IT...
THESE OUTFITS ARE ONES I MADE OUT OF CLOTHES FROM LAST YEAR AND FROM MIDDLE SCHOOL.
SEE? THAT MUST BE WHY!
"NICE BODY," SHINO! I CANNOT WAIT TO SEE YOU NEXT YEAR!
GOODNESS! PLEASE DON'T TEASE!
I HAVEN'T GROWN THAT MUCH!
!!
EARLY MORNING JOG
I DIDN'T THINK YOU GUYS WOULD GET THIS PUMPED UP!
YOU NEED TO WORK EVERY DAY TO BE FIT!
PLEASE COACH US!!
THEY GAVE UP AFTER ONE DAY.

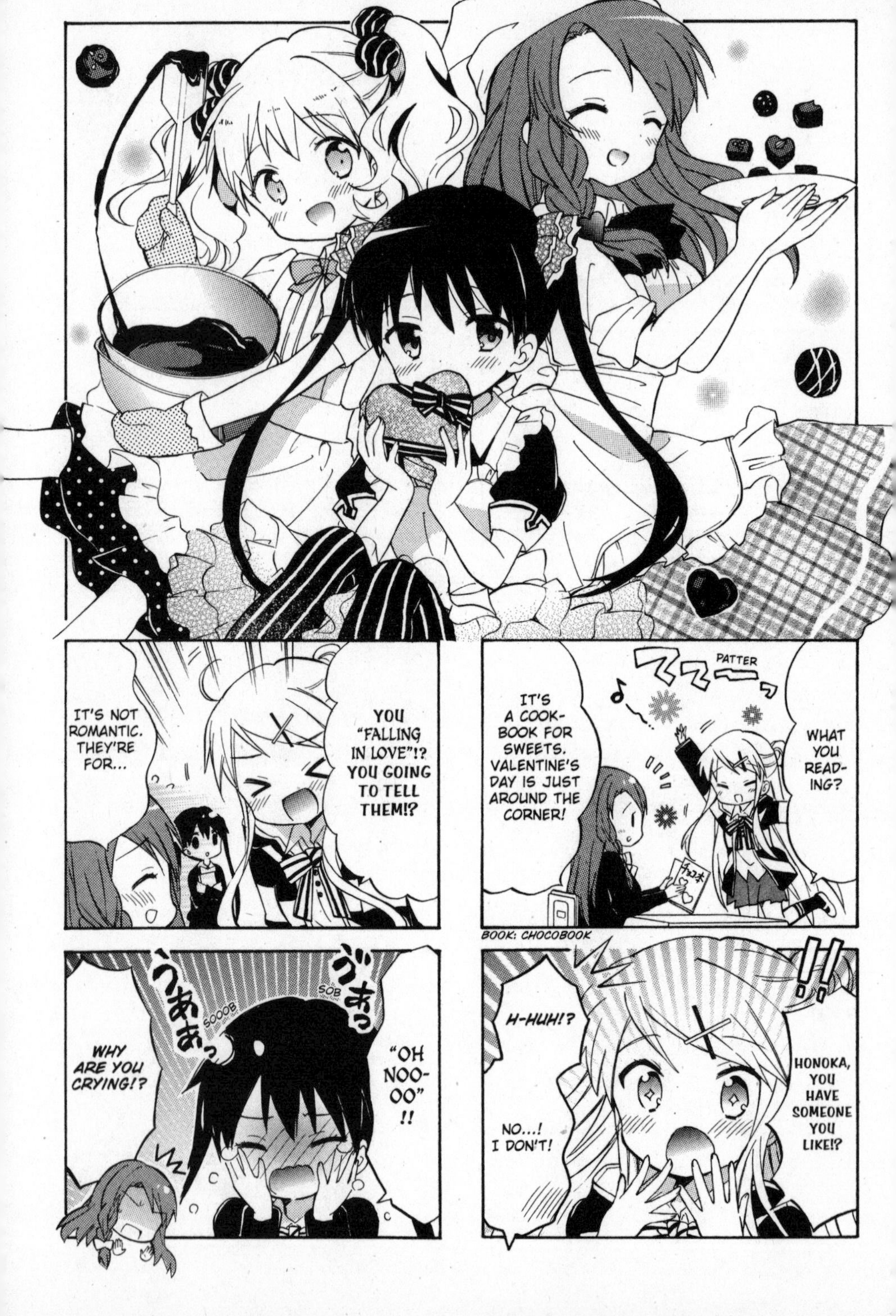
WHAT YOU READING?
PATTER
IT'S A COOKBOOK FOR SWEETS. VALENTINE'S DAY IS JUST AROUND THE CORNER!
BOOK: CHOCOBOOK
HONOKA, YOU HAVE SOMEONE YOU LIKE!?
H-HUH!?
NO...! I DON'T!
YOU "FALLING IN LOVE"!? YOU GOING TO TELL THEM!?
IT'S NOT ROMANTIC. THEY'RE FOR...
SOB
SOOOB
"OH NOOO-OO" !!
WHY ARE YOU CRYING!?

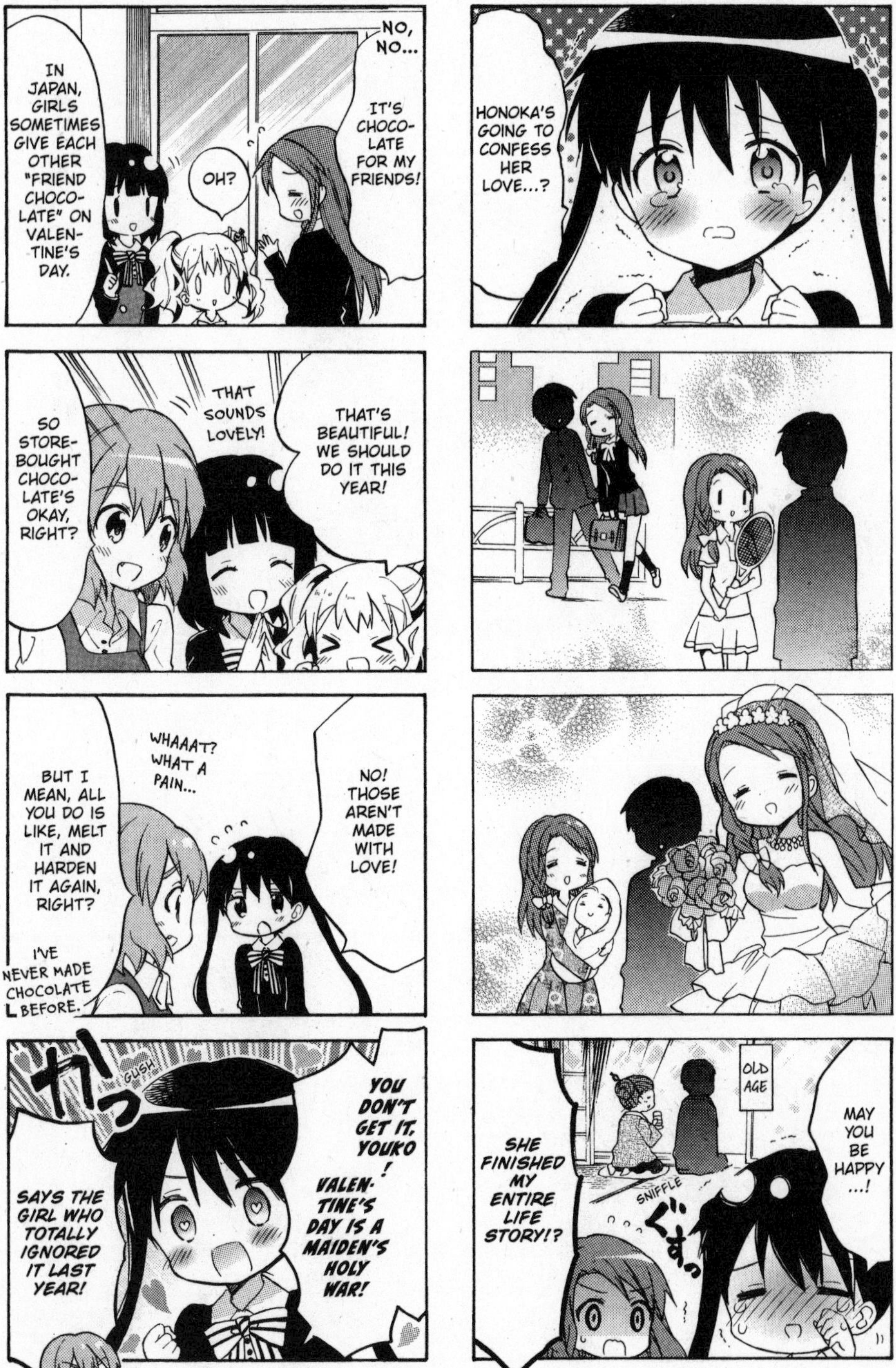
HONOKA'S GOING TO CONFESS HER LOVE...?
OLD AGE
MAY YOU BE HAPPY...!
SHE FINISHED MY ENTIRE LIFE STORY!?
SNIFFLE
NO, NO... IT'S CHOCOLATE FOR MY FRIENDS!
OH?
IN JAPAN, GIRLS SOMETIMES GIVE EACH OTHER "FRIEND CHOCOLATE" ON VALENTINE'S DAY.
THAT'S BEAUTIFUL! WE SHOULD DO IT THIS YEAR!
THAT SOUNDS LOVELY!
SO STORE-BOUGHT CHOCOLATE'S OKAY, RIGHT?
NO! THOSE AREN'T MADE WITH LOVE!
WHAAAT? WHAT A PAIN...
BUT I MEAN, ALL YOU DO IS LIKE, MELT IT AND HARDEN IT AGAIN, RIGHT?
I'VE NEVER MADE CHOCOLATE BEFORE.
YOU DON'T GET IT, YOUKO! VALENTINE'S DAY IS A MAIDEN'S HOLY WAR!
GUSH
SAYS THE GIRL WHO TOTALLY IGNORED IT LAST YEAR!

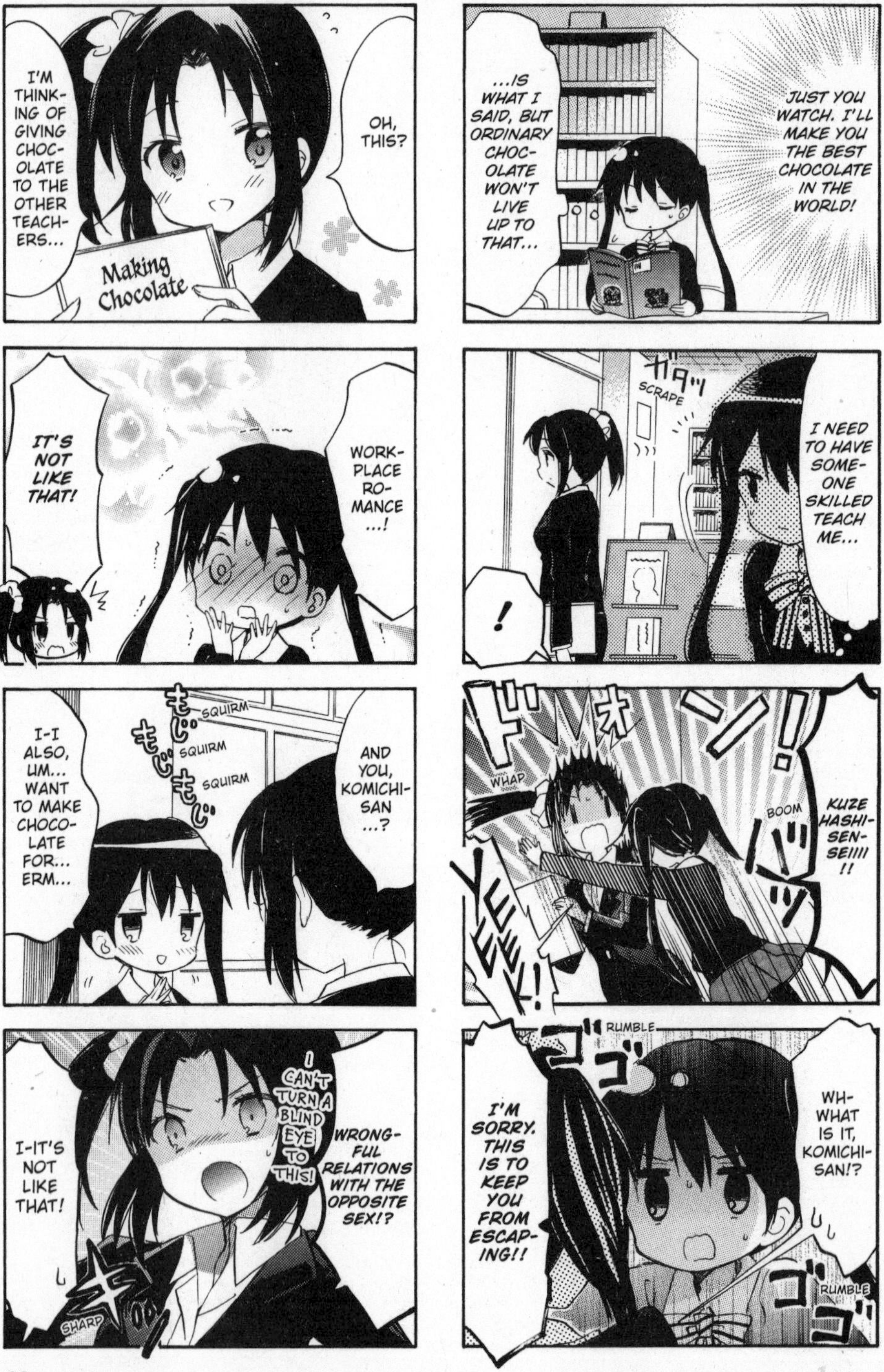
JUST YOU WATCH. I'LL MAKE YOU THE BEST CHOCOLATE IN THE WORLD!
...IS WHAT I SAID, BUT ORDINARY CHOCO-OLATE WON'T LIVE UP TO THAT...
SCRAPE
I NEED TO HAVE SOME-ONE SKILLED TEACH ME...
!
WHAP
BOOM
KUZE HASHI-SEN-SEI!!!! !!
RUMBLE
WH-WHAT IS IT, KOMICHI-SAN!?
I'M SORRY. THIS IS TO KEEP YOU FROM ESCAP-ING!!
RUMBLE
OH, THIS?
I'M THINK-ING OF GIVING CHOC-OLATE TO THE OTHER TEACH-ERS...
Making Chocolate
WORK-PLACE RO-MANCE ...!
IT'S NOT LIKE THAT!
SQUIRM
SQUIRM
SQUIRM
AND YOU, KOMICHI-SAN ...?
I-I ALSO, UM... WANT TO MAKE CHOCO-LATE FOR... ERM...
WRONG-FUL RELATIONS WITH THE OPPOSITE SEX!?
I CAN'T TURN A BLIND EYE TO THIS!
I-IT'S NOT LIKE THAT!
SHARP

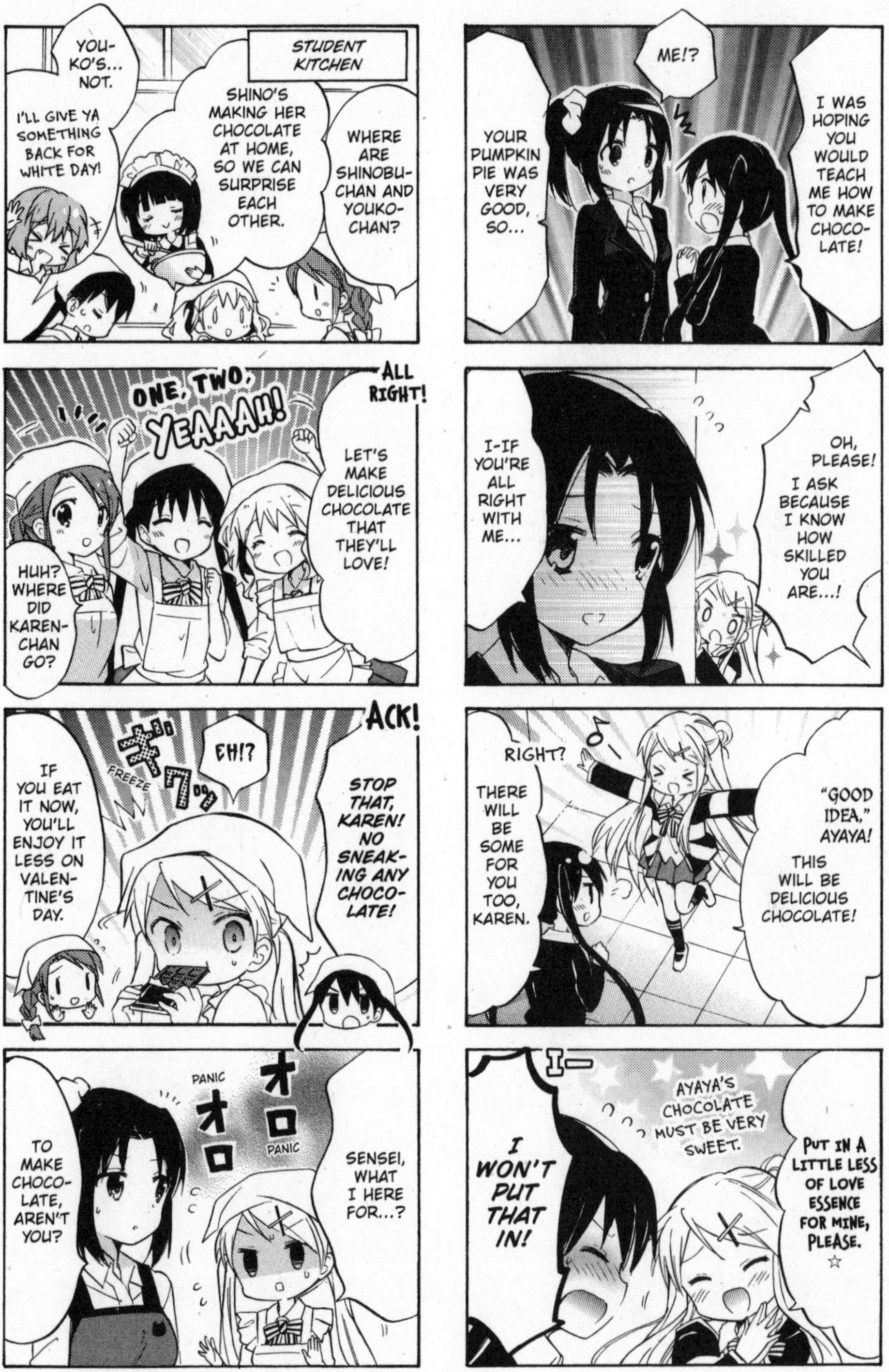
I WAS HOPING YOU WOULD TEACH ME HOW TO MAKE CHOCOLATE!
YOUR PUMPKIN PIE WAS VERY GOOD, SO...
ME!?
OH, PLEASE! I ASK BECAUSE I KNOW HOW SKILLED YOU ARE...!
I-IF YOU'RE ALL RIGHT WITH ME...
"GOOD IDEA," AYAYA! THIS WILL BE DELICIOUS CHOCOLATE!
RIGHT?
THERE WILL BE SOME FOR YOU TOO, KAREN.
PUT IN A LITTLE LESS OF LOVE ESSENCE FOR MINE, PLEASE. ☆
AYAYA'S CHOCOLATE MUST BE VERY SWEET.
I—
I WON'T PUT THAT IN!
STUDENT KITCHEN
WHERE ARE SHINOBU-CHAN AND YOUKO-CHAN?
SHINO'S MAKING HER CHOCOLATE AT HOME, SO WE CAN SURPRISE EACH OTHER.
YOU-KO'S... NOT.
I'LL GIVE YA SOMETHING BACK FOR WHITE DAY!
ALL RIGHT!
LET'S MAKE DELICIOUS CHOCOLATE THAT THEY'LL LOVE!
ONE, TWO, YEAAAH!
HUH? WHERE DID KAREN-CHAN GO?
ACK!
STOP THAT, KAREN! NO SNEAKING ANY CHOCOLATE!
EH!?
ギクッ
FREEZE
IF YOU EAT IT NOW, YOU'LL ENJOY IT LESS ON VALENTINE'S DAY.
SENSEI, WHAT I HERE FOR...?
オロ
PANIC
オロ
PANIC
TO MAKE CHOCOLATE, AREN'T YOU?

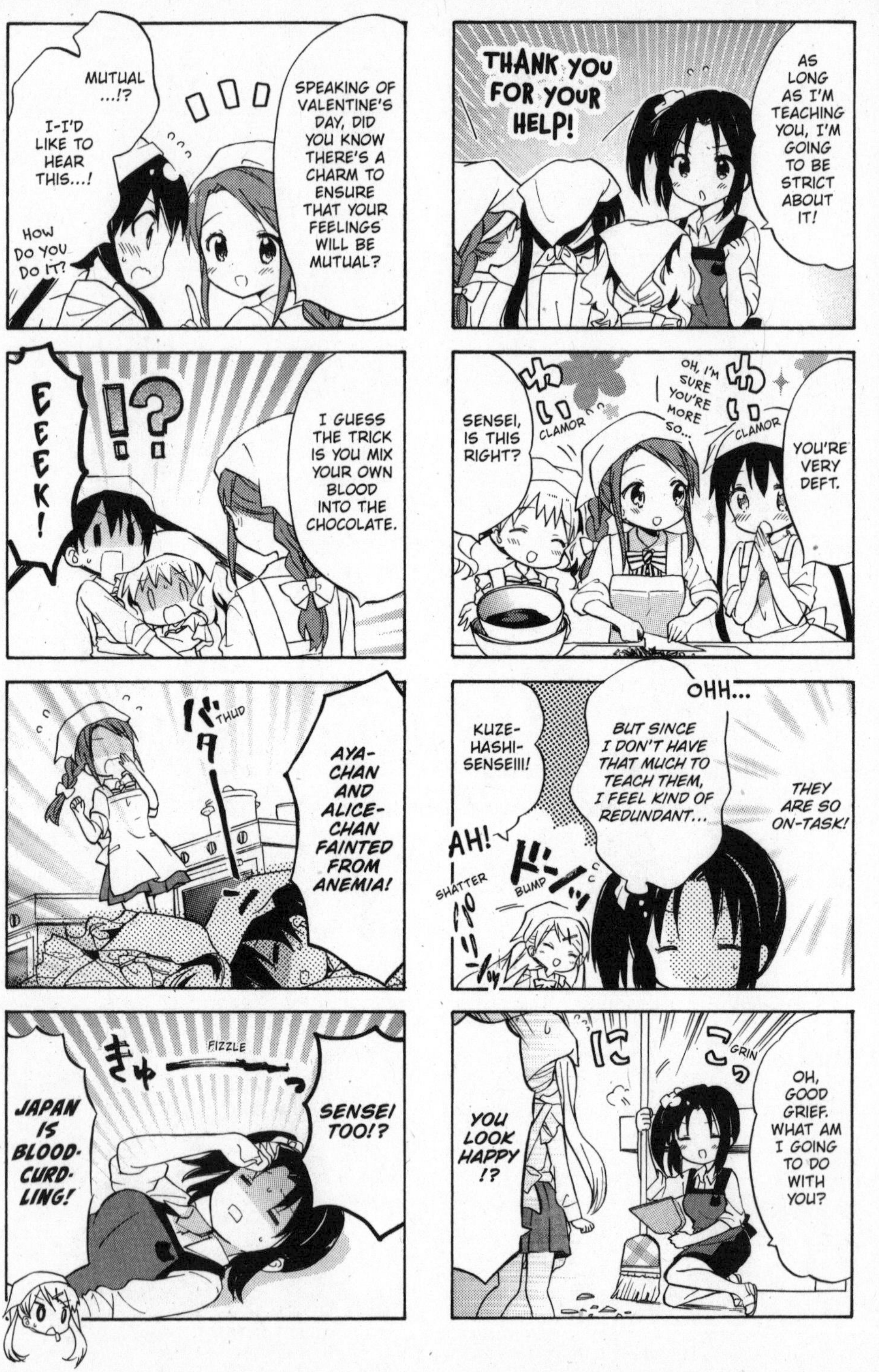

AS LONG AS I'M TEACHING YOU, I'M GOING TO BE STRICT ABOUT IT!
THANK YOU FOR YOUR HELP!
YOU'RE VERY DEFT.
CLAMOR
OH, I'M SURE YOU'RE MORE SO...
CLAMOR
SENSEI, IS THIS RIGHT?
OHH...
THEY ARE SO ON-TASK!
BUT SINCE I DON'T HAVE THAT MUCH TO TEACH THEM, I FEEL KIND OF REDUNDANT...
KUZE-HASHI-SENSEIII!
AH!
BUMP
SHATTER
GRIN
OH, GOOD GRIEF. WHAT AM I GOING TO DO WITH YOU?
YOU LOOK HAPPY!?
SPEAKING OF VALENTINE'S DAY, DID YOU KNOW THERE'S A CHARM TO ENSURE THAT YOUR FEELINGS WILL BE MUTUAL?
MUTUAL...!?
I-I'D LIKE TO HEAR THIS...!
HOW DO YOU DO IT?
I GUESS THE TRICK IS YOU MIX YOUR OWN BLOOD INTO THE CHOCOLATE.
EEEK!
AYA-CHAN AND ALICE-CHAN FAINTED FROM ANEMIA!
THUD
SENSEI TOO!?
FIZZLE
JAPAN IS BLOOD-CURDLING!

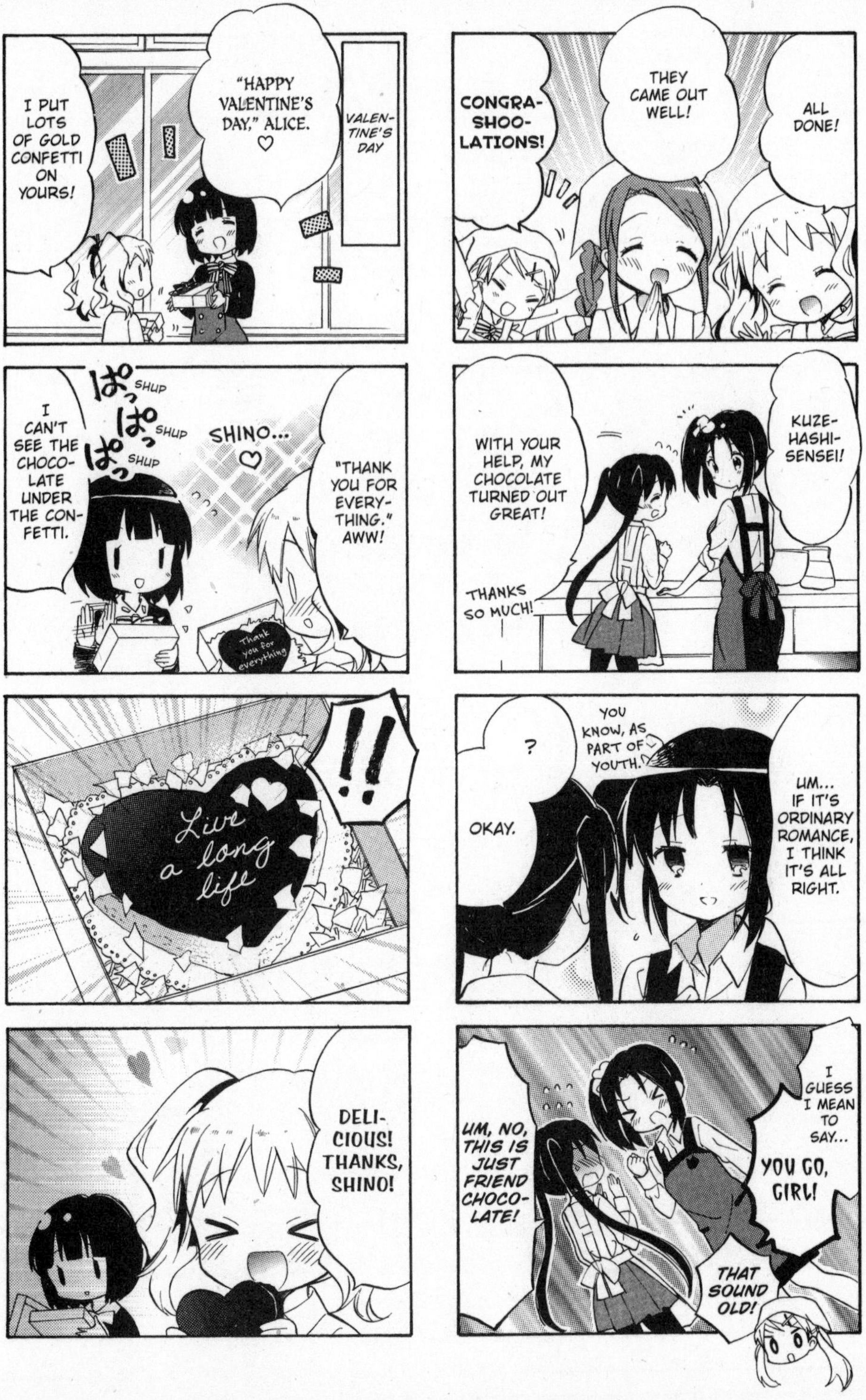
ALL DONE!
THEY CAME OUT WELL!
CONGRA-SHOO-LATIONS!
KUZE-HASHI-SENSEI!
WITH YOUR HELP, MY CHOCOLATE TURNED OUT GREAT!
THANKS SO MUCH!
UM... IF IT'S ORDINARY ROMANCE, I THINK IT'S ALL RIGHT.
YOU KNOW, AS PART OF YOUTH.♡
?
OKAY.
I GUESS I MEAN TO SAY...
YOU GO, GIRL!
UM, NO, THIS IS JUST FRIEND CHOCOLATE!
THAT SOUND OLD!
VALENTINE'S DAY
"HAPPY VALENTINE'S DAY," ALICE. ♡
I PUT LOTS OF GOLD CONFETTI ON YOURS!
"THANK YOU FOR EVERYTHING." AWW!
SHINO... ♡
ぱっ SHUP
ぱっ SHUP
ぱっ SHUP
I CAN'T SEE THE CHOCOLATE UNDER THE CONFETTI.
Thank you for everything
!!
Live a long life
DELICIOUS! THANKS, SHINO!

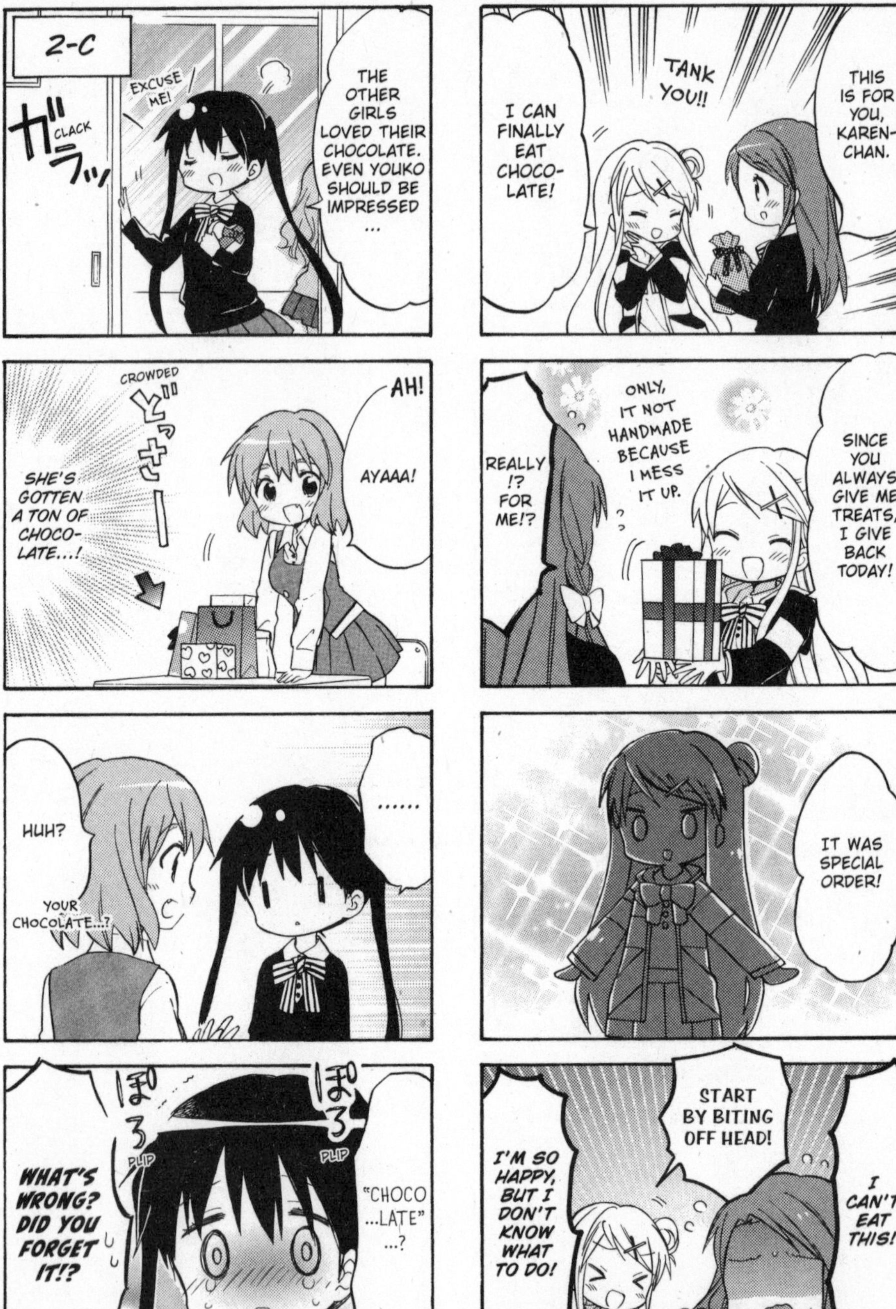
THIS IS FOR YOU, KAREN-CHAN.
TANK YOU!!
I CAN FINALLY EAT CHOCOLATE!
SINCE YOU ALWAYS GIVE ME TREATS, I GIVE BACK TODAY!
ONLY, IT NOT HANDMADE BECAUSE I MESS IT UP.
REALLY!? FOR ME!?
IT WAS SPECIAL ORDER!
I CAN'T EAT THIS!
START BY BITING OFF HEAD!
I'M SO HAPPY, BUT I DON'T KNOW WHAT TO DO!
THE OTHER GIRLS LOVED THEIR CHOCOLATE. EVEN YOUKO SHOULD BE IMPRESSED ...
2-C
EXCUSE ME!
ガラッ
CLACK
AH!
AYAAA!
どっさー
CROWDED
SHE'S GOTTEN A TON OF CHOCOLATE...!
......
HUH?
YOUR CHOCOLATE...?
ぽろ
PLIP
"CHOCO ...LATE" ...?
ぽろ
PLIP
WHAT'S WRONG? DID YOU FORGET IT!?

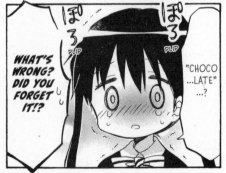

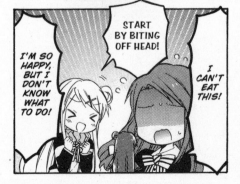

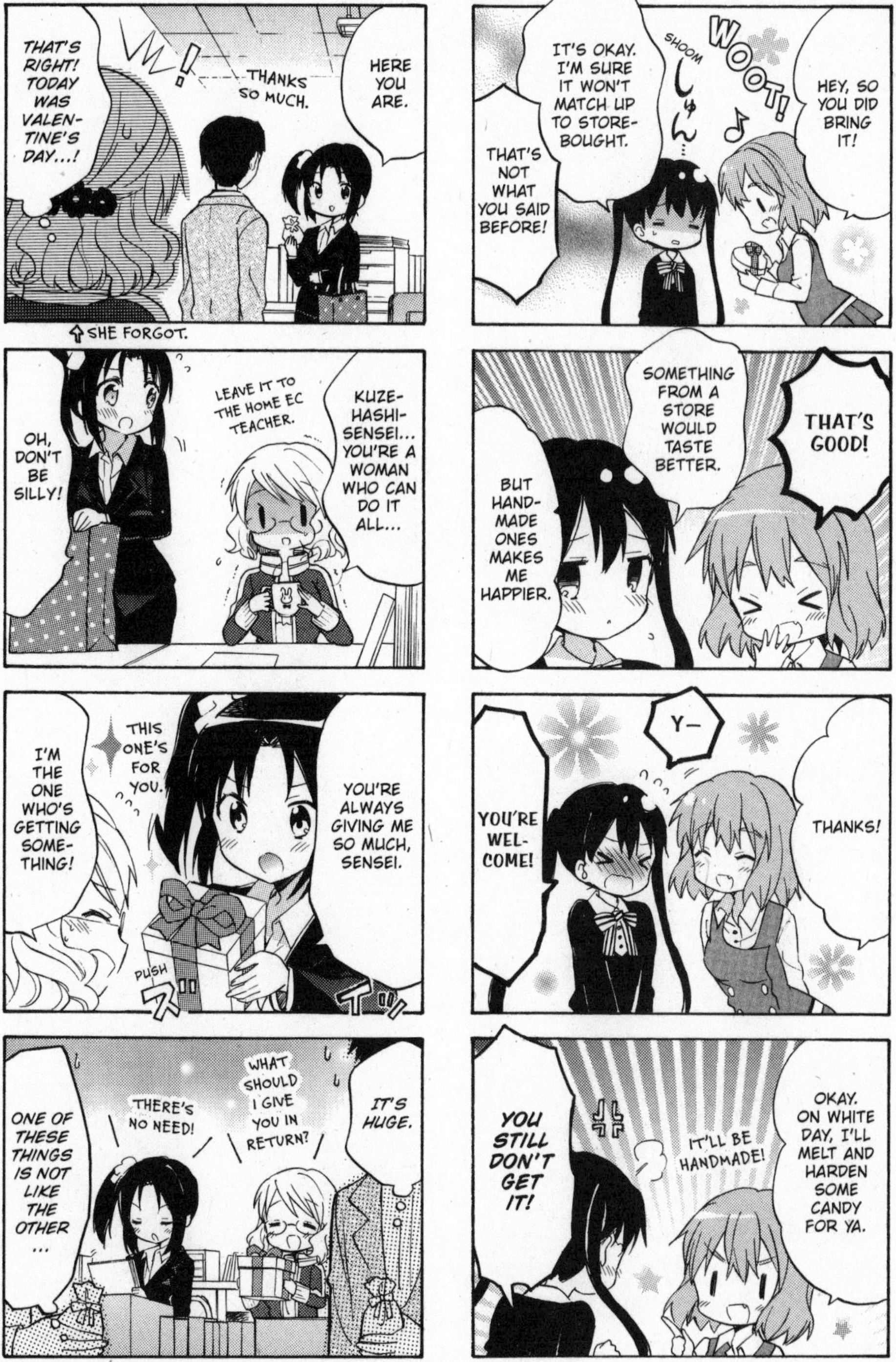
HEY, SO YOU DID BRING IT!
WOOT!
♪
SHOOM しゅん…
IT'S OKAY. I'M SURE IT WON'T MATCH UP TO STORE-BOUGHT.
THAT'S NOT WHAT YOU SAID BEFORE!
THAT'S GOOD!
SOMETHING FROM A STORE WOULD TASTE BETTER.
BUT HAND-MADE ONES MAKES ME HAPPIER.
THANKS!
Y—
YOU'RE WEL-COME!
OKAY. ON WHITE DAY, I'LL MELT AND HARDEN SOME CANDY FOR YA.
IT'LL BE HANDMADE!
YOU STILL DON'T GET IT!
HERE YOU ARE.
THANKS SO MUCH.
THAT'S RIGHT! TODAY WAS VALEN-TINE'S DAY...!
SHE FORGOT.
KUZE-HASHI-SENSEI... YOU'RE A WOMAN WHO CAN DO IT ALL...
LEAVE IT TO THE HOME EC TEACHER.
OH, DON'T BE SILLY!
YOU'RE ALWAYS GIVING ME SO MUCH, SENSEI.
THIS ONE'S FOR YOU.
I'M THE ONE WHO'S GETTING SOME-THING!
PUSH
IT'S HUGE.
WHAT SHOULD I GIVE YOU IN RETURN?
THERE'S NO NEED!
ONE OF THESE THINGS IS NOT LIKE THE OTHER...

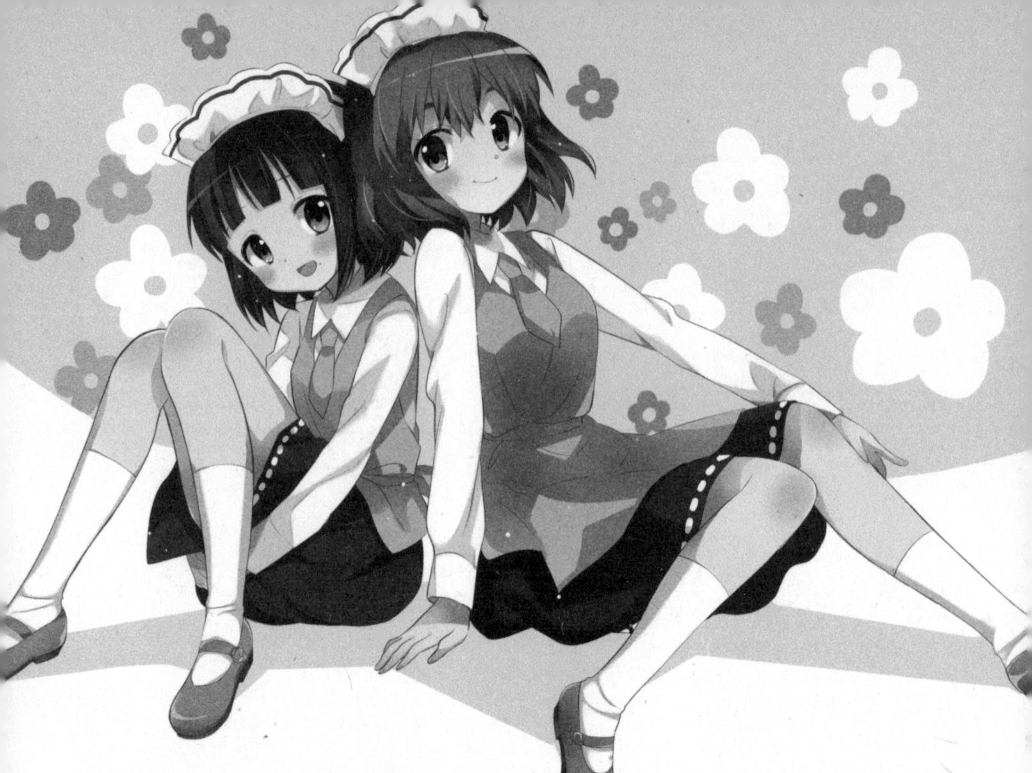

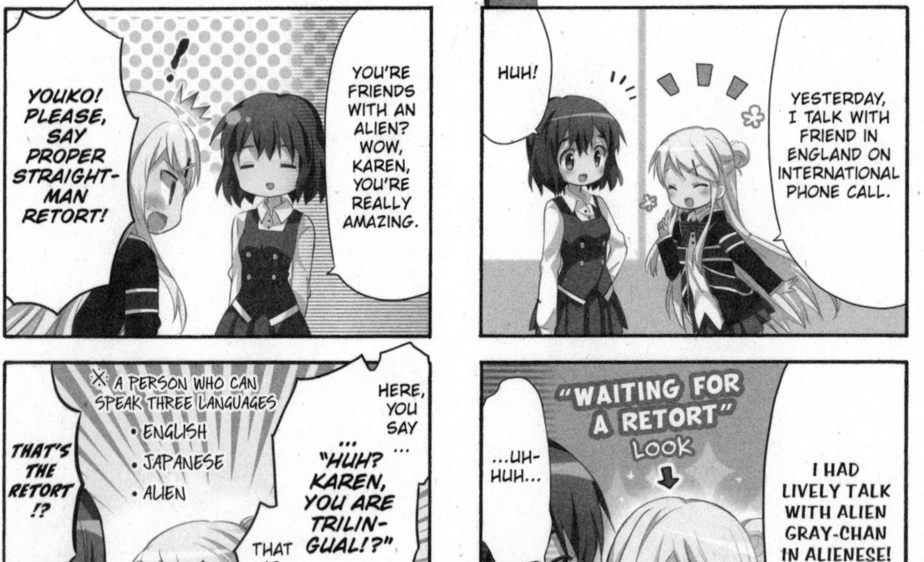

YESTERDAY, I TALK WITH FRIEND IN ENGLAND ON INTERNATIONAL PHONE CALL.
HUH!
I HAD LIVELY TALK WITH ALIEN GRAY-CHAN IN ALIENESE!
"WAITING FOR A RETORT" LOOK
...UH-HUH...
YOU'RE FRIENDS WITH AN ALIEN? WOW, KAREN, YOU'RE REALLY AMAZING.
YOUKO! PLEASE, SAY PROPER STRAIGHT-MAN RETORT!
HERE, YOU SAY ... ... "HUH? KAREN, YOU ARE TRILIN-GUAL!?"
THAT IS COR-RECT ANS-WER!
※ A PERSON WHO CAN SPEAK THREE LANGUAGES
• ENGLISH
• JAPANESE
• ALIEN
THAT'S THE RETORT !?

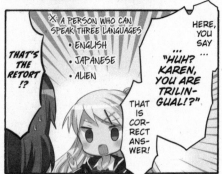

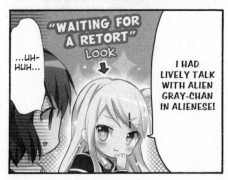

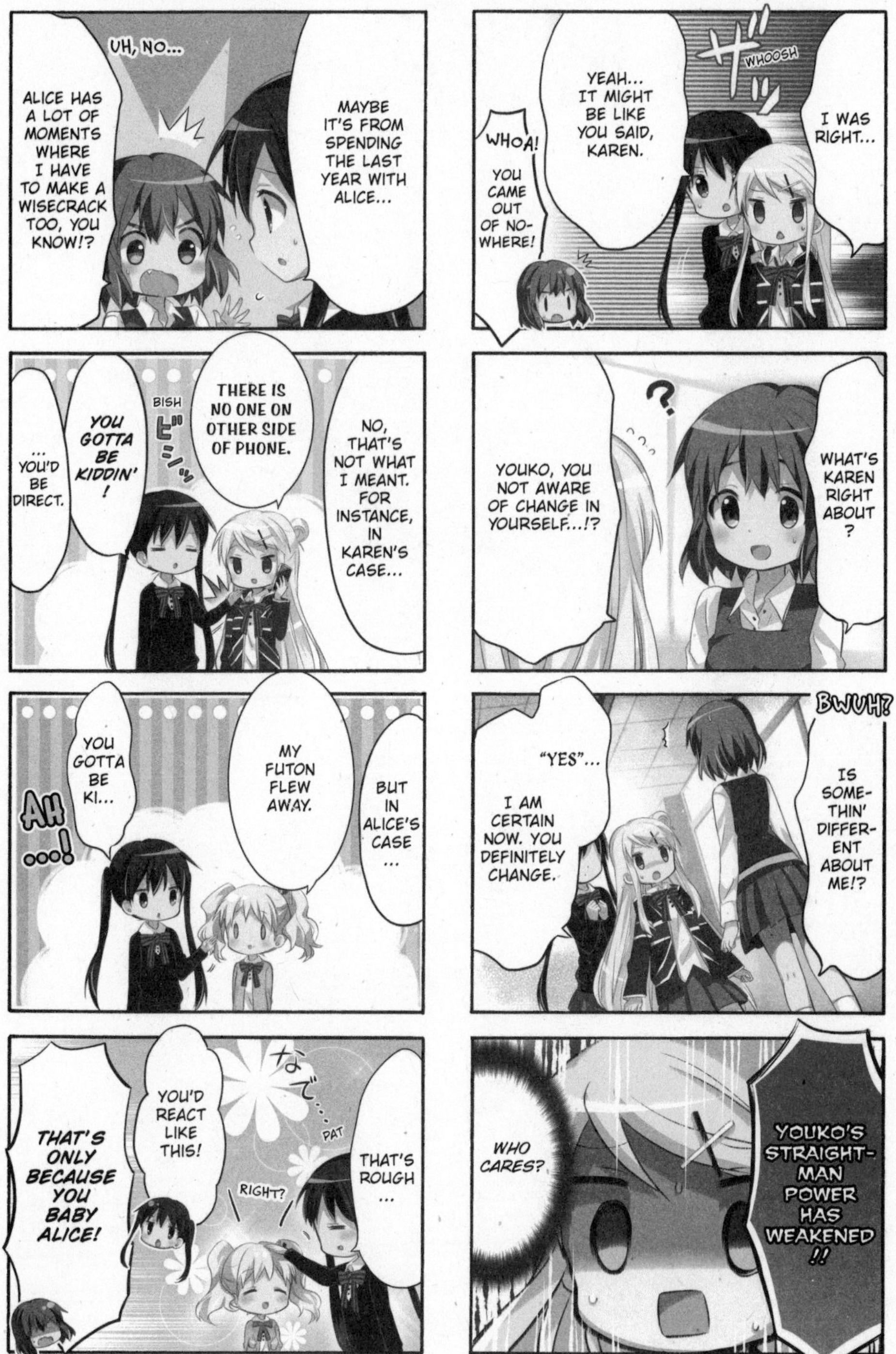
WHOOSH
I WAS RIGHT...
YEAH... IT MIGHT BE LIKE YOU SAID, KAREN.
WHOA! YOU CAME OUT OF NO-WHERE!
WHAT'S KAREN RIGHT ABOUT?
?
YOUKO, YOU NOT AWARE OF CHANGE IN YOURSELF...!?
BWUH?
IS SOME-THIN' DIFFER-ENT ABOUT ME!?
"YES"... I AM CERTAIN NOW. YOU DEFINITELY CHANGE.
YOUKO'S STRAIGHT-MAN POWER HAS WEAKENED!!
WHO CARES?
MAYBE IT'S FROM SPENDING THE LAST YEAR WITH ALICE...
UH, NO...
ALICE HAS A LOT OF MOMENTS WHERE I HAVE TO MAKE A WISECRACK TOO, YOU KNOW!?
NO, THAT'S NOT WHAT I MEANT. FOR INSTANCE, IN KAREN'S CASE...
THERE IS NO ONE ON OTHER SIDE OF PHONE.
BISH
YOU GOTTA BE KIDDIN'!
...YOU'D BE DIRECT.
BUT IN ALICE'S CASE...
MY FUTON FLEW AWAY.
YOU GOTTA BE KI...
AH...!
THAT'S ROUGH...
PAT
RIGHT?
YOU'D REACT LIKE THIS!
THAT'S ONLY BECAUSE YOU BABY ALICE!

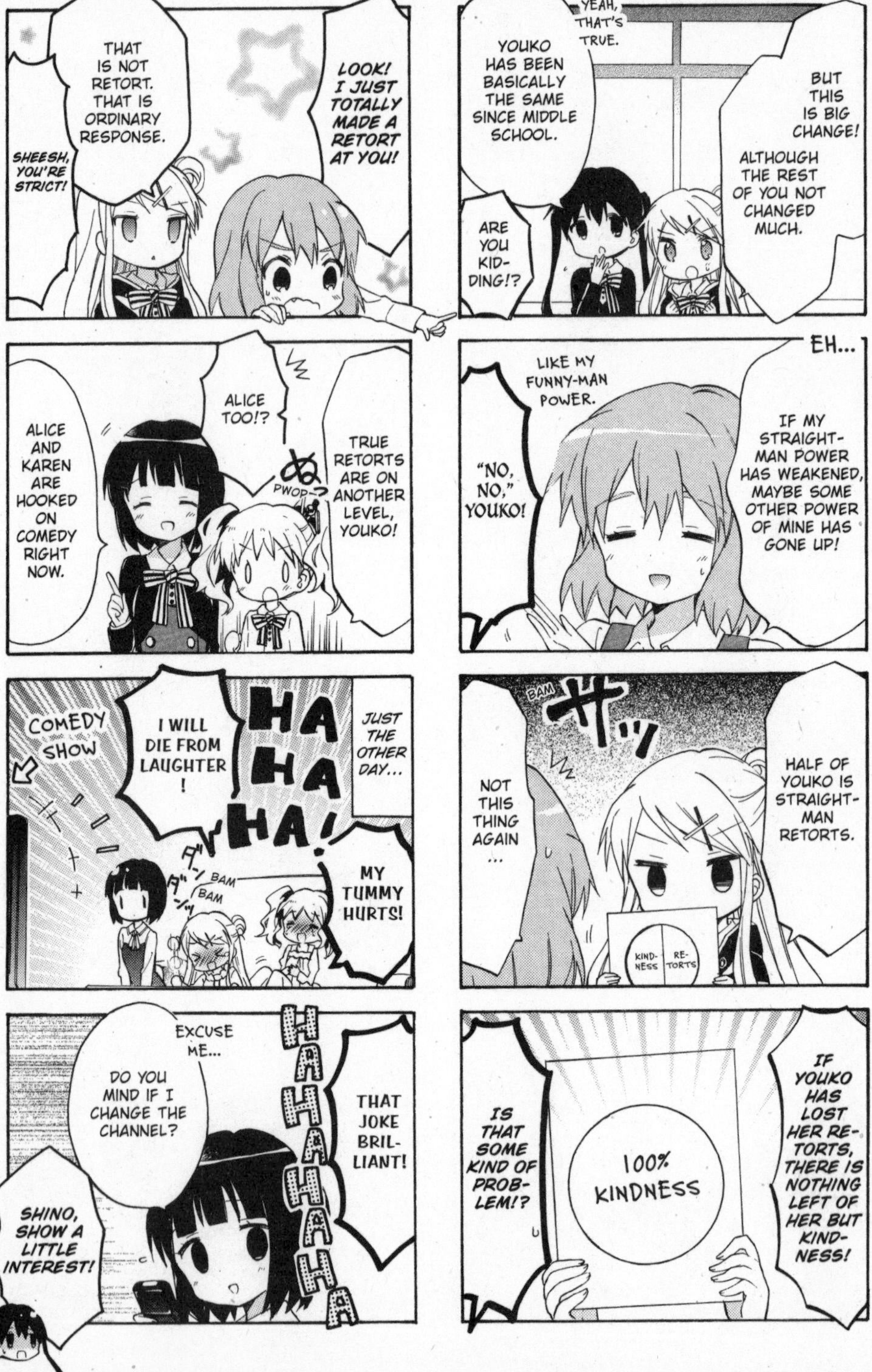
BUT THIS IS BIG CHANGE!
ALTHOUGH THE REST OF YOU NOT CHANGED MUCH.
YEAH, THAT'S TRUE.
YOUKO HAS BEEN BASICALLY THE SAME SINCE MIDDLE SCHOOL.
ARE YOU KID-DING!?
EH...
IF MY STRAIGHT-MAN POWER HAS WEAKENED, MAYBE SOME OTHER POWER OF MINE HAS GONE UP!
LIKE MY FUNNY-MAN POWER.
“NO, NO,” YOUKO!
HALF OF YOUKO IS STRAIGHT-MAN RETORTS.
BAM
NOT THIS THING AGAIN...
KIND-NESS
RE-TORTS
IF YOUKO HAS LOST HER RE-TORTS, THERE IS NOTHING LEFT OF HER BUT KIND-NESS!
100% KINDNESS
IS THAT SOME KIND OF PROB-LEM!?
LOOK! I JUST TOTALLY MADE A RETORT AT YOU!
THAT IS NOT RETORT. THAT IS ORDINARY RESPONSE.
SHEESH, YOU'RE STRICT!
TRUE RETORTS ARE ON ANOTHER LEVEL, YOUKO!
ALICE TOO!?
PWOP--
ALICE AND KAREN ARE HOOKED ON COMEDY RIGHT NOW.
JUST THE OTHER DAY...
HA HA HA HA!
I WILL DIE FROM LAUGHTER!
COMEDY SHOW
MY TUMMY HURTS!
BAM
BAM
THAT JOKE BRIL-LIANT!
HAHAHAHAHA
EXCUSE ME...
DO YOU MIND IF I CHANGE THE CHANNEL?
SHINO, SHOW A LITTLE INTEREST!

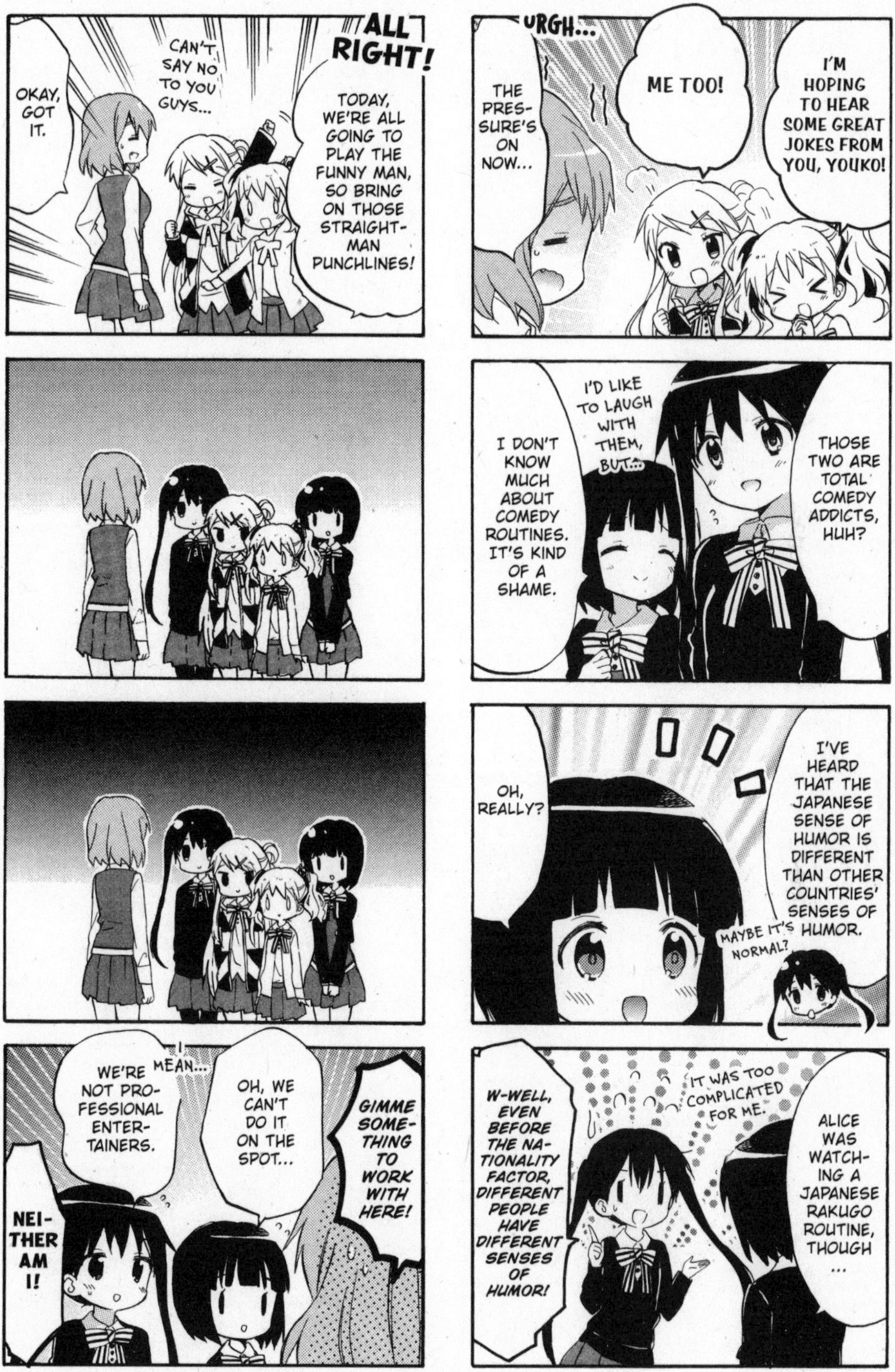
URGH...
I'M HOPING TO HEAR SOME GREAT JOKES FROM YOU, YOUKO!
ME TOO!
THE PRES-SURE'S ON NOW...
THOSE TWO ARE TOTAL COMEDY ADDICTS, HUH?
I'D LIKE TO LAUGH WITH THEM, BUT...
I DON'T KNOW MUCH ABOUT COMEDY ROUTINES. IT'S KIND OF A SHAME.
I'VE HEARD THAT THE JAPANESE SENSE OF HUMOR IS DIFFERENT THAN OTHER COUNTRIES' SENSES OF HUMOR.
MAYBE IT'S NORMAL?
OH, REALLY?
ALICE WAS WATCHING A JAPANESE RAKUGO ROUTINE, THOUGH...
IT WAS TOO COMPLICATED FOR ME.
W-WELL, EVEN BEFORE THE NATIONALITY FACTOR, DIFFERENT PEOPLE HAVE DIFFERENT SENSES OF HUMOR!
ALL RIGHT!
TODAY, WE'RE ALL GOING TO PLAY THE FUNNY MAN, SO BRING ON THOSE STRAIGHT-MAN PUNCHLINES!
CAN'T SAY NO TO YOU GUYS...
OKAY, GOT IT.
GIMME SOMETHING TO WORK WITH HERE!
OH, WE CAN'T DO IT ON THE SPOT...
I MEAN...
WE'RE NOT PROFESSIONAL ENTERTAINERS.
NEITHER AM I!

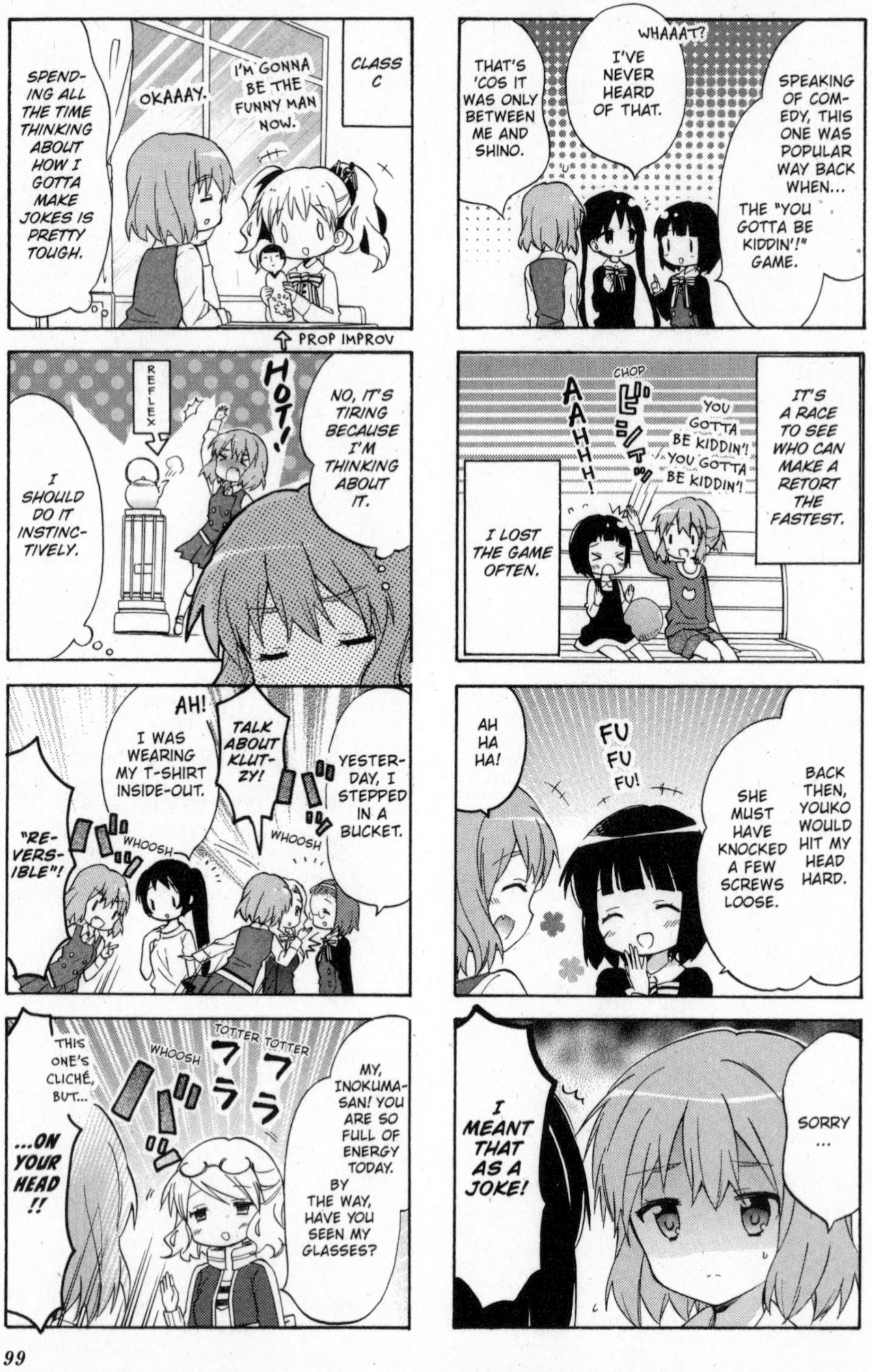
SPEAKING OF COMEDY, THIS ONE WAS POPULAR WAY BACK WHEN... THE "YOU GOTTA BE KIDDIN'!" GAME.
WHAAAT? I'VE NEVER HEARD OF THAT.
THAT'S 'COS IT WAS ONLY BETWEEN ME AND SHINO.
IT'S A RACE TO SEE WHO CAN MAKE A RETORT THE FASTEST.
YOU GOTTA BE KIDDIN'! YOU GOTTA BE KIDDIN'!
CHOP
AAHHH!
I LOST THE GAME OFTEN.
BACK THEN, YOUKO WOULD HIT MY HEAD HARD.
SHE MUST HAVE KNOCKED A FEW SCREWS LOOSE.
FU FU FU!
AH HA HA!
SORRY ...
I MEANT THAT AS A JOKE!
CLASS C
I'M GONNA BE THE FUNNY MAN NOW.
OKAAAY.
SPENDING ALL THE TIME THINKING ABOUT HOW I GOTTA MAKE JOKES IS PRETTY TOUGH.
PROP IMPROV
NO, IT'S TIRING BECAUSE I'M THINKING ABOUT IT.
HOT!
REFLEX
I SHOULD DO IT INSTINCTIVELY.
YESTERDAY, I STEPPED IN A BUCKET.
WHOOSH
TALK ABOUT KLUTZY!
AH!
I WAS WEARING MY T-SHIRT INSIDE-OUT.
WHOOSH
"REVERSIBLE"!
MY, INOKUMA-SAN! YOU ARE SO FULL OF ENERGY TODAY. BY THE WAY, HAVE YOU SEEN MY GLASSES?
TOTTER TOTTER
WHOOSH
THIS ONE'S CLICHÉ, BUT...
...ON YOUR HEAD!!

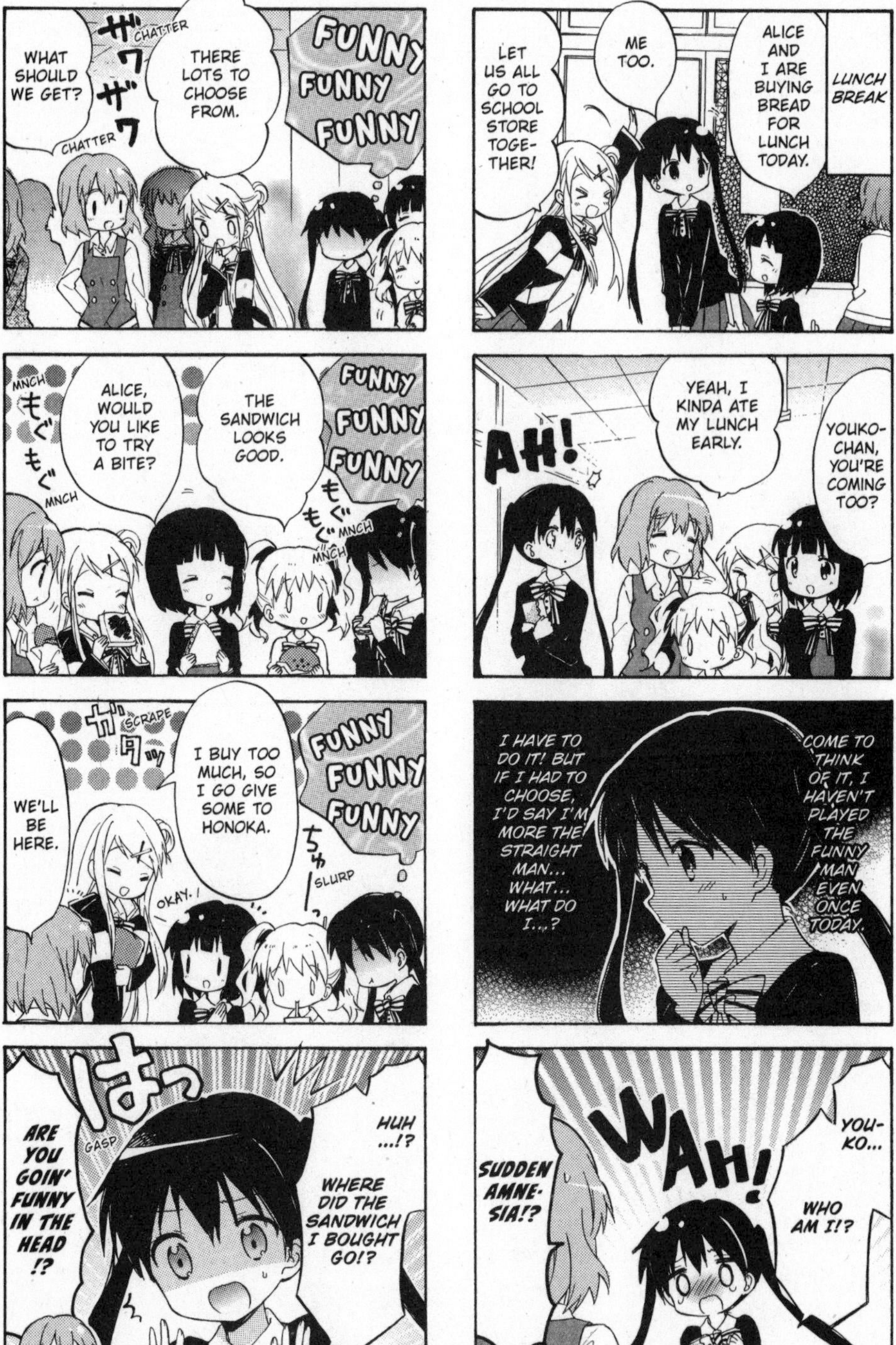
LUNCH BREAK
ALICE AND I ARE BUYING BREAD FOR LUNCH TODAY.
ME TOO.
LET US ALL GO TO SCHOOL STORE TOGE-THER!
YOUKO-CHAN, YOU'RE COMING TOO?
YEAH, I KINDA ATE MY LUNCH EARLY.
AH!
COME TO THINK OF IT, I HAVEN'T PLAYED THE FUNNY MAN EVEN ONCE TODAY.
I HAVE TO DO IT! BUT IF I HAD TO CHOOSE, I'D SAY I'M MORE THE STRAIGHT MAN... WHAT... WHAT DO I...?
YOU-KO...
WHO AM I!?
WAH!
SUDDEN AMNE-SIA!?
FUNNY FUNNY FUNNY
THERE LOTS TO CHOOSE FROM.
ザワ CHATTER
ザワ CHATTER
WHAT SHOULD WE GET?
FUNNY FUNNY FUNNY
もぐもぐ MNCH MNCH
THE SANDWICH LOOKS GOOD.
ALICE, WOULD YOU LIKE TO TRY A BITE?
もぐもぐ MNCH MNCH
FUNNY FUNNY FUNNY
I BUY TOO MUCH, SO I GO GIVE SOME TO HONOKA.
ガタッ SCRAPE
WE'LL BE HERE.
ちゅー SLURP
OKAY.
HUH ...!?
WHERE DID THE SANDWICH I BOUGHT GO!?
はっ GASP
ARE YOU GOIN' FUNNY IN THE HEAD!?

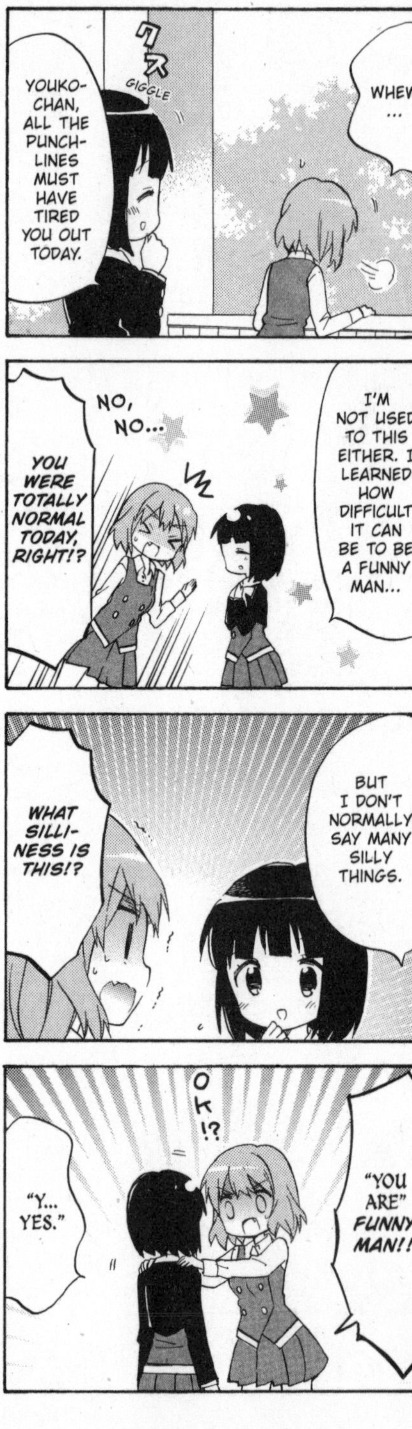
WHEW ...
クス GIGGLE
YOUKO-CHAN, ALL THE PUNCH-LINES MUST HAVE TIRED YOU OUT TODAY.
I'M NOT USED TO THIS EITHER. I LEARNED HOW DIFFICULT IT CAN BE TO BE A FUNNY MAN...
NO, NO...
YOU WERE TOTALLY NORMAL TODAY, RIGHT!?
BUT I DON'T NORMALLY SAY MANY SILLY THINGS.
WHAT SILLI-NESS IS THIS!?
OK!?
"YOU ARE" FUNNY MAN!!
"Y... YES."
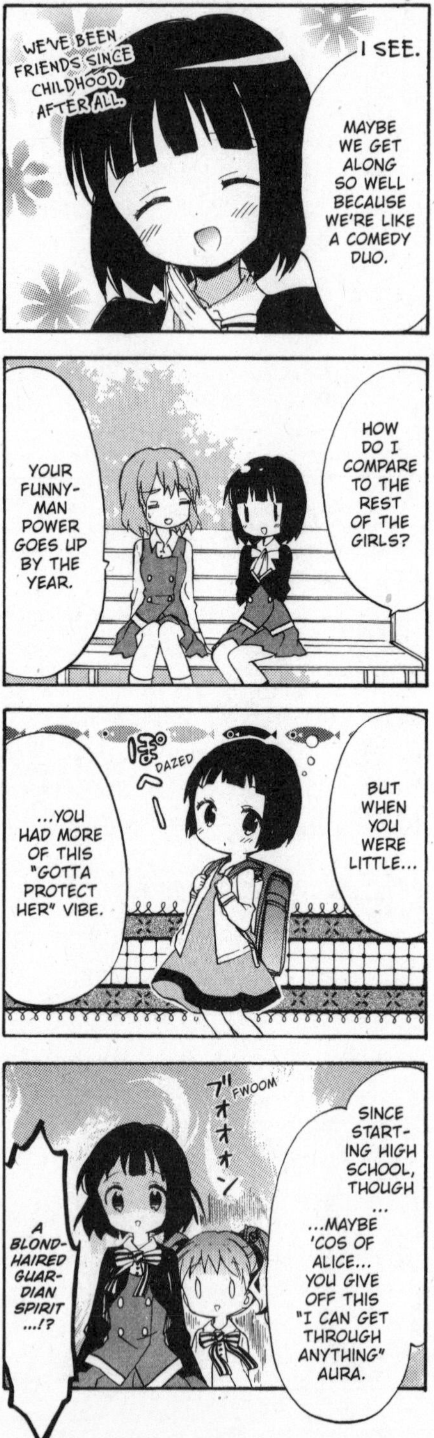
I SEE.
MAYBE WE GET ALONG SO WELL BECAUSE WE'RE LIKE A COMEDY DUO.
WE'VE BEEN FRIENDS SINCE CHILDHOOD, AFTER ALL.
HOW DO I COMPARE TO THE REST OF THE GIRLS?
YOUR FUNNY-MAN POWER GOES UP BY THE YEAR.
BUT WHEN YOU WERE LITTLE...
ぽへー DAZED
...YOU HAD MORE OF THIS "GOTTA PROTECT HER" VIBE.
ブオオオン FWOOM
SINCE START-ING HIGH SCHOOL, THOUGH ...
...MAYBE 'COS OF ALICE... YOU GIVE OFF THIS "I CAN GET THROUGH ANYTHING" AURA.
A BLOND-HAIRED GUAR-DIAN SPIRIT ...!?

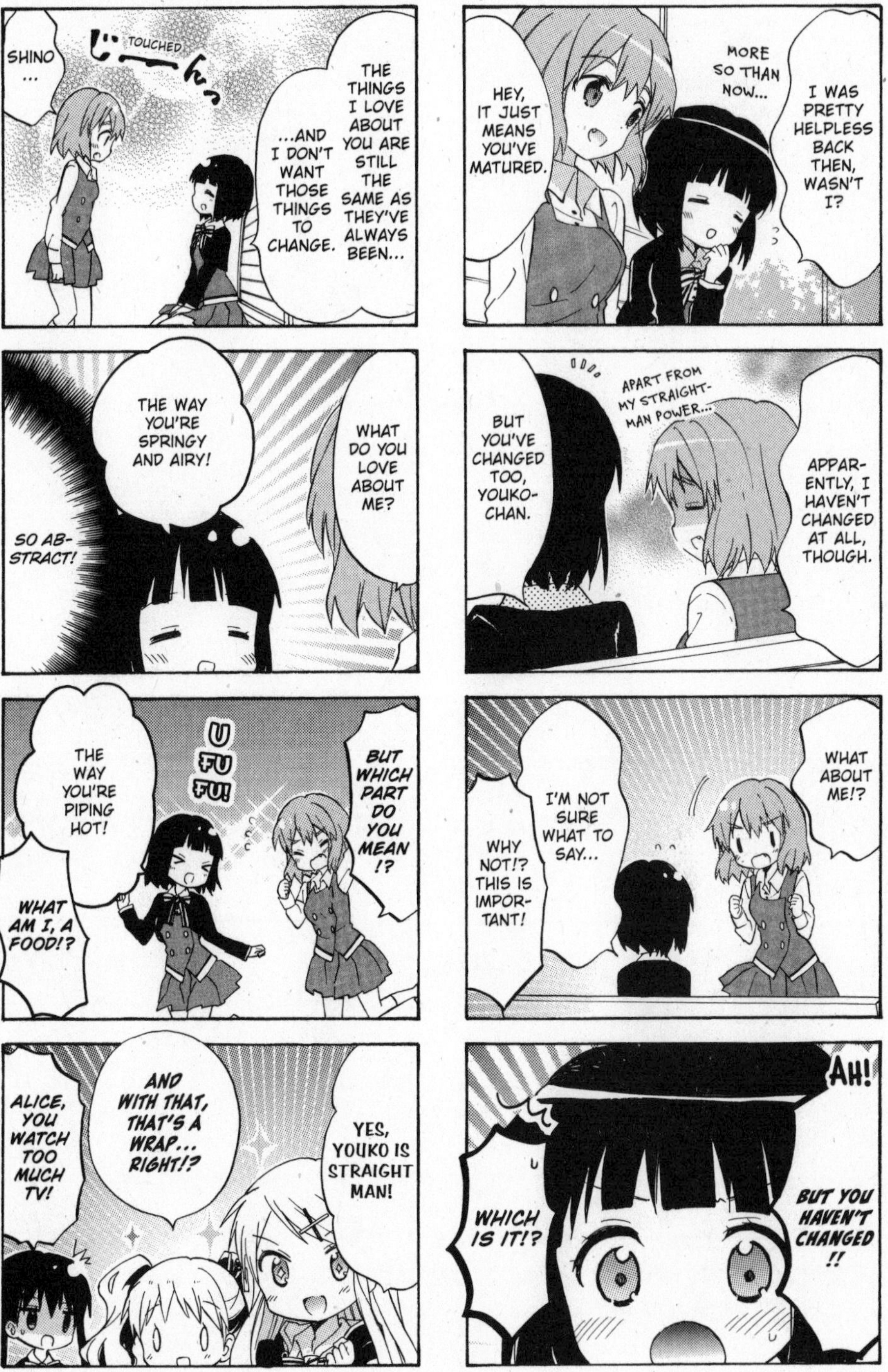
I WAS PRETTY HELPLESS BACK THEN, WASN'T I?
MORE SO THAN NOW...
HEY, IT JUST MEANS YOU'VE MATURED.
APPARENTLY, I HAVEN'T CHANGED AT ALL, THOUGH.
APART FROM MY STRAIGHT-MAN POWER...
BUT YOU'VE CHANGED TOO, YOUKO-CHAN.
WHAT ABOUT ME!?
I'M NOT SURE WHAT TO SAY...
WHY NOT!? THIS IS IMPORTANT!
AH!
BUT YOU HAVEN'T CHANGED !!
WHICH IS IT!?
THE THINGS I LOVE ABOUT YOU ARE STILL THE SAME AS THEY'VE ALWAYS BEEN...
...AND I DON'T WANT THOSE THINGS TO CHANGE.
じーーんっ
TOUCHED
SHINO...
WHAT DO YOU LOVE ABOUT ME?
THE WAY YOU'RE SPRINGY AND AIRY!
SO ABSTRACT!
BUT WHICH PART DO YOU MEAN !?
U FU FU!
THE WAY YOU'RE PIPING HOT!
WHAT AM I, A FOOD!?
YES, YOUKO IS STRAIGHT MAN!
AND WITH THAT, THAT'S A WRAP... RIGHT!?
ALICE, YOU WATCH TOO MUCH TV!

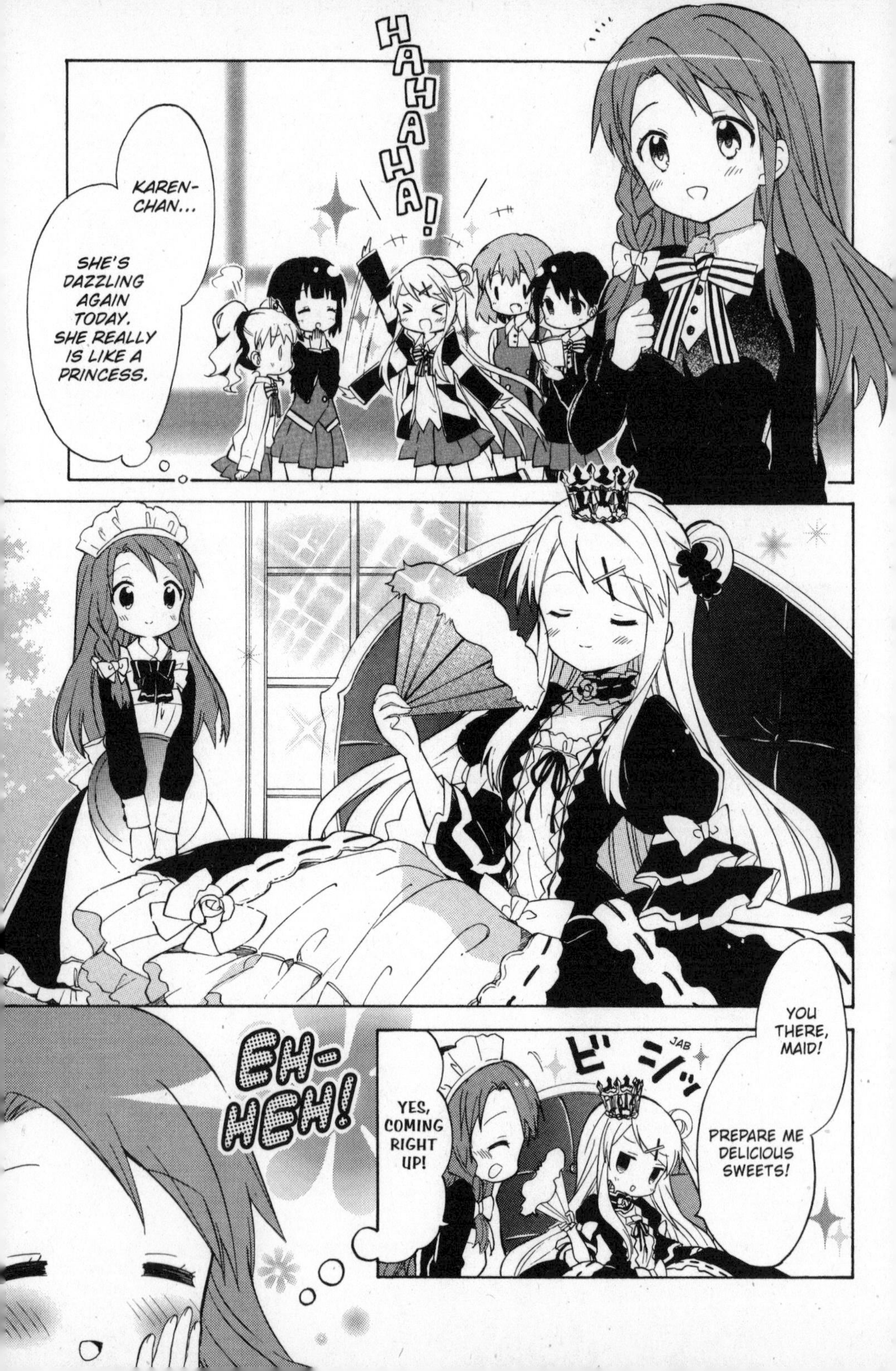
HAHAHAHA!
KAREN-CHAN... SHE'S DAZZLING AGAIN TODAY. SHE REALLY IS LIKE A PRINCESS.
YOU THERE, MAID! PREPARE ME DELICIOUS SWEETS!
JAB
ビシッ
YES, COMING RIGHT UP!
EH-HEH!

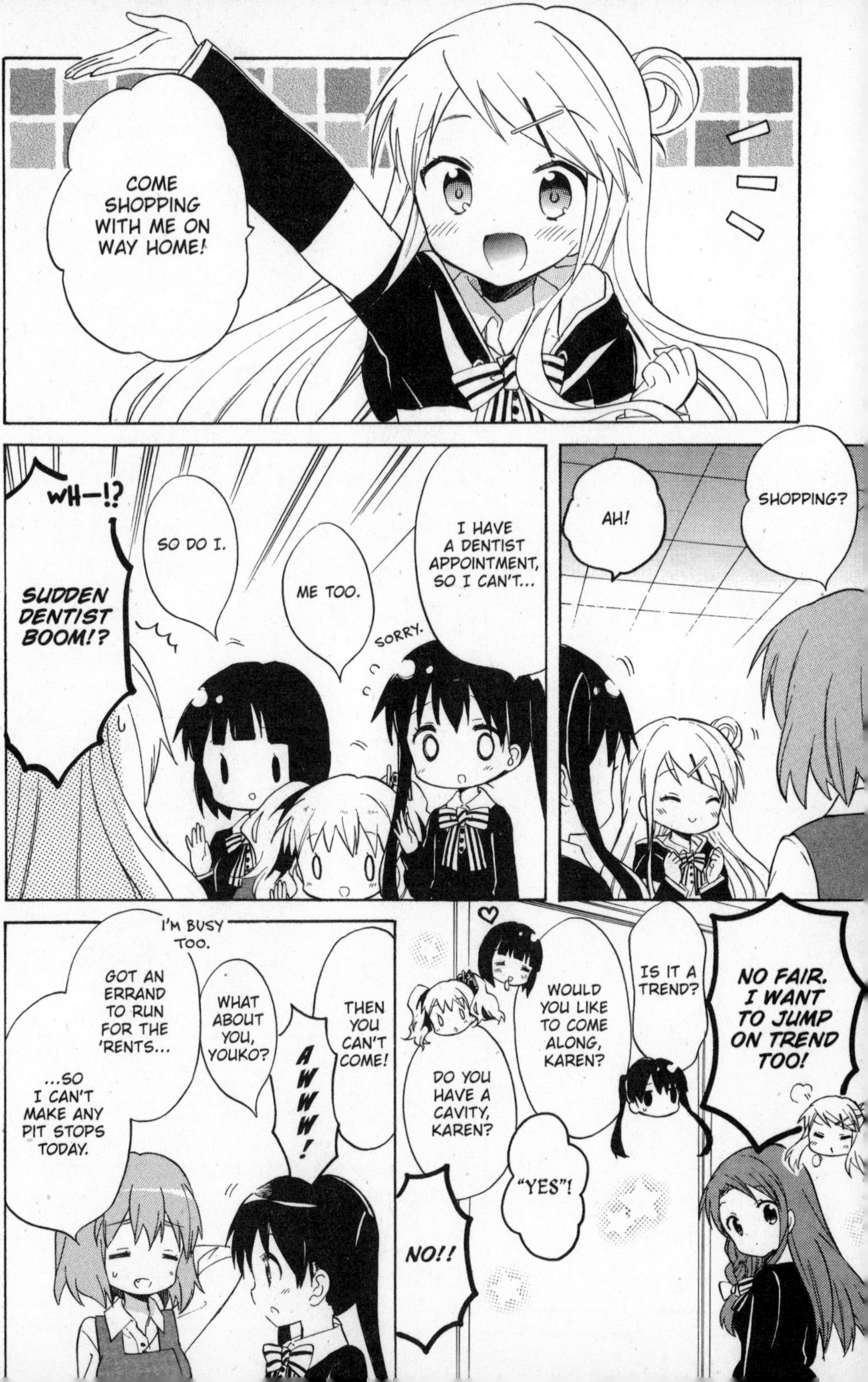

COME SHOPPING WITH ME ON WAY HOME!
SHOPPING?
AH!
I HAVE A DENTIST APPOINTMENT, SO I CAN'T...
SORRY.
ME TOO.
SO DO I.
WH—!?
SUDDEN DENTIST BOOM!?
NO FAIR. I WANT TO JUMP ON TREND TOO!
IS IT A TREND?
WOULD YOU LIKE TO COME ALONG, KAREN?
DO YOU HAVE A CAVITY, KAREN?
"YES"!
NO!!
THEN YOU CAN'T COME!
AWWW!
WHAT ABOUT YOU, YOUKO?
I'M BUSY TOO.
GOT AN ERRAND TO RUN FOR THE 'RENTS...
...SO I CAN'T MAKE ANY PIT STOPS TODAY.

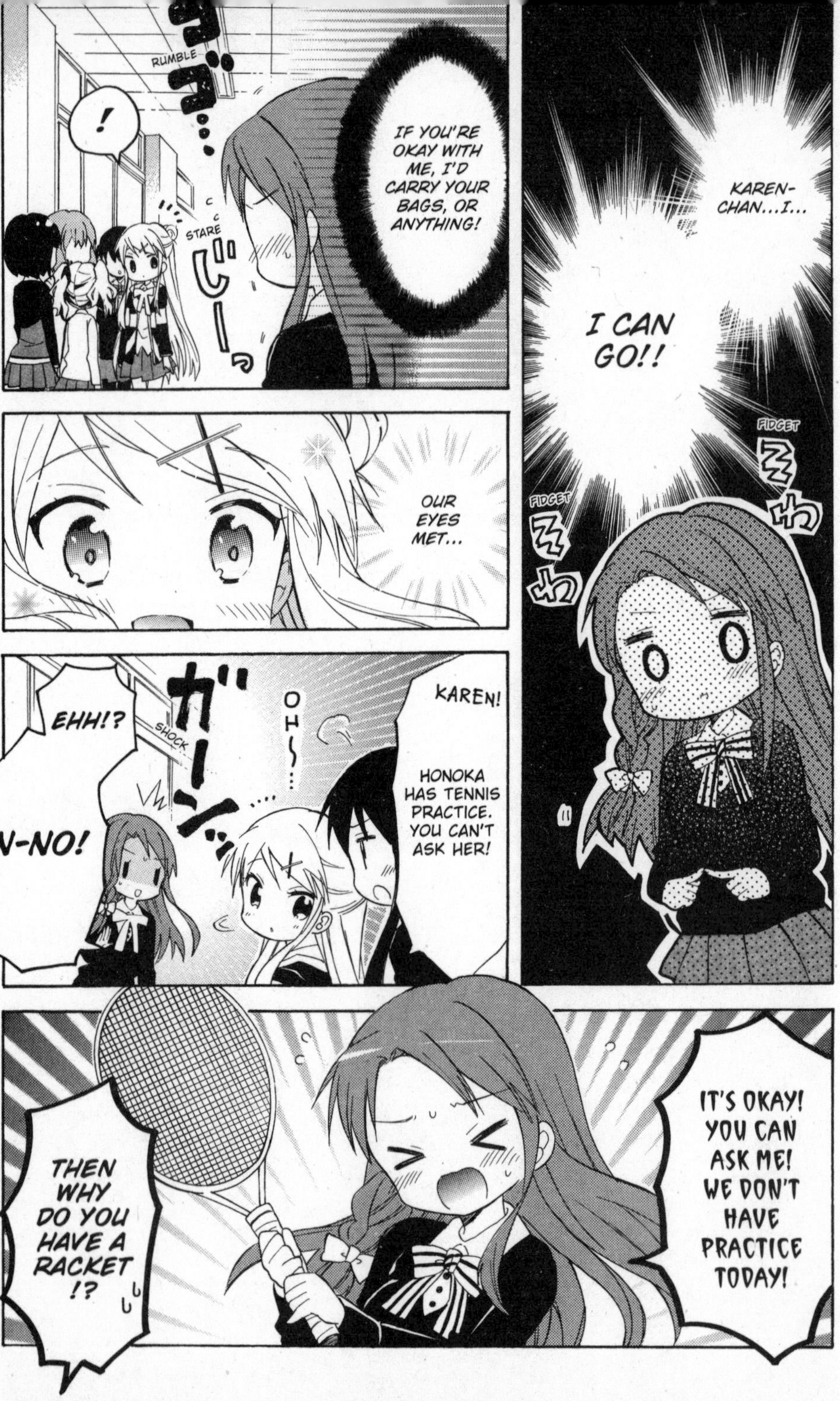
KAREN-CHAN...I...
I CAN GO!!
FIDGET
FIDGET
IF YOU'RE OKAY WITH ME, I'D CARRY YOUR BAGS, OR ANYTHING!
RUMBLE
!
STARE
OUR EYES MET...
KAREN!
HONOKA HAS TENNIS PRACTICE. YOU CAN'T ASK HER!
OH~...
SHOCK
EHH!?
N-NO!
IT'S OKAY! YOU CAN ASK ME! WE DON'T HAVE PRACTICE TODAY!
THEN WHY DO YOU HAVE A RACKET!?

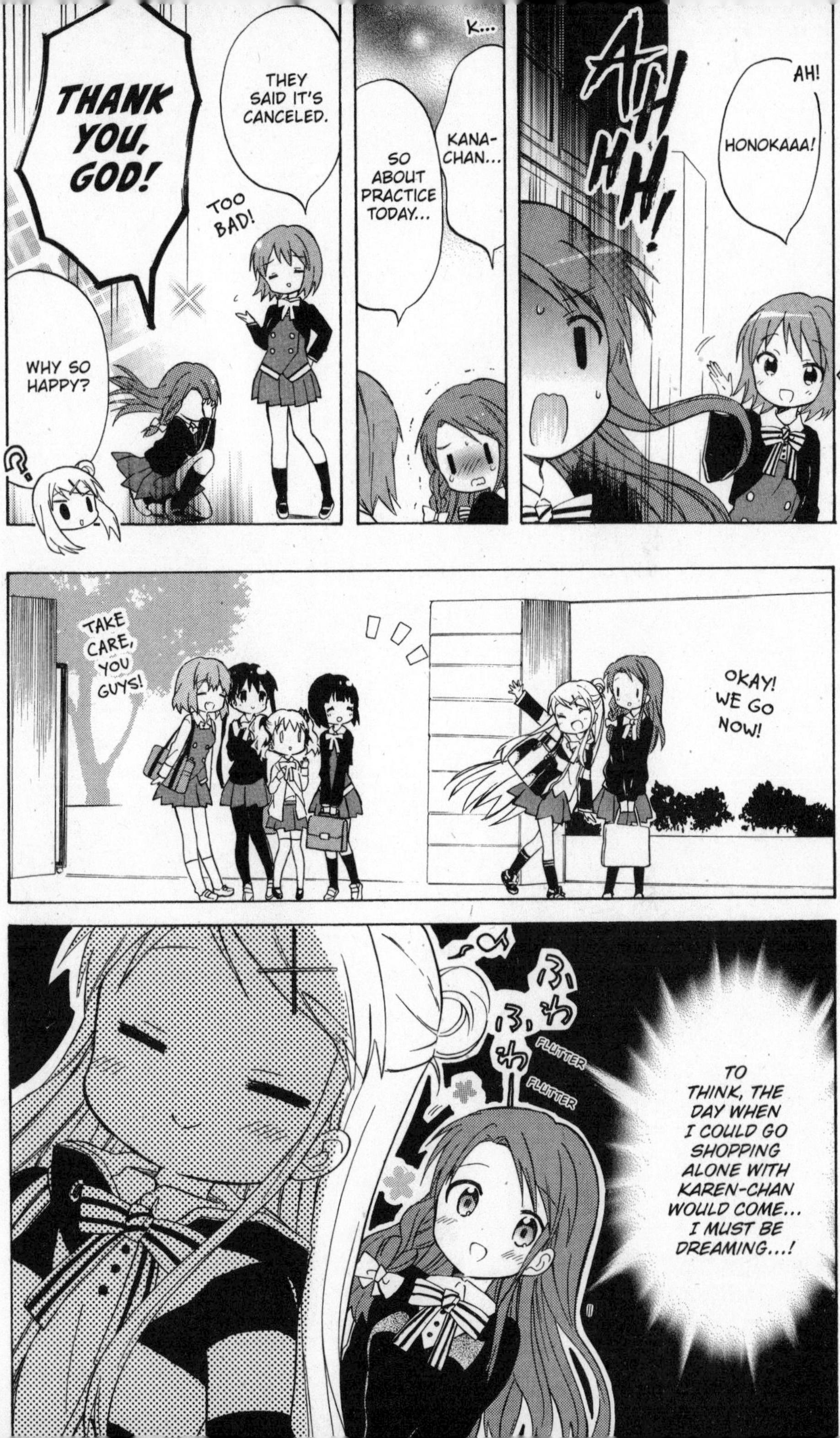
AH!
HONOKAAA!
TENNIS TEAM MEMBER
AHHH!
K...
KANA-CHAN...
SO ABOUT PRACTICE TODAY...
THEY SAID IT'S CANCELED.
TOO BAD!
THANK YOU, GOD!
WHY SO HAPPY?
OKAY! WE GO NOW!
TAKE CARE, YOU GUYS!
ふわふわ
FLUTTER FLUTTER
TO THINK, THE DAY WHEN I COULD GO SHOPPING ALONE WITH KAREN-CHAN WOULD COME... I MUST BE DREAMING...!

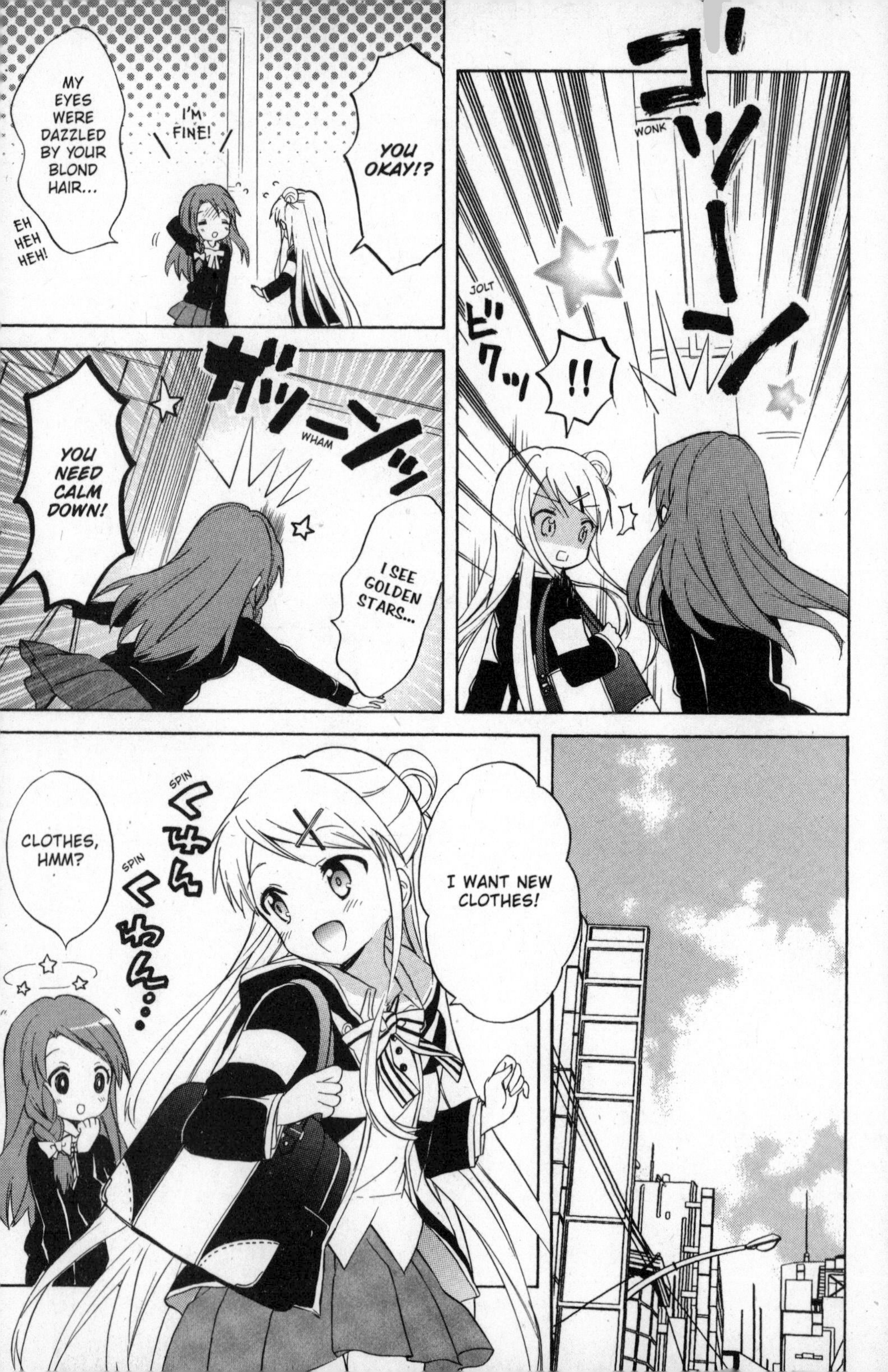

WONK
JOLT
!!
YOU OKAY!?
I'M FINE!
MY EYES WERE DAZZLED BY YOUR BLOND HAIR...
EH HEH HEH!
WHAM
YOU NEED CALM DOWN!
I SEE GOLDEN STARS...
I WANT NEW CLOTHES!
SPIN
SPIN
CLOTHES, HMM?

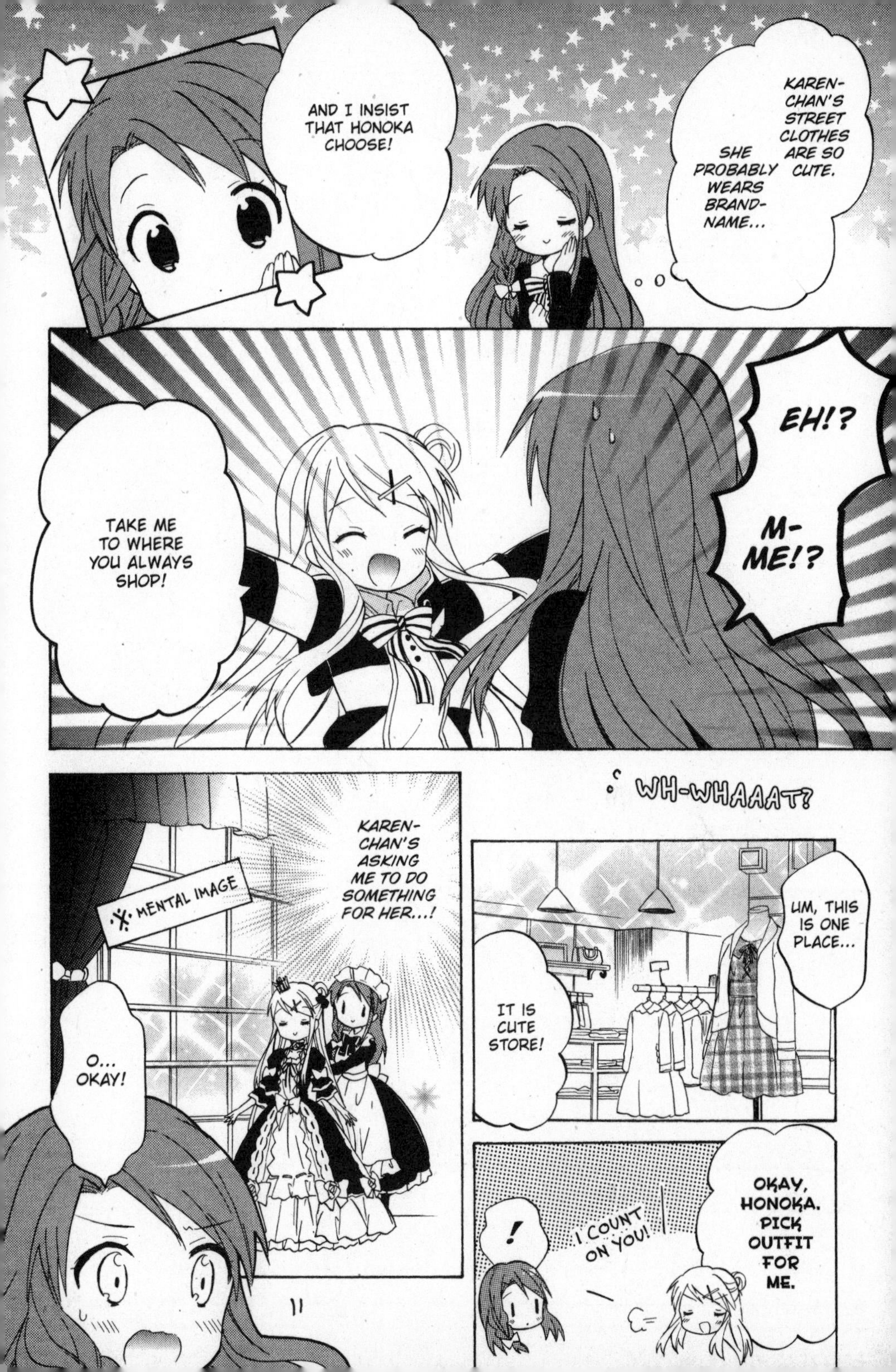
KAREN-CHAN'S STREET CLOTHES ARE SO CUTE.
SHE PROBABLY WEARS BRAND-NAME...
AND I INSIST THAT HONOKA CHOOSE!
EH!?
M-ME!?
TAKE ME TO WHERE YOU ALWAYS SHOP!
WH-WHAAAT?
UM, THIS IS ONE PLACE...
IT IS CUTE STORE!
OKAY, HONOKA. PICK OUTFIT FOR ME.
I COUNT ON YOU!
!
KAREN-CHAN'S ASKING ME TO DO SOMETHING FOR HER...!
※ MENTAL IMAGE
O... OKAY!

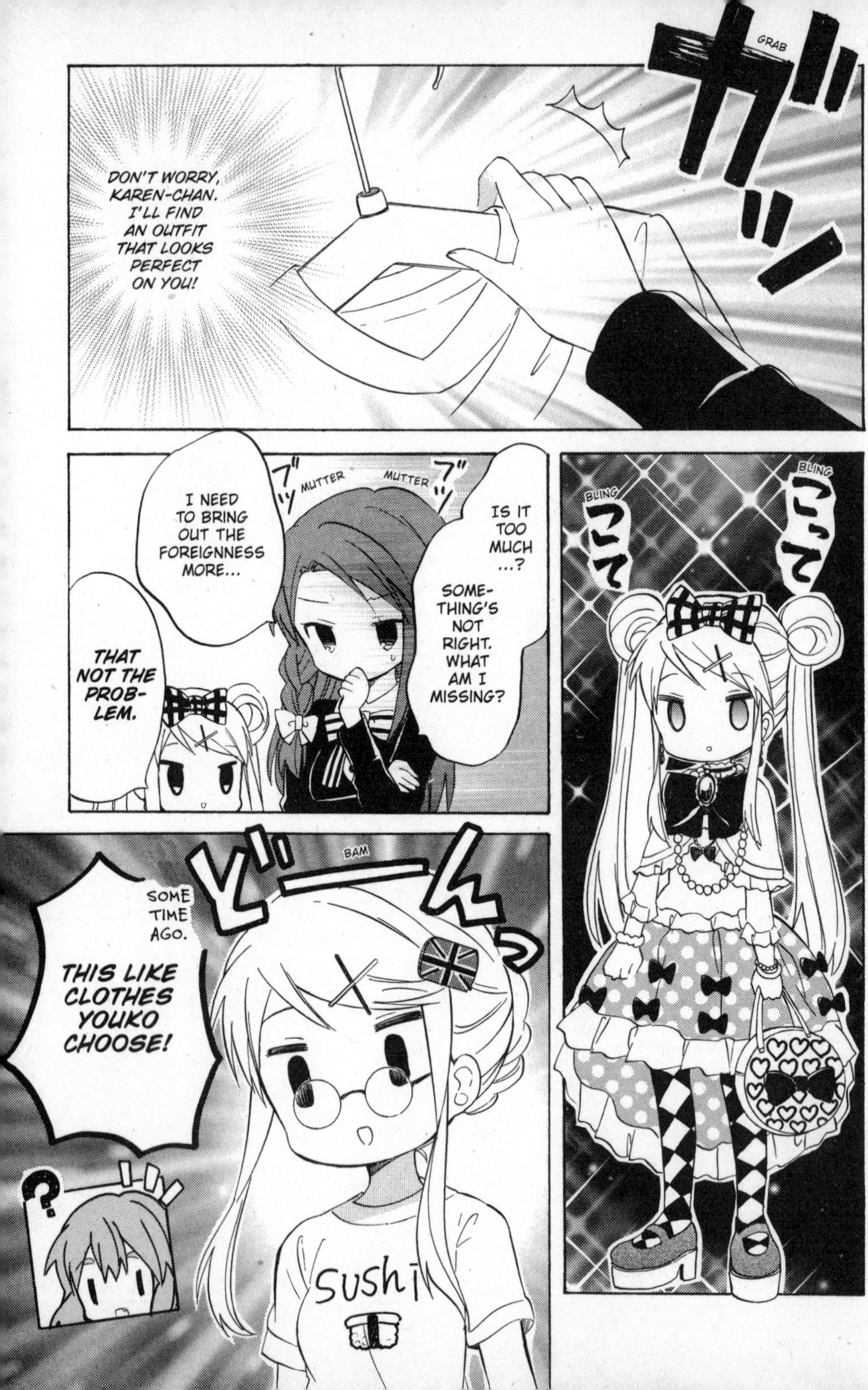
GRAB
DON'T WORRY, KAREN-CHAN. I'LL FIND AN OUTFIT THAT LOOKS PERFECT ON YOU!
BLING
BLING
IS IT TOO MUCH ...?
SOME-THING'S NOT RIGHT. WHAT AM I MISSING?
MUTTER
MUTTER
I NEED TO BRING OUT THE FOREIGNNESS MORE...
THAT NOT THE PROB-LEM.
BAM
SOME TIME AGO.
THIS LIKE CLOTHES YOUKO CHOOSE!
SUSHi

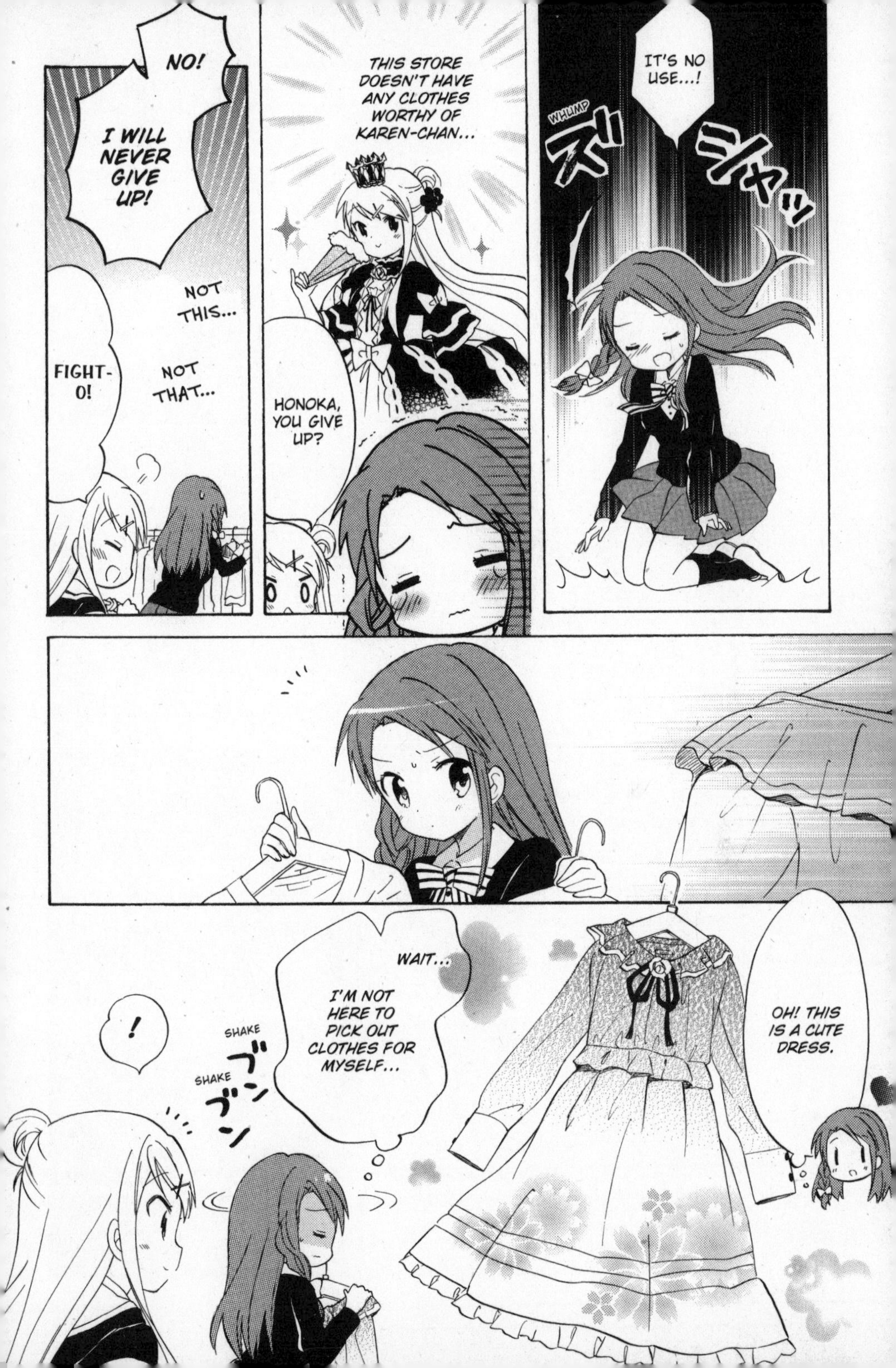
IT'S NO USE...!
WHUMP
ズシャッ
THIS STORE DOESN'T HAVE ANY CLOTHES WORTHY OF KAREN-CHAN...
HONOKA, YOU GIVE UP?
NO!
I WILL NEVER GIVE UP!
NOT THIS...
NOT THAT...
FIGHT-O!
OH! THIS IS A CUTE DRESS.
WAIT...
I'M NOT HERE TO PICK OUT CLOTHES FOR MYSELF...
SHAKE
SHAKE
ブンブン
!

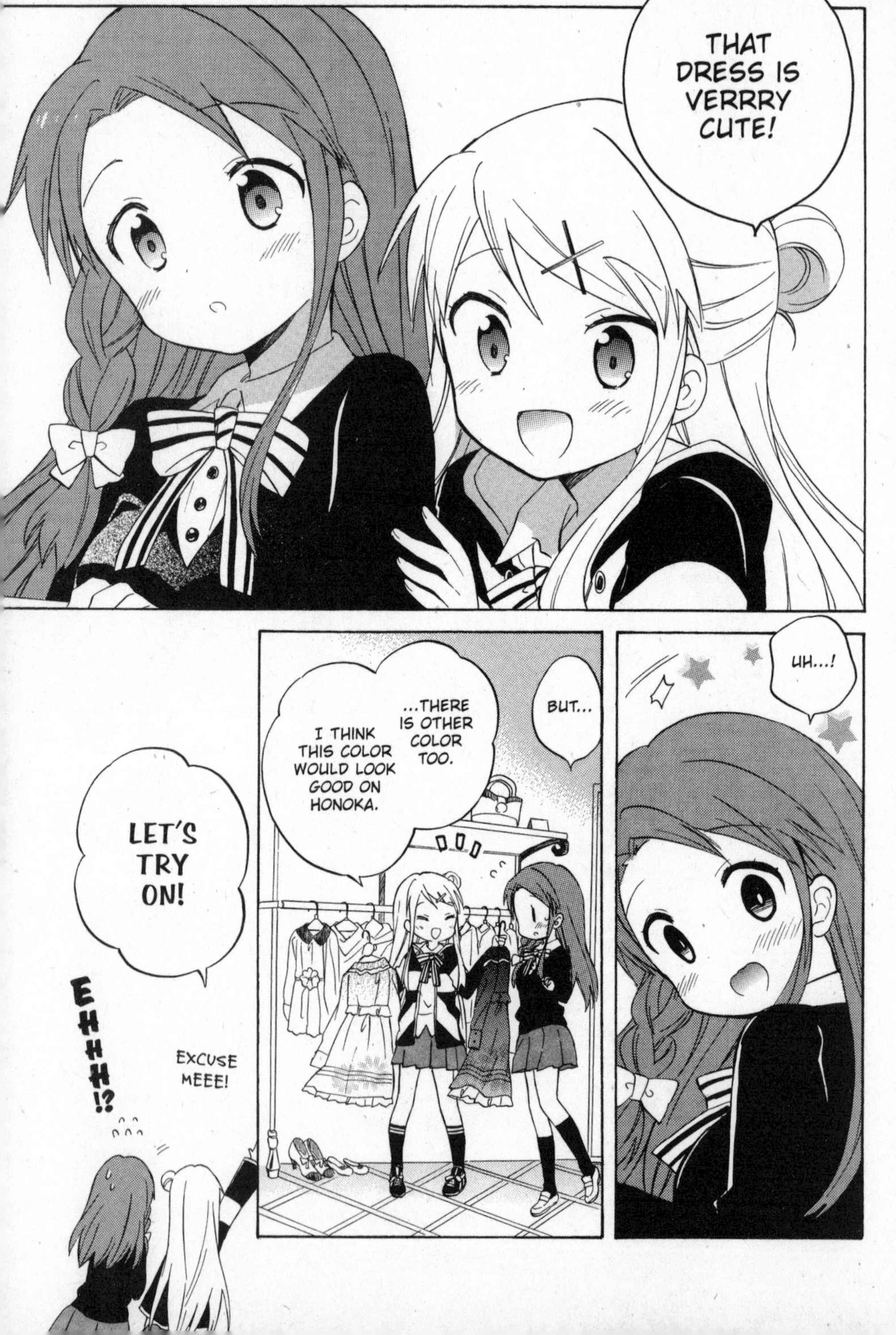
THAT DRESS IS VERRRY CUTE!
UH...!
BUT...
...THERE IS OTHER COLOR TOO.
I THINK THIS COLOR WOULD LOOK GOOD ON HONOKA.
LET'S TRY ON!
EHHHH!?
EXCUSE MEEE!

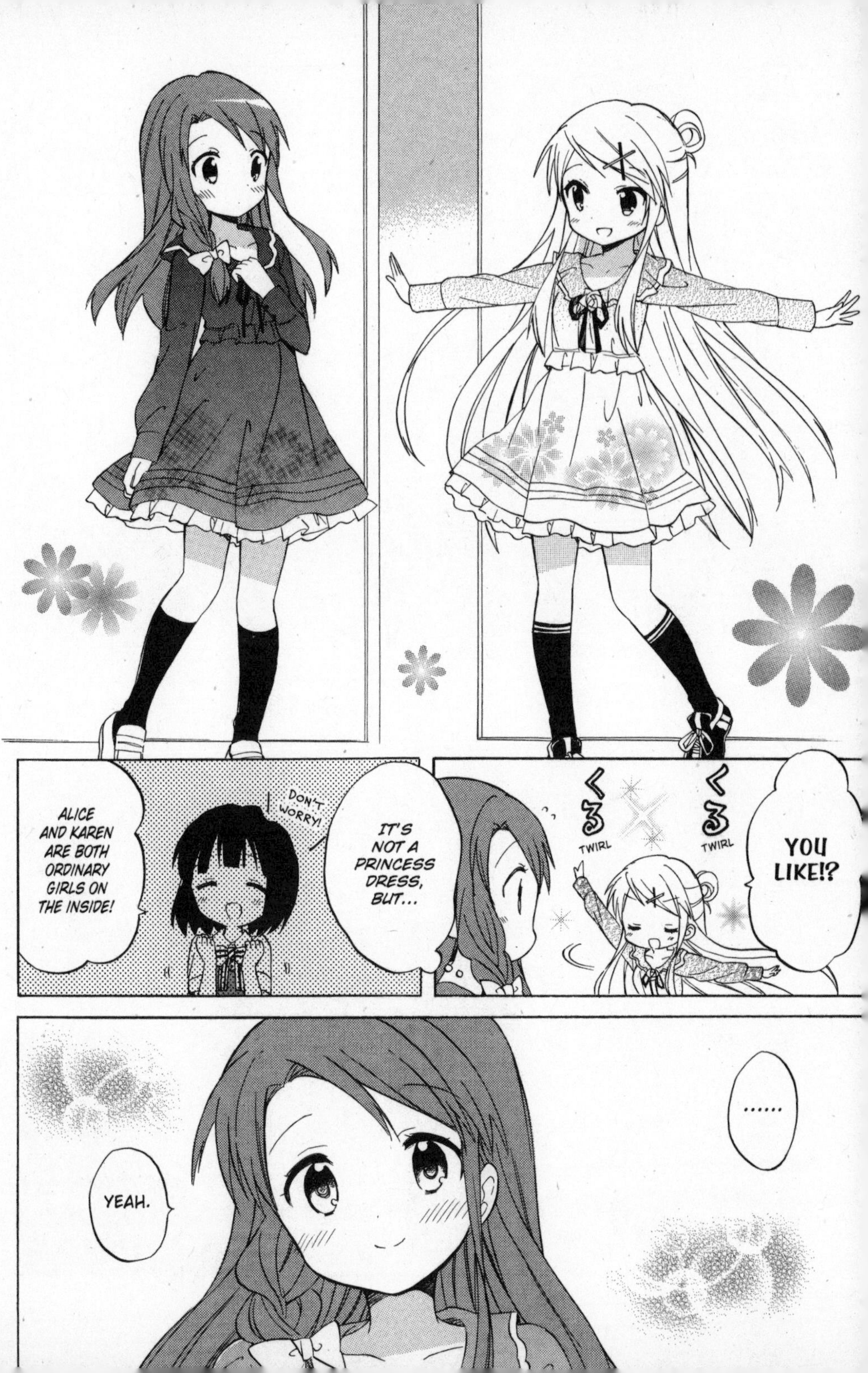

YOU LIKE!?
くる TWIRL
くる TWIRL
IT'S NOT A PRINCESS DRESS, BUT...
DON'T WORRY!
ALICE AND KAREN ARE BOTH ORDINARY GIRLS ON THE INSIDE!
......
YEAH.

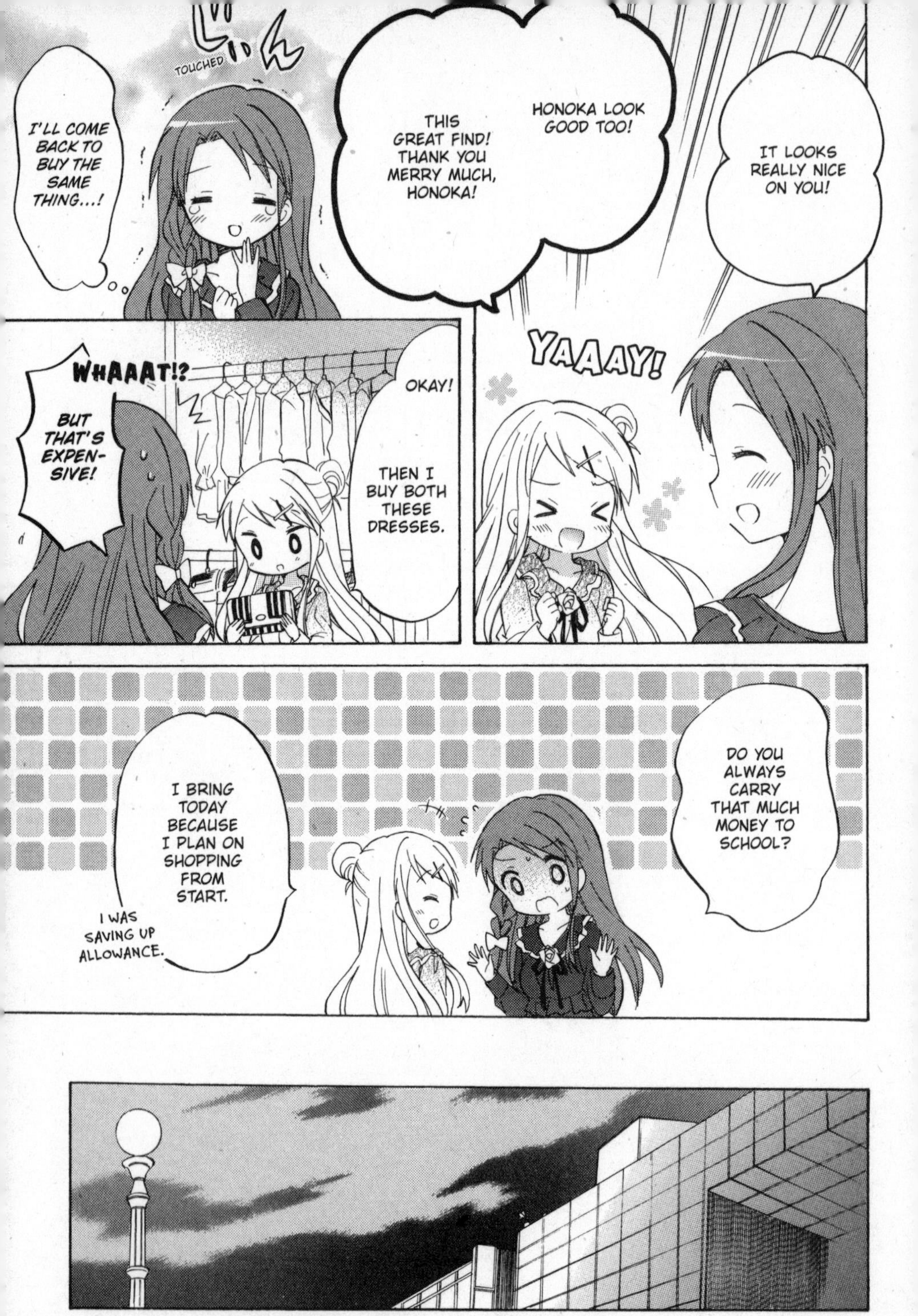
IT LOOKS REALLY NICE ON YOU!
YAAAY!
HONOKA LOOK GOOD TOO!
THIS GREAT FIND! THANK YOU MERRY MUCH, HONOKA!
TOUCHED
I'LL COME BACK TO BUY THE SAME THING...!
OKAY!
THEN I BUY BOTH THESE DRESSES.
WHAAAT!?
BUT THAT'S EXPEN-SIVE!
DO YOU ALWAYS CARRY THAT MUCH MONEY TO SCHOOL?
I BRING TODAY BECAUSE I PLAN ON SHOPPING FROM START.
I WAS SAVING UP ALLOWANCE.

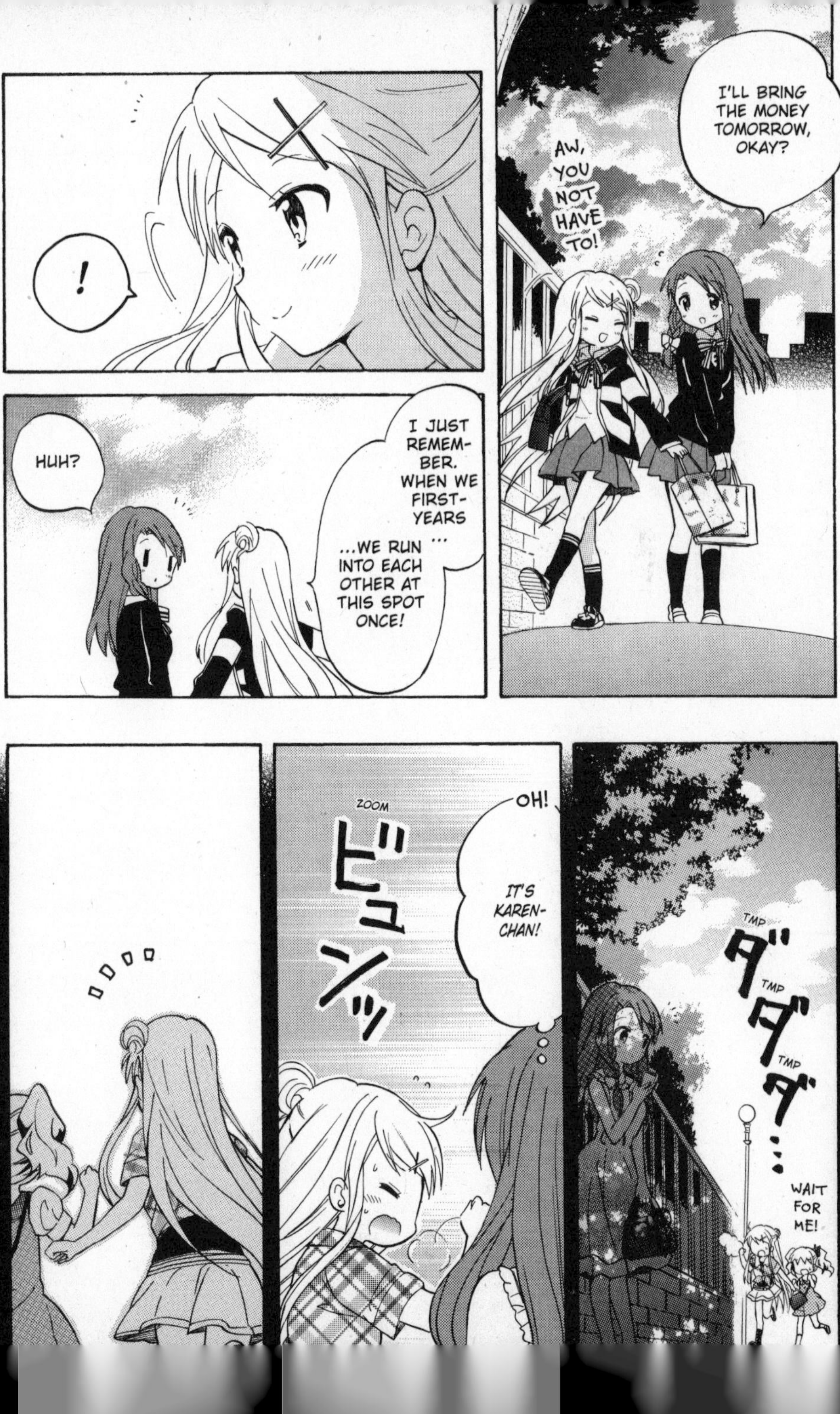
I'LL BRING THE MONEY TOMORROW, OKAY?
AW, YOU NOT HAVE TO!
!
I JUST REMEMBER. WHEN WE FIRST-YEARS ...
...WE RUN INTO EACH OTHER AT THIS SPOT ONCE!
HUH?
TMP
TMP
TMP
ダダダ…
WAIT FOR ME!
OH!
IT'S KAREN-CHAN!
ZOOM
ビュンッ

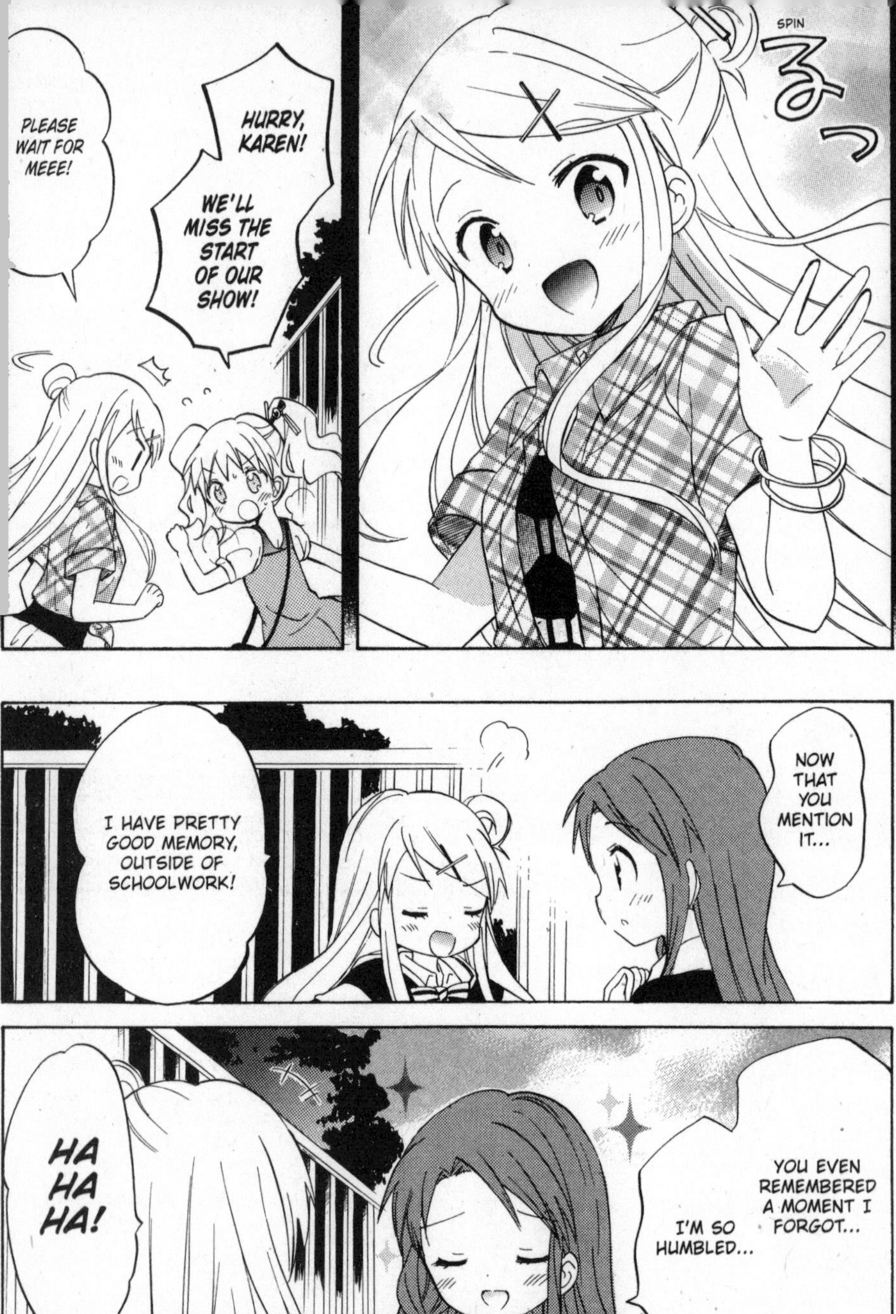
SPIN
HURRY, KAREN!
WE'LL MISS THE START OF OUR SHOW!
PLEASE WAIT FOR MEEE!
NOW THAT YOU MENTION IT...
I HAVE PRETTY GOOD MEMORY, OUTSIDE OF SCHOOLWORK!
YOU EVEN REMEMBERED A MOMENT I FORGOT...
I'M SO HUMBLED...
HA HA HA!

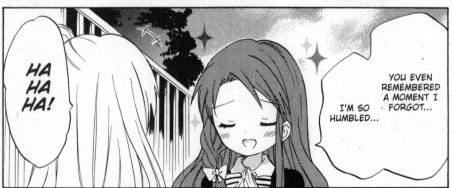

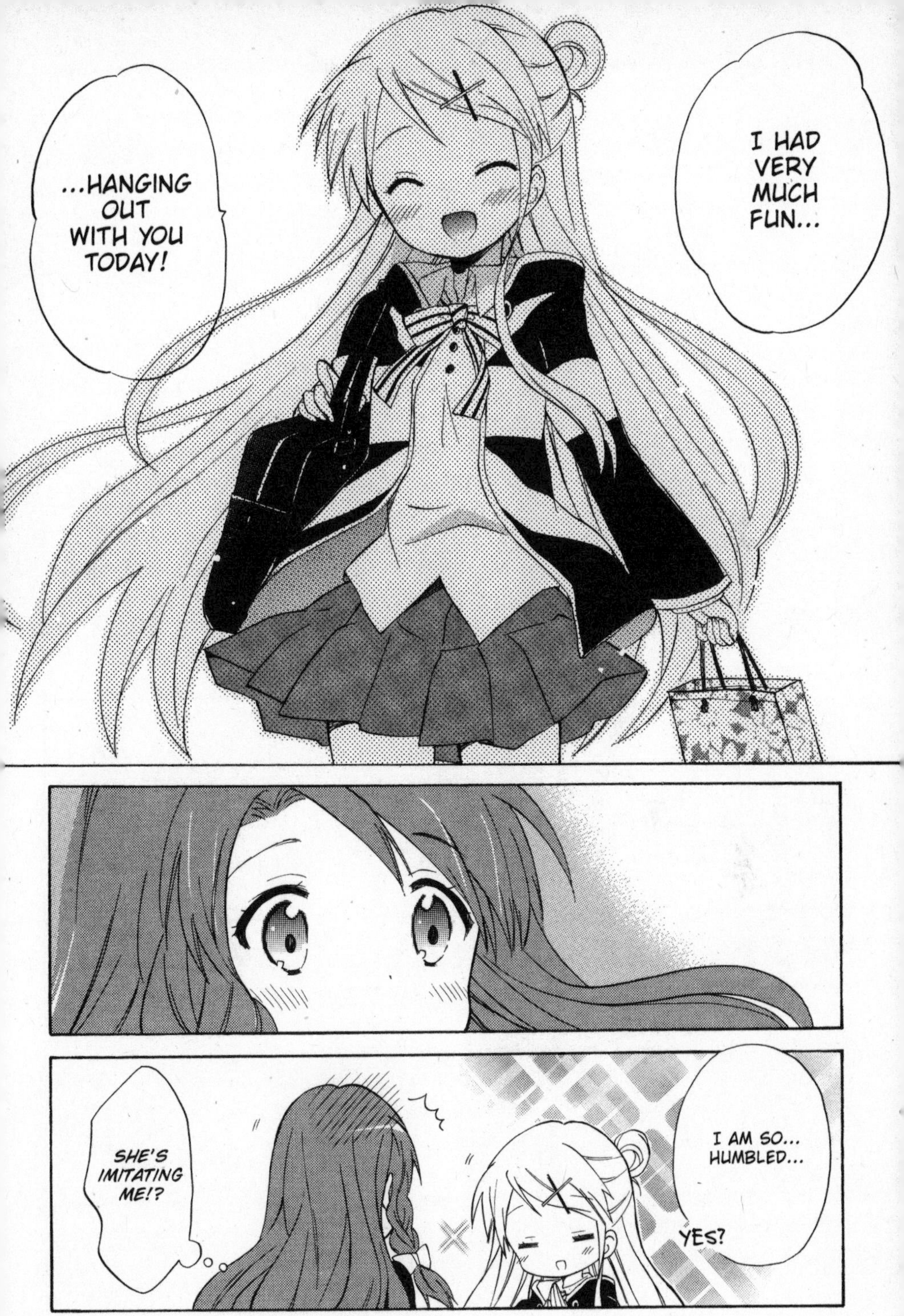
I HAD VERY MUCH FUN...
...HANGING OUT WITH YOU TODAY!
I AM SO... HUMBLED...
YES?
SHE'S IMITATING ME!?

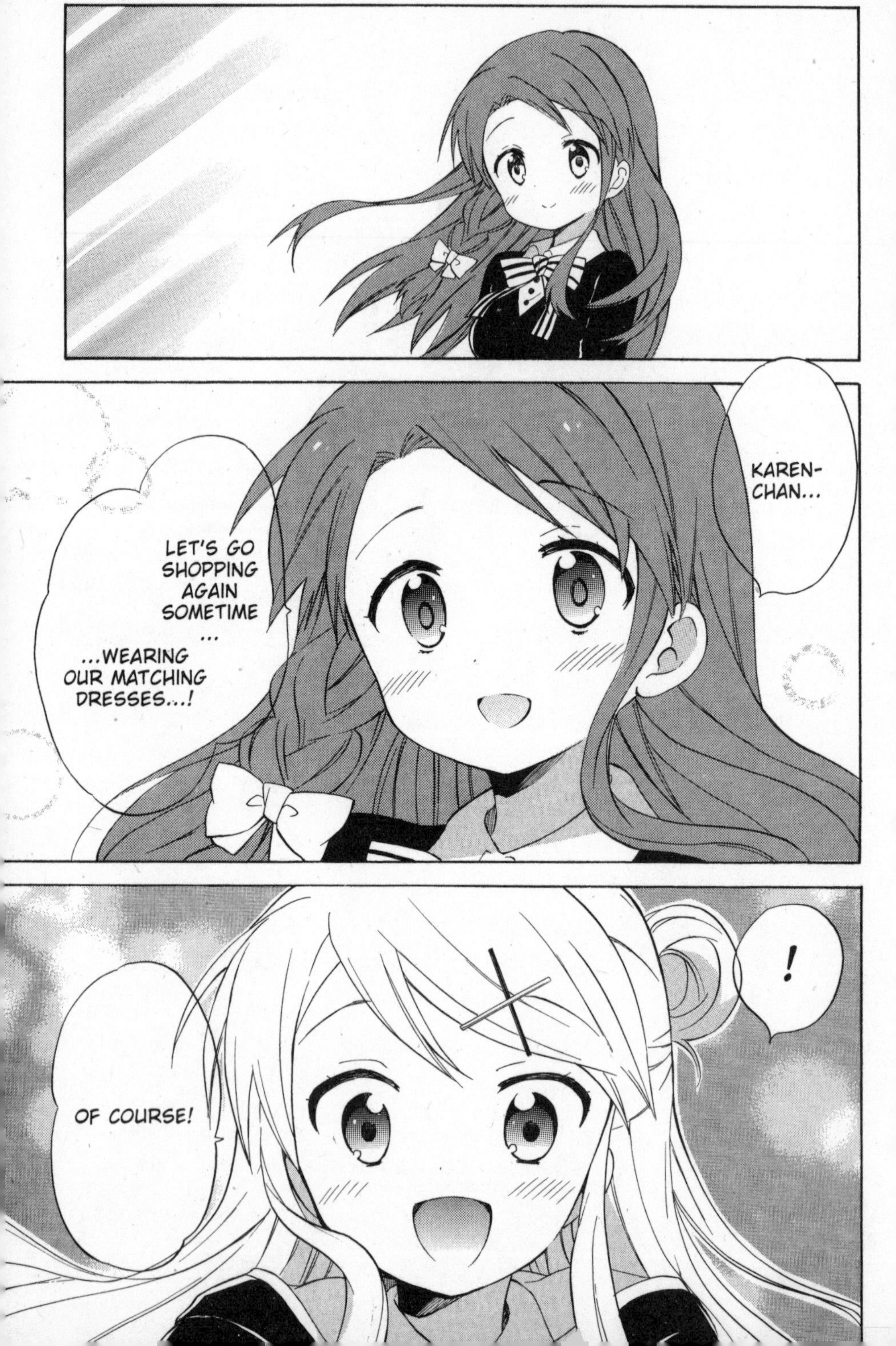
KAREN-CHAN...
LET'S GO SHOPPING AGAIN SOMETIME ... ...WEARING OUR MATCHING DRESSES...!
!
OF COURSE!

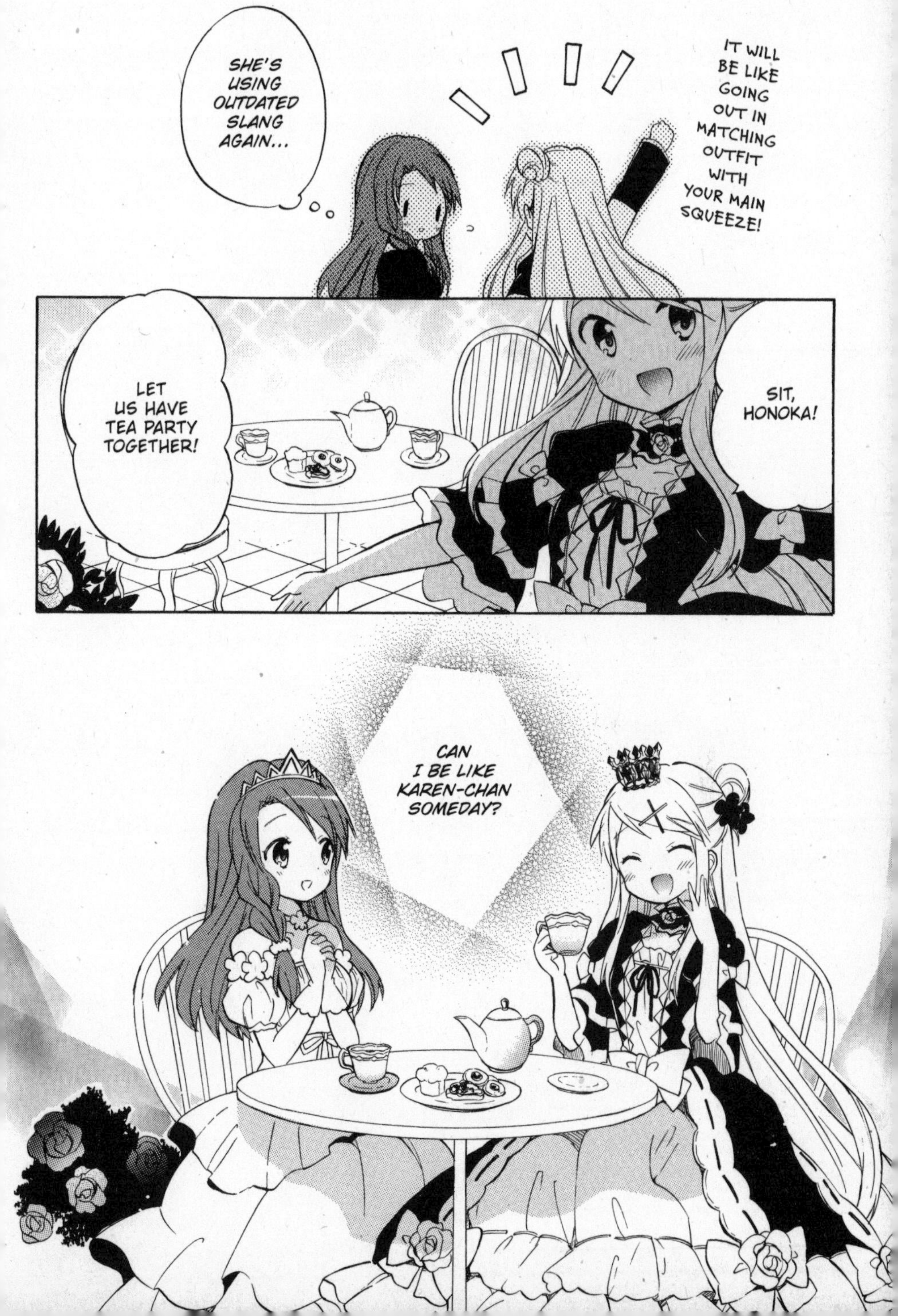
IT WILL BE LIKE GOING OUT IN MATCHING OUTFIT WITH YOUR MAIN SQUEEZE!
SHE'S USING OUTDATED SLANG AGAIN...
SIT, HONOKA!
LET US HAVE TEA PARTY TOGETHER!
CAN I BE LIKE KAREN-CHAN SOMEDAY?

Afterword

Thank you so much for picking up Volume 6.

We're at Volume 6...! Incredible.

To all of the staff on the second season of the anime,

thanks for your hard work.

Thank you to everyone who watched it!

Truly, thank you so much for the fun time.

Well, I hope we'll meet again in Volume 7.

Next time, I think they'll be third-years?

The series will still go on for a while, so I hope

you'll continue to support it!

Special Thanks ♪ My editor, Hideki Satomi-sama; the anime staff and voice cast; all the people who've supported me; all of my readers!

Hara ✿

PLEASE CHECK OUT THE YUI HARA ARTBOOK, PARADE!

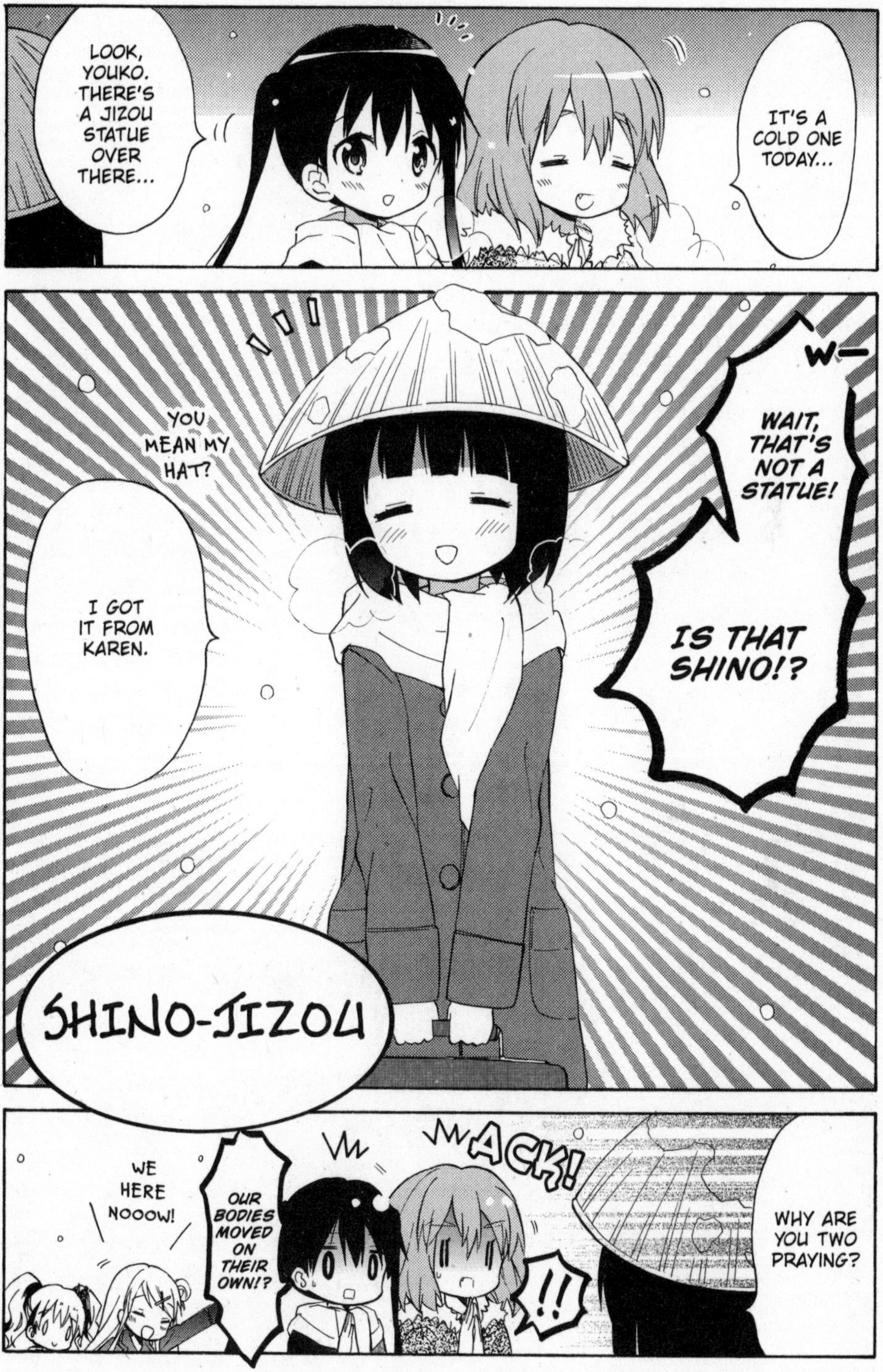
IT'S A COLD ONE TODAY...
LOOK, YOUKO. THERE'S A JIZOU STATUE OVER THERE...
W—
WAIT, THAT'S NOT A STATUE!
IS THAT SHINO!?
YOU MEAN MY HAT?
I GOT IT FROM KAREN.
SHINO-JIZOU
WHY ARE YOU TWO PRAYING?
WACK!
!!
OUR BODIES MOVED ON THEIR OWN!?
WE HERE NOOOW!

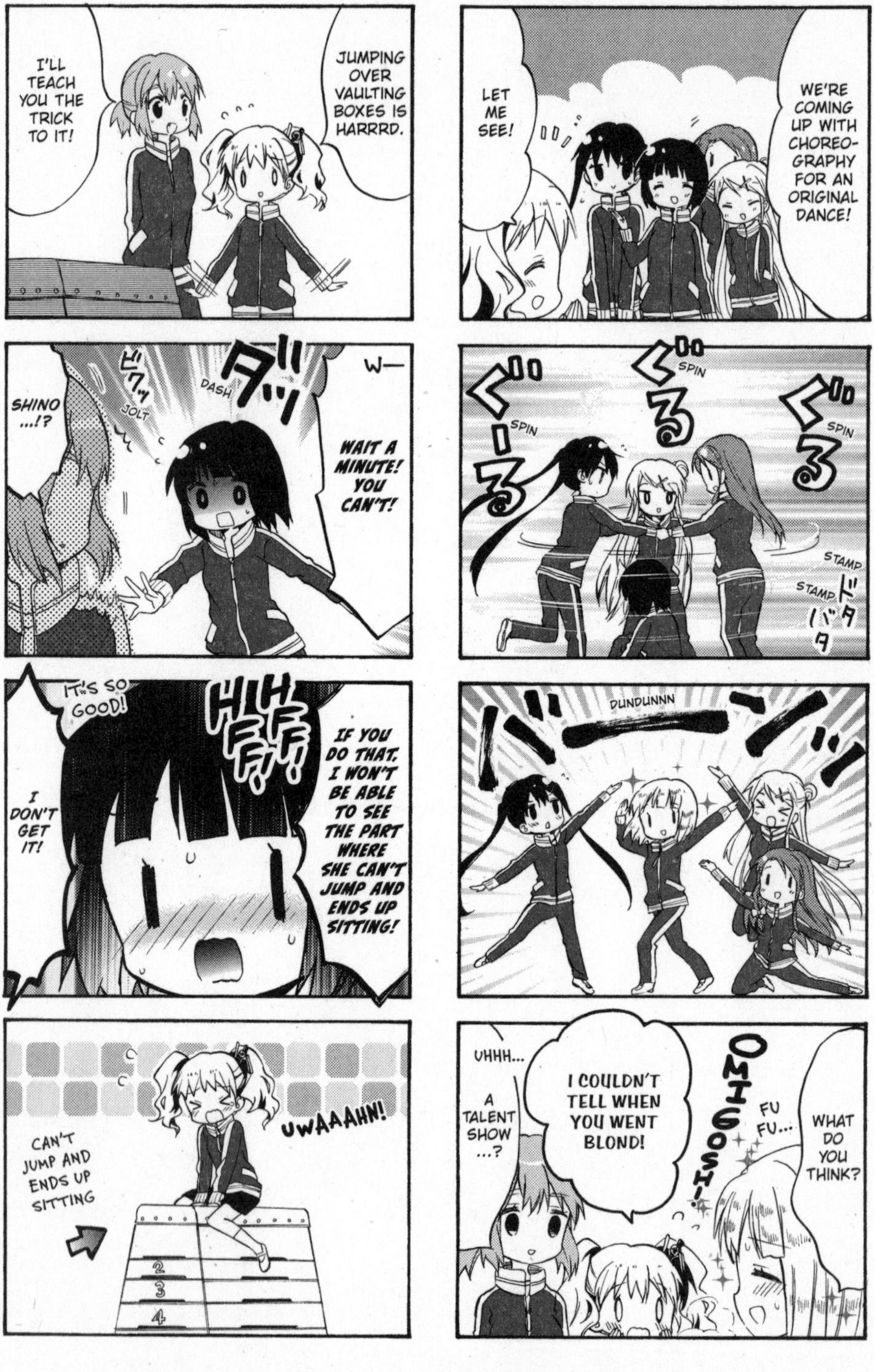

WE'RE COMING UP WITH CHOREOGRAPHY FOR AN ORIGINAL DANCE!
LET ME SEE!
ぐるぐる SPIN
ぐるぐる SPIN
ぐるぐる SPIN
STAMP STAMP ドタバタ
バーーン DUNDUNNN
WHAT DO YOU THINK?
FU FU...
OMIGOSH!
I COULDN'T TELL WHEN YOU WENT BLOND!
UHHH...
A TALENT SHOW ...?
JUMPING OVER VAULTING BOXES IS HARRRD.
I'LL TEACH YOU THE TRICK TO IT!
W—
ダッ DASH
WAIT A MINUTE! YOU CAN'T!
ビクッ JOLT
SHINO ...!?
IF YOU DO THAT, I WON'T BE ABLE TO SEE THE PART WHERE SHE CAN'T JUMP AND ENDS UP SITTING!
HIHFFF!
IT'S SO GOOD!
I DON'T GET IT!
UWAAAHN!
CAN'T JUMP AND ENDS UP SITTING
2
3
4

kiniro
mosaic

Translation Notes

PAGE 4
Visiting someone who isn't well (whether they're in the hospital or at home) is called *omimai*. Visitors will often bring a gift, such as flowers or fruits.

PAGE 7
In Japan's bathing culture, it's traditional to first wash yourself off with a shower, and then sit in a very hot bath to soak for a while. Children are taught to **count to one hundred** before getting out of the tub.

PAGE 8
In Japanese, the phrase Aya uses to mean **"a quick dip"** is *karasu no gyouzui* (literally "a crow's bath," an idiom for "a quick bath"). Youko doesn't recognize the idiom, and thinks that maybe Aya said "*Karasu-chan no gyouza*"—their teacher "Karasu-chan's gyouza dumplings." Shino corrects her and tells her the meaning of *karasu no gyouzui*.

PAGE 17
In Japanese, the idiom used for Karen **"seeing the light"** is *me kara uroko*, which literally means "scales (fall) from one's eyes."

PAGE 18
Translated as **"tough love,"** in Japanese, Karasu-sensei asks Kuzehashi-sensei if she's using *suparuta* with Karen—a "Spartan," or extra-strict teaching style.

PAGE 24
When Youko says **"grill time"** instead of "kill time" because food's on her mind, in Japanese, she uses the word *hitsumabushi* (a Nagoya dish of grilled eel over rice) instead of *himatsubushi* ("killing time").

PAGE 28
Cinemas in Japan also sell promotional movie merchandise, including nice **booklets** with premium content such as interviews, photos, etc.

PAGE 29
Three-three-seven is a clapping rhythm for cheer groups.

PAGE 35
In Japanese, Honoka says *"meido no miyage da yo"* ("I'll take this with me to my grave"). But Karen doesn't seem to know the idiom, and hears *meido* as the Japanese pronunciation of the English word **"maid."**

PAGE 47
Japanese manzai is a comedy style performed by a duo—a straight man (*tsukkomi*) and a funny man (*boke*). In this case, Aya was the funny man, and
Youko the straight man.

PAGE 50
For New Year's, two **pine branches** (*kadomatsu*/"gate pine") are placed in front of homes as spiritual anchors (*yorishiro*) to usher the gods into one's home. The number **nine** is bad luck because its pronunciation (*ku*) is a homonym for agony/suffering.

PAGE 59
In *The Tale of the Bamboo Cutter*, an old bamboo cutter finds a thumb-sized baby in a mysterious stalk of bamboo. He and his wife raise the baby as **Princess Kaguya.** The old man later finds gold inside of the bamboo he cuts, and becomes rich; as Princess Kaguya grows up, she becomes normal-sized and extraordinarily beautiful. Suitors come to court her, but she gives them impossible tasks so she can refuse to marry them. Eventually, she reveals that she is not of this world and must return to her home, the moon, leaving her adoptive parents behind.

PAGE 60

According to Japanese tradition, if your first dream of the new year is lucky, you have a lucky year ahead of you. So it's no wonder Shinobu is upset about her dream...

PAGE 62

Hot pot is a dish popular in East Asian countries, featuring a pot of broth in which all kinds of ingredients, such as meat, vegetables, tofu, and seafood can be placed and boiled at the table.

Shino isn't familiar with them, but the hot pot "roles" that Alice and her mother call off are real Japanese, and pretty punny. The **hot pot magistrate** (*nabe bugyou*) is the person who dictates what goes into the hot pot, and how long it cooks. The **scummy local governor** (*aku daikan*) role is named after the evil local governor character archetype in historical fiction—*aku* means "evil," but it's also a homonym for "soup scum." Finally, the **waiting towngirl** is *machimusume*, where *machi* can mean both "waiting" and "town," and *musume* means "girl."

PAGE 63

Mystery hot pot (*yaminabe*, "hot pot-in-the-dark") is a potluck hot pot game—all the participants bring ingredients for the hot pot, but they don't tell the others what they're bringing, and the ingredients commonly include foods that shouldn't belong in hot pot. It's also cooked in the dark, so no one sees what goes in it until it's too late...

PAGE 66

The **oden performance** (*odengei*) is a classic comedy skit from the 1980s, in which piping hot oden is pushed toward someone protesting and they react to it in funny, overblown ways as it's force-fed to them, touched onto their face, etc. The original skit was performed by entertainers "Beat" Takeshi Kitano and Tsurutarou Kataoka.

PAGE 80
As can be seen in the panel above Alice, *kokeshi* are handmade wooden dolls of Japanese origin. These dolls have no arms or legs, and are very slender, much like Shino hopes to be...

PAGE 82
The other type of Shino Alice mentions is a **"Kintarou** Shino," named after "Golden Boy Kintarou," a very famous young man in Japanese folklore. The characters in his name can be translated as "Golden Boy," hence the title. Shino repeats Alice's "Shino is Shino" phrase, but puts her own twist on it, saying "Gold is gold" using the *kin* character from Kintarou's name. The boy is known for being rather plump, so Shino's not fond of the comparison.

PAGE 88
There are a few different "categories" of chocolate given on Valentine's Day in Japan (and it's predominantly given out by girls and women, unlike in countries where both men and women are expected to give gifts). Honoka and the girls are talking about *tomo choko*, or **"friend chocolate."** *Giri choko* is **"obligation chocolate"** given to friends, coworkers, and so on; it doesn't have romantic meaning. *Honmei choko* (**"true feeling chocolate"**) is given to the person you have romantic feelings for, and is often more elaborate or expensive than *giri choko*.

PAGE 90
On **White Day** (March 14), men who received gifts on Valentine's Day are supposed to give a gift in return.

PAGE 92
Translated as **"You go, girl,"** in Japanese, Kuzehashi-sensei tells Aya to *ganba*, a slangy way to say *ganbare* ("do your best"/"good luck"). As Karen comments, it's a little bit behind the times now.

PAGE 96
The Japanese for **"my futon flew away"** is more punny because of the repetition of "futon": *futon ga futtonda.* It's sort of like saying, "I scream for ice cream."

PAGE 98
In **rakugo** performances, a traditional comedy style that began in the Edo period, a single *rakugo* storyteller sits on the stage in the formal *seiza* position and tells a long, comical tale, using only a fan and small cloth as props, and their voice and movements to act out all of the characters.

PAGE 118
Translated as **"going out with your main squeeze,"** in the original Japanese, Karen uses the word *abekku* ("a couple on a date," from the French *avec*). As Honoka comments, it's an outdated word.

PAGE 120
Jizou is the guardian deity of children, particularly children who have passed away before their parents. His straw hat features prominently in the story of *Kasa Jizou*, in which an old man and his wife make straw hats to sell for food, but the old man ends up putting the hats on the Jizou statues to protect them from the snow. His good deeds are rewarded in the end, as the statues bring him and his wife a veritable feast upon his return home.

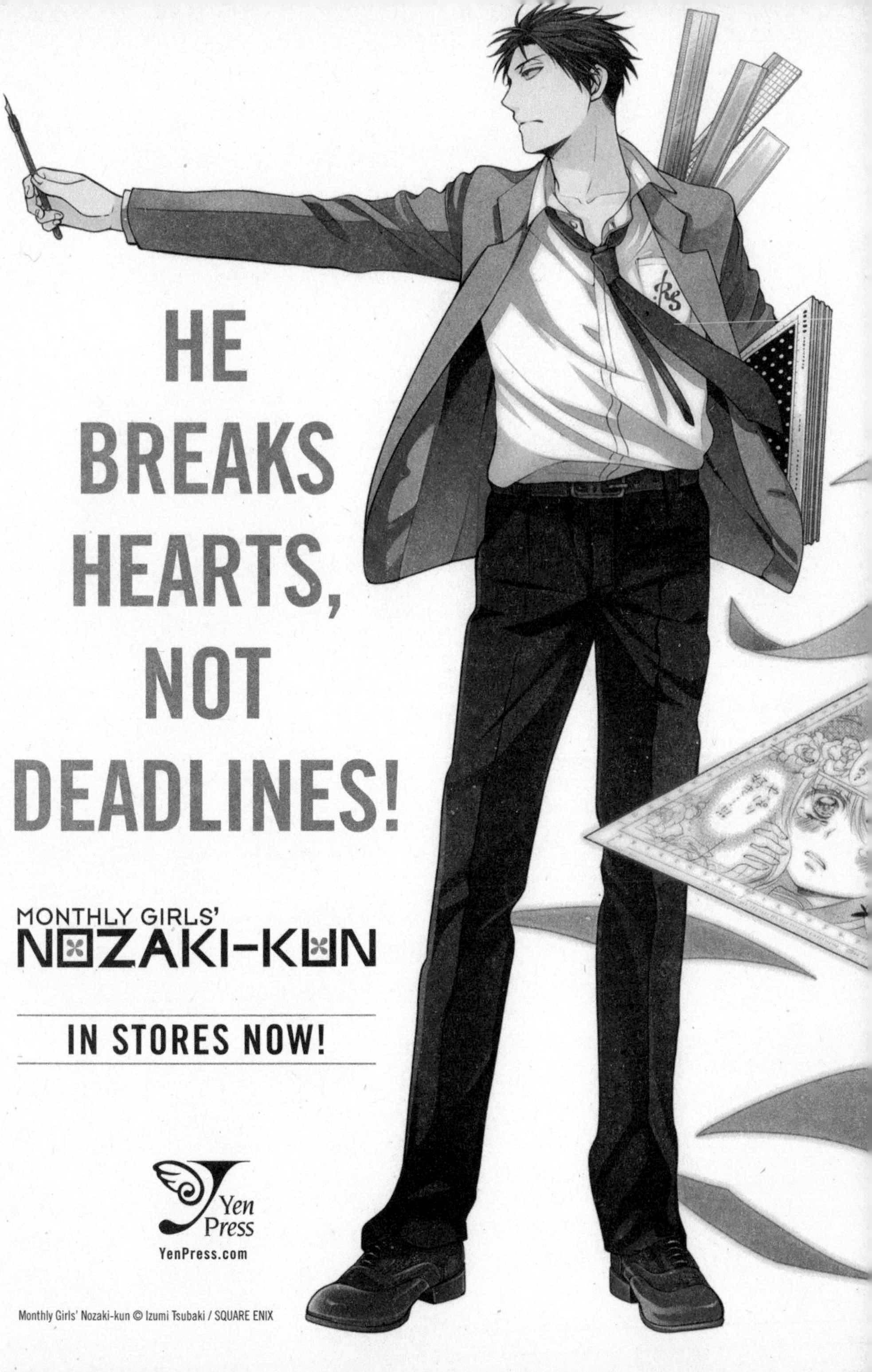
HE BREAKS HEARTS, NOT DEADLINES!
MONTHLY GIRLS'
NOZAKI-KUN
IN STORES NOW!
Yen Press
YenPress.com
Monthly Girls' Nozaki-kun © Izumi Tsubaki / SQUARE ENIX

Karino Takatsu, creator of
SERVANT x SERVICE, presents:

My Monster Girl's Too Cool For You

**Burning adoration melts
her heart...literally!**

In a world where *youkai* and
humans attend school together,
a boy named Atsushi Fukuzumi
falls for snow *youkai* Muku Shiroishi. Fukuzumi's passionate feelings
melt Muku's heart...and the rest of her?! The first volume of an
interspecies romantic comedy you're sure to fall head over heels for
is now available!!

Read new installments of this series every month at the same time as Japan!

CHAPTERS AVAILABLE NOW AT E-TAILERS EVERYWHERE!

YenPress.com   © Karino Takatsu/SQUARE ENIX CO., LTD.

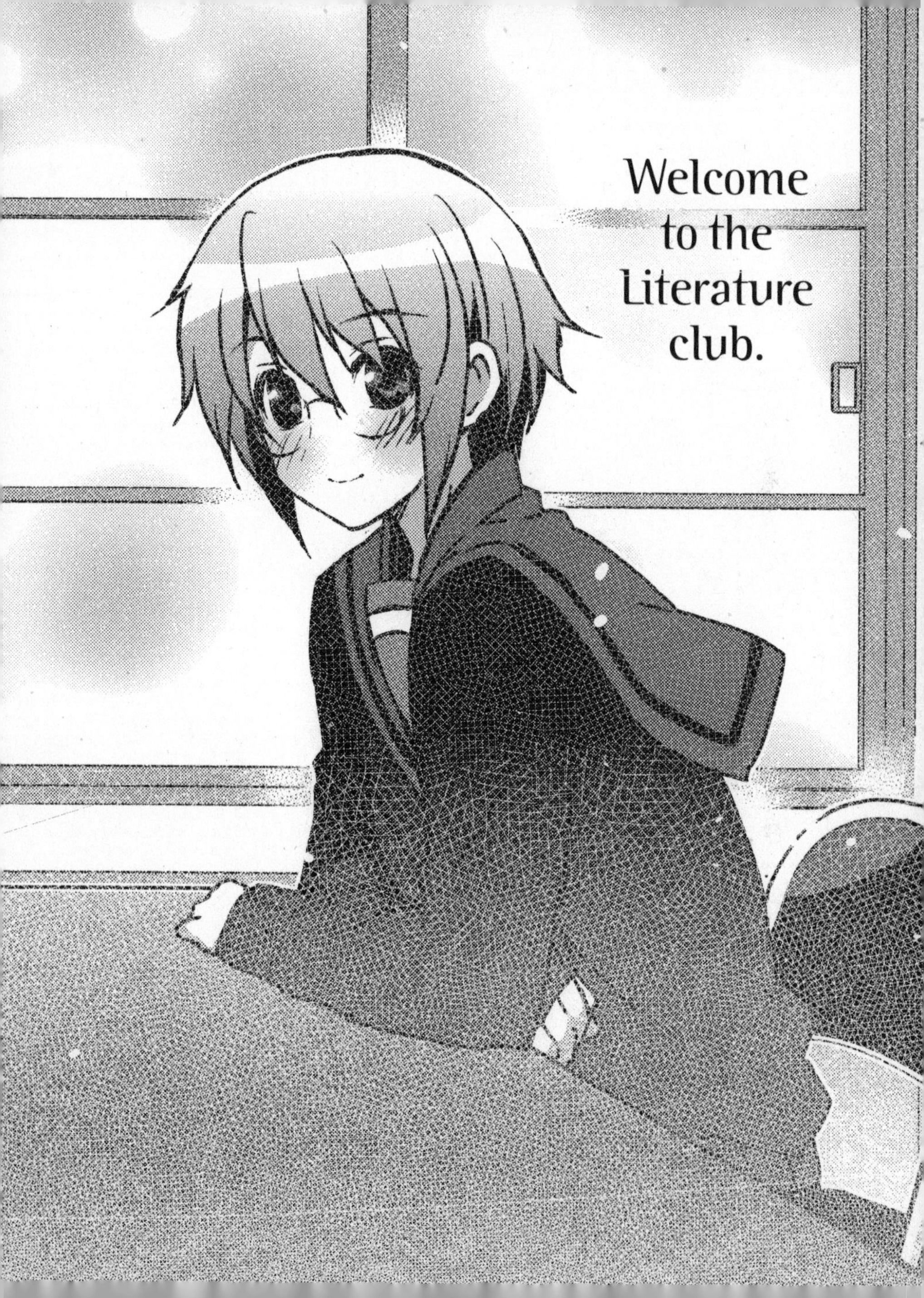
Welcome to the Literature club.

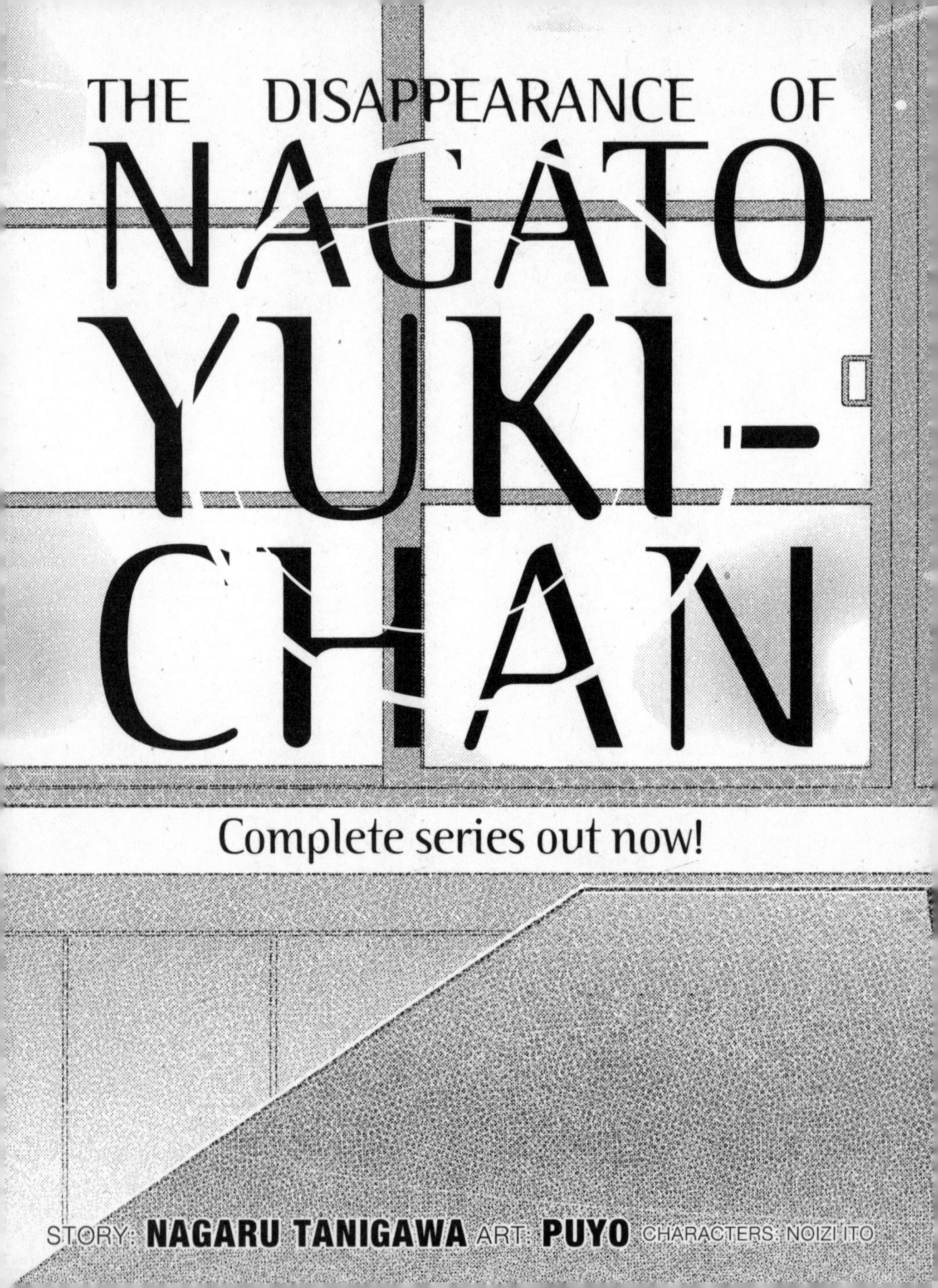
THE DISAPPEARANCE OF
NAGATO YUKI-CHAN
Complete series out now!
STORY: NAGARU TANIGAWA ART: PUYO CHARACTERS: NOIZI ITO

The Phantomhive family has a butler who's almost too good to be true...

...or maybe he's just too good to be human.

Black Butler

YANA TOBOSO

VOLUMES 1-23 IN STORES NOW!

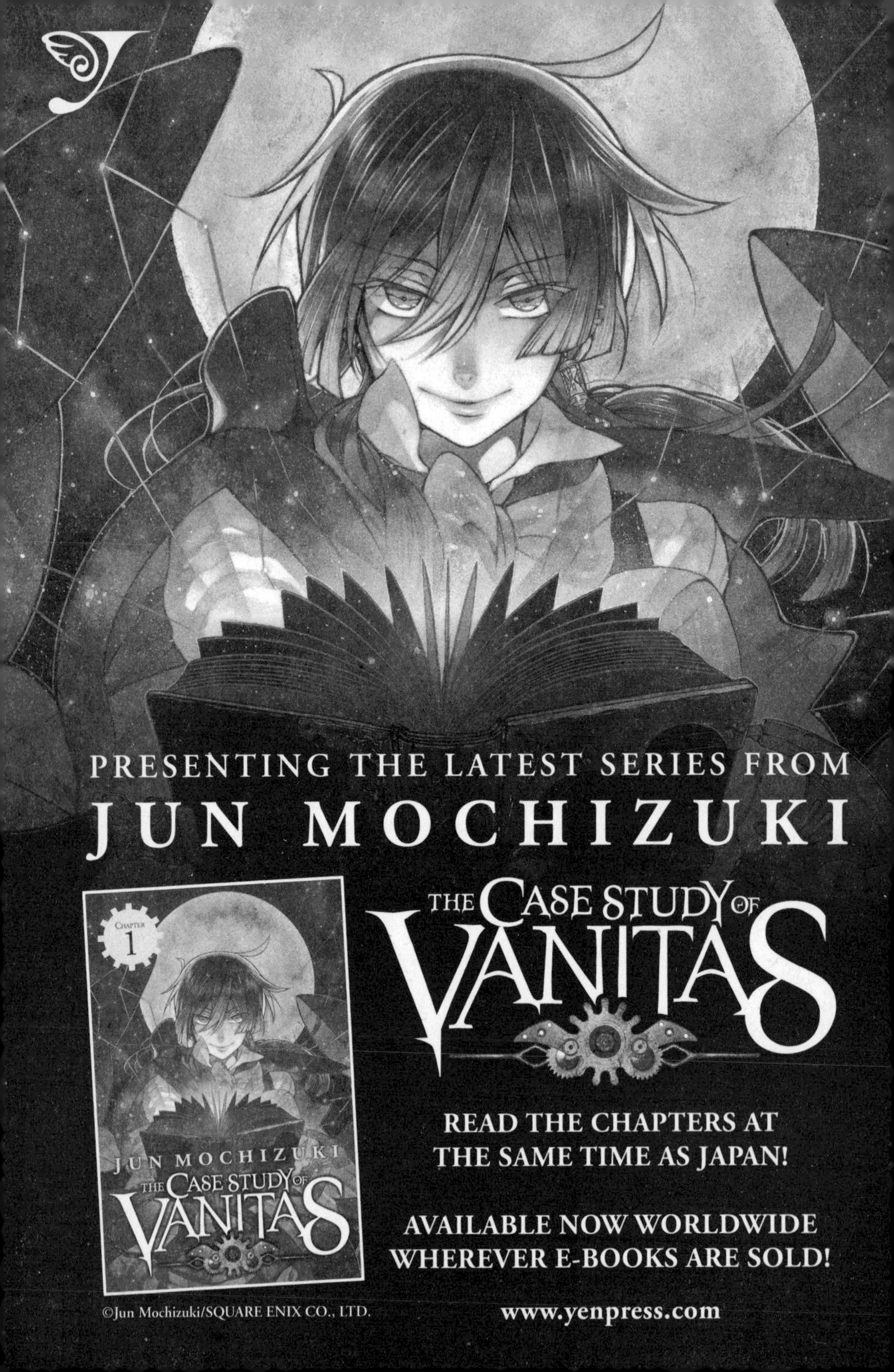
PRESENTING THE LATEST SERIES FROM
JUN MOCHIZUKI
CHAPTER 1
JUN MOCHIZUKI
THE CASE STUDY OF VANITAS
THE CASE STUDY OF VANITAS
READ THE CHAPTERS AT
THE SAME TIME AS JAPAN!
AVAILABLE NOW WORLDWIDE
WHEREVER E-BOOKS ARE SOLD!
©Jun Mochizuki/SQUARE ENIX CO., LTD.
www.yenpress.com

ENJOY EVERYTHING.

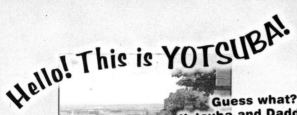

Hello! This is YOTSUBA!

Guess what? Guess what? Yotsuba and Daddy just moved here from waaaay over there!

And Yotsuba met these nice people next door and made new friends to play with!

The pretty one took Yotsuba on a bike ride!
(Whoooa! There was a big hill!!)

And Ena's a good drawer!
(Almost as good as Yotsuba!)

And their mom always gives Yotsuba ice cream!
(Yummy!)

And...
And... OHHHH!

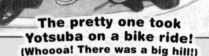

k i n i r o 🟦 m o s a i c

Y u i

BAYA

Translation: Amanda Haley
Lettering: Rochelle Gancio

KINIRO MOSAIC VOL. 6
© 2015 Yui Hara. All rights reserved. First published in Japan in 2015 by HOUBUNSHA CO., LTD., Tokyo. English translation rights in United States, Canada, and United Kingdom arranged with HOUBUNSHA CO., LTD. through Tuttle-Mori Agency, Inc., Tokyo.

English translation © 2018 by Yen Press, LLC

Yen Press
1290 Avenue of the Americas
New York, NY 10104

Visit us at yenpress.com
facebook.com/yenpress
twitter.com/yenpress
yenpress.tumblr.com
instagram.com/yenpress

First Yen Press Edition: April 2018

Yen Press is an imprint of Yen Press, LLC.
The Yen Press name and logo are trademarks of Yen Press, LLC.

The publisher is not responsible for websites (or their content) that are not owned by the publisher.

Library of Congress Control Number: 2016946069

ISBNs: 978-0-316-43358-7 (paperback)
        978-0-316-43359-4 (ebook)

10 9 8 7 6 5 4 3 2 1

WOR

Printed in the United States of America